THE UK'S NUCLEAR SCANDAL

The true history of Britain's nuclear weapons test
experiments 1952 to 1967 – a Cold War legacy of
power, prestige and profit for the few at the cost of
global collateral health damage for the many

Dennis Hayden

on behalf of the
Combined History Archive of Nuclear Veterans

FOR THE BETRAYED

*Dedicated to the memory of all who loyally served
at UK nuclear weapon test locations*

From Indoctrinated Innocence...

In vegetation sparse off Nullarbor,
Where a blistering sun beats down,
Lies Maralinga, the 'land of thunder',
Man-made marvel, atomic town.
From above a crystal seeming,
Buildings aluminium gleaming
Beneath an Australian ocean sky.
Around the town lies burnished ground:
Scorched scrub, mulga and
Eucalyptus tree, roots probing
Waters rarely found.
Irony smiles: was this once beneath the sea?

*Written by the author Dennis Hayden as a 21-year-old, shortly
after arriving at Maralinga in 1965*

Contents

Acknowledgements

I would like to thank all the nuclear veterans, academics and others who jointly hold archive and other documents, many of which have been noted by the Combined History Archive of Nuclear Veterans and used in the writing of this book.

Thanks are due in particular to Ian Anderson, a legal practitioner on three continents in civil, criminal and human rights cases, including chemical and radiation cases (nuclear tests and accidents), for reviewing drafts of this book's progress. Without Ian's interest and support over many decades, this book may never have been written.

The following people are also thanked for having been a tremendous inspiration during the past three decades or more:

Dr Keith Baverstock, for his 2004 critique of NRPB significantly flawed and biased studies using epidemiological rather than blood tests; Susie Boniface, nuclear veteran supporter and freelance journalist; Professor Chris Busby, for being the UK's leading expert on low dose low level radiation and much else, e.g. winning tribunal cases for nuclear veterans; Ken McGinley, the father of British nuclear veteran campaigning since the 1980s; Alan Owen, the son of a nuclear veteran campaigner and founder of LABRATS International, for his Global Health Survey 2020; Joe Pasquini, probably the last of the RAF nuclear cloud flyers and tireless campaigner, who sadly passed away shortly before publication of this book; Dai Williams, an independent academic with long support of the nuclear veterans' campaign for justice; and David Whyte, tenacious independent nuclear veteran campaigner who uses freedom of information as a vexation to the MOD.

Also a special mention for Drs Alice Stewart and Rosalie Bertell; for Michael Meacher MP, Environment Minister, for being sacked just for including independent scientists on a radiation committee; and to too many others who, for seeking truth and challenging the bias of government scientific censorship on matters nuclear, have had their careers and/or lives wrecked or diminished or made more difficult in the process.

Most love and admiration goes to Archie Ross, Barry Smith and all the others who fought to the end of their lives for justice and recognition for those who participated in the nuclear weapon tests, their widows and families.

During the writing of this book in 2021, three nuclear veteran campaign leaders lost their lives:

Roy Sefton, fellow member of the Action Executive of the CVFI, who enabled a world-first independent blood test study by the New Zealand Nuclear Test Veterans Association beyond the control of the UK MOD; Alan Batchelor, fearless and faithful vice president of the Australian Nuclear Veterans Association;

and the UK's tenacious campaigning nuclear widow and CVFI colleague, Shirley Denson. Their selfless campaigning from the 1980s will never, ever be forgotten.

Also, thanks to Alison Thompson, The Proof Fairy, for her helpful and professional work and advice regarding the publication of this book.

Last but not least, thanks to my wife Dawn for her patience, support and love for almost fifty years.

Foreword

It is difficult to do justice in a short number of words to this truly remarkable book, which takes readers into the 'dark abyss' of the military/spy complex known as the British Ministry of Defence by meticulously documenting its psychotic lack of ethics and morality in defending one of Britain's most notorious peacetime violations of the Nuremberg Code.

Since the early 20th century, ionizing radiation was known to affect the very building blocks of life, namely atoms, which form molecules and living cells.

Despite this, *The UK's Nuclear Scandal* shows how post-World War II political expediency drove Britain to condemn approximately 30,000 young, healthy British and Commonwealth servicemen and their unborn children to the unprotected effects of ionizing radiation in experiments to develop atomic and nuclear weapons.

Like later government experiments with sarin gas on young unsuspecting troops, these healthy servicemen deployed at Australian and Pacific bomb test sites were not informed of the serious long-term health effects to themselves and their unborn children from internal radiation by inhaling plutonium and other alpha emitters released by the experimental detonations. Though accompanying scientists wore respirators and radiation suits, they were issued only with shorts and light shirts. Decades later, their bones and those of their dead children would be secretly removed for government analysis.

This book documents the deceit and farcical chicanery of

this Defence Ministry to bamboozle the media and courts with junk science to show its experimental tests were safe – well, at least for its well protected scientists. In doing so it raises the disturbing issue of political manipulation of science and scientists through research funding allocations, 'D' notices and the Official Secrets Act.

This book is a 'must read' for anyone interested in the actual state of human rights in contemporary Britain.

Ian Anderson, legal practitioner on three continents

Preface

"All truth at first is ridiculed, then it is vehemently denied and finally it becomes self-evident."
Francois Voltaire (1694 - 1778)

The impetus for this book began for me in early 1966. As a 21-year-old RAF junior technician I was flown back to the UK just a month before completion of a 12-month tour of duty at Maralinga, a British nuclear weapon test site in South Australia. On arrival back in England, I ended up as a patient at the military hospital, RAF Halton.

By mid-1969 I was taken off air movement squadron load team flying duties, which had involved international travel, and graded medically unfit for any further RAF service except 'light' desk work restricted to the UK only.

During the period between 1969 and 1974, I spent about 100 days in various military hospitals. I was informed by military doctors I had no chance of further promotion. My RAF career was finished. Future promotion prospects were over. My contracted years of enlistment expired in March 1974 and I returned to civilian life.

Just before leaving the RAF, a cost-saving benefit occurred for the MOD. Because I wasn't medically discharged, this enabled them to deny me any pension for my 12 years of military service from 1962 to 1974.

In civilian life, I had a lot of catching up to do. After a two-year RAF administrative apprenticeship, I'd spent 14 years in a situation where no pension provision was able to be accrued. Luckily, I still had the strength to carry a briefcase and wield a pen.

In 1992, the linked health conditions of acute recurring iritis and ankylosing spondylitis were assessed by the Department of Health and Social Security (DHSS) as attributable to my military service. Two years or so later, war pension claims policy was placed under control of the Ministry of Defence's Veterans Agency with policy enforced by a newly created politician of obfuscation: a Minister for Veterans.

It appears that gaps in the treatment of nuclear veterans had to be plugged by the pen-pushing bean counters of Whitehall.

By this time the MOD was fully aware of the fact that I was an 'awkward' nuclear veteran. That is, by asking questions I was regarded as a vexation which, as with all nuclear veterans or their widows, whether campaigning or not 'rocking the boat', meant the shutters were closed on justice. Pension appeal tribunals had begun to spiral downwards into kangaroo courts of bias and denial, a position they have remained in to this day.

I received a weasel-worded letter around 1994 stating that although I had been awarded a 20% war disability pension by DHSS doctors, this award was not recognised by the MOD Veterans Agency as having any link to my time at Maralinga. Despite the 1973 Armed Forces Act reforms, I was barred from any pension consideration for my 12 years of service because the act did not come into force until 1975 and, in any event, I had left the RAF in 1974 – conveniently, for them, without a medical discharge.

When dealing with the superannuated bureaucrats and officials of the Ministry of Defence, all nuclear veterans, or widows of veterans, or genetically impaired offspring of nuclear veterans are treated with contempt.

However, I consider myself one of the lucky survivors of

the nuclear weapon test experiments. Compared to the suffering of many, my concerns are trivial. Members of the armed forces who attended such locations have inherited a wide and varied legacy of illnesses. My own health problems, including part surgical removal of an enlarged thyroid in 1985, have been at the lower end of the scale of legacy ill health compared to those at the upper end of exposure to radiation.

For example, Lance Corporal Derek Redman was an extremely fit young man "built like a brick out- house with no medical history of diabetes," according to his brother and parents. Derek served in the Royal Engineers at Christmas Island, the UK's major nuclear weapon test location in the Pacific, where he fell ill and died within hours. His body was sealed in a coffin and quickly buried at sea by a hastily assembled military burial squad. By this means, no post-mortem examination could be convened to explain the causal link for his untimely death at the age of 27.

Derek Redman's military medical papers recorded his death as being due to severe diabetes. Professor Partha Kar, consultant endocrinologist at Portsmouth Hospital NHS Trust, confirmed in a report in the *Daily Mirror* by Sue Boniface: "The only way we can be certain diabetes caused this man's death is with a post-mortem."

Many nuclear veterans died of leukaemia in their 30s, within seven years of returning from UK bomb tests. These and many other premature deaths happened before the veterans had begun to form associations in the UK, Australia, New Zealand and Fiji to campaign for justice. A squadron leader who flew through radioactive clouds at Christmas Island and died in 1963 of leukaemia – attributed by a consultant to radiation exposure – had his case for compensation denied with the excuse that nuclear test service is not classed as war service.

Dead men cannot speak. The bureaucrats at the MOD realise this and so have waged a war of attrition against the veterans until we all are dead. They have contrived a sanitised version of nuclear history: radiation is safe, and it is harmless. But no one today is fooled regarding the toxicity of invisible-to-the-eye airborne pathogens that know no borders.

Introduction

"War is a racket. It always has been. It is the only one in which profits are reckoned in dollars and the losses in lives."
US Marine Corps General Smedley D Butler (1881 to 1940)

War is indeed a nasty and vicious business. Whether war is waged by conventional weapons or by chemical, biological or nuclear weapons, the armed forces of both sides take the brunt of the damage. It remains, as General Butler wrote in 1935, always the armed forces, often conscripts, and bystanding civilians who pay the enormous tax bill in deaths and injury.

Nothing has changed.

From 1952 to 1967, combined UK and Commonwealth armed forces in the Pacific and Australia took part in one of the most notorious mass violations of human rights by any western democratic nation.

Other nuclear weapon states have followed the same path of shame in varying degrees with regard to their treatment of nuclear test veterans. It appears to be an international problem.

However, this book focuses only on the UK's nuclear record from the point of view of archive and other documents of events from 1945 to date.

The 30,000-plus men, mainly from the UK, Australia, New Zealand and Fiji, of whom about 35% were young national service conscripts, were part of a programme of nuclear test experiments. This cohort of men were used, abused and then abandoned to a fate of radiation-induced legacy ill health, premature death and genetic damage after giving loyal service to the nation.

This book is a record of the historic lack of integrity, ethics,

9

morality and recognition shown by successive UK governments with regard to the nuclear tests.

It is an indictment against desk-bound, superannuated bureaucrats, officials and politicians who have never dug a trench; never stood in close proximity to the shockwave of gamma radiation of a nuclear detonation; never had to live, work and breathe in areas of residual radioactive fallout; never flown an aircraft through a radioactive mushroom cloud; and never been made to crawl through the toxic dust of ground zero at a bomb test location – all hazardous duties carried out for the nation without any respirators, masks or other personal protection equipment or any vaccine capable of giving immunity.

Superannuated bureaucrats have never had to return to loved ones with significantly translocated chromosomes in their DNA and with a range of legacy health issues. Knowledge of how to diagnose radiation exposure has been ignored by officials. Early remedial treatments for radiation-induced illnesses have been denied.

This book is an indictment of the deception of those who make policy to deny any duty of care by the use of a simple lie that radiation is harmless, which is made into a big lie, to be repeated until eventually it is believed by the officials themselves.

It is a fantasy land where the emperor wears no clothes.

This is a scandal of an establishment devoid of integrity which, over the past decades, has become ever more self-evidently exposed.

The appendix of this book gives a list of references which may be of interest not only to readers but also to nuclear historians who, like veterans, are banned access to information regarding the true history of the nuclear tests.

This book need not ever have been written. Since the 1980s, an honourable settlement of claims could have been made on many occasions... but has been dismissed.

The Badge
Combined Services, Maralinga 1965-1966.
The author's incentive for founding the
Combined Veterans' Forum (CVF), later to become the
Combined Veterans' Forum International (CVFI).

Chapter 1:1945 and the Race for Nuclear Weapons

"They were deliberating amongst themselves as to how they could give wings to death so that it could, in a moment, penetrate everywhere, both near and far."
The Labyrinth of the World, 1623

Two atomic bombs were dropped on Japan. The first bomb, on 6 August 1945, destroyed the city of Hiroshima. Two days later, a second bomb destroyed Nagasaki. The yields of both were small by later standards of mass destruction. The populations of the two Japanese cities suffered nuclear fallout from this devastating new weapon of war.

Both nuclear weapons had the American 'stars and stripes' stamped on them. But this is not the full story, which eventually led to the British nuclear bomb test programme of 1952 to 1967.

Throughout history, war is well known as 'the mother of all inventions'. It always has been.

In 1935, the clouds of war were gathering. Winston Churchill had noted the danger to fragile western democracies before most politicians. Britain had been bankrupted by the First World War of 1914-18. Across the Atlantic, the political leadership of the far wealthier United States of America had every intention of keeping out of any war. They intended to remain neutral and continue making money.

So, what changed US policy?

It all hinged on the degree of fear of war – or a nation's

desire for peace and prosperity.

Winston Churchill's perception of a rapidly changing world was born of a combination of military and political experience. As a young man, he had served as an officer with British forces in late 19th century Sudan and, later, as a war correspondent in the Boer War.

By the 1930s, he had experienced high political office in a wide range of military spheres: First Lord of the Admiralty 1911-16; Minister of Munitions 1917; Minister of War 1918; and Minister of Air 1919-21. Britain, in the 1930s, had a man highly attuned to how the winds of war were blowing. He warned of the dangers, but the desire for peace by government outweighed its fear of war.

In the United States a highly decorated Marine Corps General, Smedley D Butler, who retired in 1931, had also noted and understood the dangers of war looming on the horizon. In 1935 he wrote:

"The mad dogs of Europe are on the loose. Hitler, with his rearmament of Germany and his constant demand for more arms, is an equal if not greater menace to peace. France only recently has increased the terms of military service for its youth from a year to eighteen months... Secretly, each nation is studying and perfecting newer and ghastlier means of annihilating its foes wholesale. Victory or defeat will be determined by the skill and ingenuity of our scientists."

And so it proved to be the case.

To achieve the "ghastlier means" of mass destruction of an enemy was not entirely a technology born out of the skill and ingenuity of the United States. This awesome new weapon of mass destruction, a nuclear bomb, was the result of a gathering of the finest scientific brains available. These experts, of many

14

nationalities, were assembled together in secrecy at Los Alamos, an isolated former ranch ideally placed in the desert of New Mexico, USA.

The far-sighted, much decorated US General Butler died in 1940. If he had lived to see the advent of nuclear weapons, it's likely he would have abhorred the damage such weapons would wreak upon the men who tested them or used them. He would have loathed the collateral damage wreaked upon innocent civilians.

The now known environmental impact of nuclear weapons is far greater and far more long-lasting than the ghastliness of conventional, biological or chemical weapons used in the First World War.

It was considered by many in 1945 that these awesome weapons were at least safer in the hands of democracies rather than having been developed by totalitarian Germany or Japan.

This is true to the extent that democracies are expected to have higher moral and ethical standards than totalitarian states. This supposition, however, did not help Japan's collaterally killed and damaged civilians when two small atomic bombs dropped out of the sky over Hiroshima and Nagasaki.

How could nuclear bomb testing be achieved safely for the military personnel and at the same time at minimum cost to the nations involved?

The answer appears to be by use of an edict adopted by totalitarians and other political leaderships for over 200 years, best explained by the French dictator Napoleon Bonaparte (1769-1821), which he found helpful for waging total aggressive war against nations, and which others have adopted ever since.

To ensure most power, prestige and profit remained in the

hands of an 'inside group' of military officers, industrialists, bankers and officials, Napoleon said: "All men are enamoured by decorations; they positively hunger for it."

Napoleon had concluded that when young men have patriotism stuffed down their throats and the promise of medals, they will tolerate anything: conscription, poor food, pay and conditions. This, of course, is a maxim that ensures greater profits for those at the top of any military industrial war machine.

In 1943, the scientists building the first atomic weapons to be used for the bombing of Japan secretly began arriving at Los Alamos. The assembled scientists were an international elite of intellectuals. Some saw the atomic bomb as a means to end the Second World War. Others viewed it as the opening of a Pandora's box of horror.

Among these brilliant minds was William Penney (later Lord Penney), then aged 34. His enthusiasm when discussing, in graphic detail, the worst destructive aspects of a nuclear bomb detonation – the fireball, the number of casualties incinerated etc. – plus his cheerful matter-of-fact smile quickly earnt him the nickname 'The Smiling Killer'. He went on to head the British nuclear bomb tests from 1952 to 1967.

Also present at Los Alamos was Joseph Rotblat, a physicist and acknowledged expert on the effects of radiation, who came to Britain in 1932 to work on 'Tube Alloys', the codename for the British atomic bomb project that commenced in the 1930s. In contrast to Penney, after Los Alamos and the bombing of Japan Rotblat worked tirelessly for nuclear disarmament.

Therefore, the nuclear arms race had its genesis in the 1930s. Once the use of uranium as a weapon was seen as a possibility, the development of nuclear weapons was inevitable, relentless and unstoppable. The speed in historic terms is breath-taking. It took a mere 27 years from the armistice ending the First World War in 1918 to the first atmospheric bomb test of the Manhattan Project: codenamed 'Trinity', detonated on 16 July 1945.

In historic terms this is probably the shortest time, i.e. only one human generation, for unleashing a global tragedy on humanity.

Britain in the 1930s was in fact ahead of the United States in its understanding of nuclear technology. However, the reverse was true concerning the strength of both nations' economies. Britain had been bankrupted by the attrition of the First World War. The 1920s' depression and another war looming did not help.

On the other hand, the US had the capital needed to develop advanced weapons of war but a policy of neutrality held its politicians from doing so.

In the late 1930s, the Danish physicist Neils Bohr had published his work on uranium fission. Scientists in Britain began to examine the powers that could be released by such a uranium fission bomb and this led to the MAUD Committee of scientists.

But Winston Churchill had decided it would be several years before such a possibility could be achieved. However, he had underestimated the ingenuity and enthusiasm of two refugee scientists working at the University of Birmingham since the early 1930s: a German, Rudolph Peierls, and an Austrian, Otto Frisch.

The first report of the MAUD Committee to Churchill's

war-torn cabinet in 1940 about the uranium fission bomb said: "Even if the war should end before all the bombs were ready, the effort would not be wasted, except in the unlikely event of complete disarmament, since *no nation would care to risk being caught without weapons of such decisive possibilities.*"

When revealing a copy of the report to the US President Roosevelt, he agreed. The US government was also impressed by how technically advanced their British scientific colleagues were and in particular how advanced was the political perception of the post-war implications for atomic weapons. Churchill persuaded Roosevelt to set up the Manhattan bomb project and reply proposing joint collaboration.

The Americans now knew how atomic bombs could be made and also why they were deemed to be a necessary weapon of war.

Yet in late 1940, Britain's politicians still felt unease about surrendering her nuclear secrets. Above all, in the long term, many believed too much information to the Americans was unwise because of America's long held neutral position in the war.

Some politicians with imperial views of a dwindling empire believed nuclear weapons would give Britain the power to police the world. With the benefit of hindsight, that seems incredible considering the position Britain was in at the time.

However, within six months the situation had changed dramatically. The Japanese bombing of the US pacific fleet at anchor in Pearl Harbour on 7 Dec 1941 changed the United States' political perception. Fear of a huge Japanese fleet off the west coast quickly committed the USA to the need for the decisive possibilities given by atomic weapon production.

The US poured astronomical amounts of money, materials

and manpower into the bomb project. The Manhattan Project to build Trinity, the world's first nuclear bomb, meant the scientists at Los Alamos wanted for nothing. The reality of making atomic bombs forged quickly ahead.

Roosevelt and Churchill signed the Quebec Agreement in 1943, giving British scientists a chance to join the Americans at the Los Alamos headquarters to ensure the race to build the bomb would happen before the end of the Second World War.

Another factor for the speed of completion of the nuclear bomb project at Los Alamos was because Hitler had also noted the awesome power of nuclear weapons. His efforts to produce 'heavy water' (i.e. water formed of oxygen and deuterium), a vital ingredient of nuclear bomb making, was thankfully sabotaged by the joint efforts of Norwegian partisans and British commandoes in operations between October 1942 and February 1943.

The entire inventory of heavy water produced during the German occupation of Norway – over 500 kg (1102 lb) – was destroyed, along with equipment critical to the operation of the vital electrolysis chambers.

As a result, Hitler switched his war effort to V1 and V2 rockets, capable of being launched from platforms hidden in occupied mainland Europe to rain down on the British Isles. The so-called 'doodlebugs' were a desperate effort to win the war. The flying bombs caused extensive damage and civilian deaths but could be intercepted and thrown off course. It is dreadful to imagine the outcome if the rockets had carried atomic weapons.

In real time, it is hard to imagine that, only seven years after the end of the Second World War, over 30,000 British and Commonwealth servicemen would be involved in the development of Britain's own nuclear deterrent.

The young men due to participate in the British weapon tests were all children of an empire that covered the globe and were justifiably filled with patriotism. In 1952, Britain may no longer have had the largest navy in the world but we still had the best.

Unlike today's generation, the heroes for young men of the day had military backgrounds or were others revered for heroic duty or sacrifice. Like their parents, uncles and grandparents, these young men were used to deprivation and hardship. They were in fact an ideal cohort to be used, abused and then abandoned at minimum cost, if needed.

They had no idea where they were heading as participants in the nuclear test programme. They had no knowledge of the impact of radiation on the human body. They implicitly trusted their leaders, who said radiation was harmless. They were all lied to. For well before 1952, archive documents clearly show the hazards of radiation were well known to the British Government.

Like the 1940s' Manhattan Project, the British nuclear test was to be a rushed affair. However, one significant difference existed and was noted by authors Denys Blakeway and Sue Lloyd-Roberts regarding the costs: it was a 'shoestring and chewing gum affair', carried out on the other side of the world, for which many people may still be paying with their lives. (*Fields of Thunder: Testing Britain's Bomb*, Unwin 1985.)

The need for a nuclear deterrent with a Union Jack stamped upon it commenced very swiftly after the end of WWII. In 1946,

Sir Winston Churchill yet again perceived Britain – a bankrupted democracy after five years of total war, its citizens still on wartime rationing – was now yet again in a situation of great fragility and peril.

Germany was a nation divided by the Western Allies and Russia into four zones of post-war administration. The British, French and US had three zones in West Germany and the Russians had control of East Germany, Poland, Czechoslovakia and the Baltic States.

Berlin, the capital of Germany, was an island inside the Russian zone of occupancy with only road access available to the Western powers. The city had been divided in half between the Allies and Russia.

At a speech at Fulton, USA on 4 March 1946, Churchill used the phrase 'iron curtain' for the first time to describe the line cut through Europe, from the Baltic to Trieste, on the Adriatic Sea. This split, however, was most graphically shown by the dividing wall in Berlin.

The tension in the air at this time was pulpable.

In 1948 the Russians, by now referred to more often as the United Soviet Socialist Republic (USSR), closed road access for the Western Allies into Berlin. The only way the people of West Berlin could be provided with all the necessities of life was by what became known as the 'Berlin airlift' by NATO nations' transport aircraft. This was a direct and unacceptable challenge to the Western defence pact made by NATO by the Warsaw Pact of the USSR.

This event could undoubtedly be regarded as the commencement of the Cold War: a war heralding a clash of ideologies between democracy and communism.

On 21 September 1949, Russia successfully detonated a nuclear bomb. This came as a huge shock to the US and British Governments.

The Russian bomb test shouldn't have been a surprise. The Russians had only followed the example of the Western Allies. They had rounded up physicists and other necessary experts from the lands they now occupied to quickly became the second nuclear weapon power.

The die was cast. The 30,000-plus children of the generations who had loyally served in British and Commonwealth forces during the First and Second World Wars were all now to be thrown under the 'wings of death' of the British nuclear weapons test experiments, which lasted 15 years, from 1952 to 1967. The nuclear arms race had now begun in earnest with three nuclear powers – the USA, USSR and Great Britain – in contention for power and prestige.

The first British bomb test, set for 1952, was originally planned to recklessly take place on an island off the coast of Scotland, in order to cut costs. However, the Prime Minister of Australia, Sir Robert Menzies, who was noted at the time as 'enamoured by decorations', quickly seized the opportunity for power, prestige and profit to come Australia's way.

This pristine southern continent was offered on a plate to Britain to be used for atmospheric atomic bomb tests. Menzies falsely reassured the worried public and Australian press that such testing would be of 'no conceivable harm' to Australian servicemen or the population. This was a convenient and expedient lie. The tone had been set for betrayal.

A huge flotilla sailed south from Britain. The underfunded 'shoestring and chewing gum' British nuclear weapon programme task force was underway to the island of Monte Bello, off the northwest coast of Australia. This was the choice for Britain's bid to become the third nuclear power.

The world now entered the Cold War era of M.A.D. – Mutual Annihilative Destruction. In the 1950s and 1960s, over a thousand nuclear weapons were detonated in the atmosphere of the planet.

The yield of the explosions of each increased to a thousand-fold. The explosive power from the nuclear tests exceeded the total for the two world wars combined. The impact was long lasting and damage to the environment was huge.

By the mid-1960s, deceased new-born babies were shown, by global post-mortem analysis, to have in their bones radioactive strontium-90 – a 28-year half-life beta radioisotope from nuclear bomb test fallout.

This was just one result of the opened Pandora's box of horror. More was yet to come.

Chapter 2: The Need-To-Know Effects of Radiation

"What is needed is adequate support to the research programs designed to define more accurately the risks from human exposure to ionising radiation."
Dr Karl Morgan, the father of health physics *(1978)*

Ever since the end of the UK's nuclear weapon tests, and according to the Defence People Secretariat of the Ministry of Defence (DPS-MOD) overseeing policy towards nuclear veterans, the effects of radiation are harmless. This is a lie. The statement "There is no peer-reviewed evidence of excess disorders or mortality among nuclear test veterans as a group or their families which could be causally linked to participation in the atmospheric tests or exposure to radiation as a result of that presence" is another lie.

This is the answer given to any nuclear veteran or widow, any Member of Parliament, any investigative journalist or member of the public asking questions about the effects of radiation. All who ask questions on this subject are lied to.

This negative ethos comes straight from the perverted pantheon of Adolf Hitler's loathing of truth: that is, 'if you are going to lie, make it a big lie and then repeat it often enough until everyone believes it, including yourself.'

The effect of radiation is the 'prime causal link' for sickness and death in nuclear veterans (2009 Limitation Trial verdict summary). All who have died prematurely and suffered legacy ill health from participation in the British bomb tests are denied justice.

We cannot entirely blame the politicians and bureaucrats of successive governments. The deception is something they've inherited. On the other hand, many have done precious little to address the concerns of nuclear veterans and their families.

The young men from Britain and the Commonwealth, including conscripts, who travelled to serve at British nuclear weapon testing sites between 1952 and 1967 knew absolutely nothing about the dangers – but have always wanted answers.

The following are some of the questions posed by young men going to British nuclear weapon tests in Australia and the Pacific, amended from Mario Petrucci's *Heavy Water Poems*, Enitharmon Press, 2004.

> Where are we going?
> *Wherever you are sent.*
> What will we do there?
> *What you are told.*
> How bad will it be?
> *No worse than we tell you it is.*
> But how will you repay us?
> *With nothing; you are persona non grata.*
> What will we tell others?
> *Nothing, or you'll face prosecution.*

The above are the only meaningful answers nuclear test veterans have received since 1967. We obeyed orders and trusted those who gave them to be honest with regard to the effects of radiation. Over half a century of deliberate obstruction, all trust has been lost. We have been betrayed and abandoned.

We first began to suspect our betrayal in the 1980s. We only knew for certain in 2009, due to science: we have the mark of the bomb in our DNA. We have been given no recognition other than being treated as a vexation for seeking the truth; denied legal aid, blood tests and access to evidence. We are, in fact, loyal servicemen who have been disenfranchised as *personae non gratae.*

In 2021, we no longer care. The need-to-know effects of radiation is part of science. Science should never be biased, ignored or dismissed. But the truth has been perverted for political reasons by advice that is significantly flawed and biased.

The advice given to the Secretary of State for Defence, other ministers, the Pension Appeal Tribunal and for Freedom of Information tribunal decisions etc. is significantly biased. The advice does not consider all scientific papers regarding the effects of radiation. The advice given only looks at science that agrees with the Government's sustained policy of denial.

The document used for advice on the effects of radiation is the *Service Personnel and Veterans Agency (SPVA) Statement on Radiation Policy.* Close analysis of this document by the Combined Veterans' Forum International (CVFI) in 2011 found advice to ministers and others is reliant on only 23 carefully selected scientific papers dating from 1942 to 1999. Of these, 18 (i.e. 78%) were more than 16 years old.

None of the papers used to advise ministers and others mention advances since the 1960s of diagnostic science capable of showing the degree of chromosomal translocations in the blood (genetic damage induced by exposure to radiation). None of the papers mention the 'crucial and pivotal' legacy of ill health and premature deaths of veterans from inhaled or ingested radioactive fallout particles, which are the seeds of serious legacy illness and death. Once inside the body, lodged in tissue and acting as internal emitters, body cells, organs, bone and blood are irradiated and damaged.

The SPVA, which produced the Statement on Radiation Policy in 2011, is a department of the MOD's Veterans Agency and overseen by a senior official, Dr Anne Braidwood. When cross-examined as an expert witness for the MOD in 2013 by lawyer Neil Sampson, acting on behalf of nuclear veterans, she said she knew nothing about radiation entering the body by inhalation, ingestion or a cut in the skin as a cause of damage. (See Chapter Ten – The Legal Fight.)

This expedient lack of knowledge is astounding because, since at least 1920, the effects of radiation gaining access to the inside of the body have been known to be extremely toxic and life threatening.

Radium is an alpha radiation, discovered by husband and wife team Pierre (1859-1906) and Marie Curie (1867-1934), who jointly received the Nobel award for physics in 1903. Mme Curie went on to also win the Nobel award for chemistry in 1911. The daughter of a Warsaw university physicist, she came from Poland to Paris to study at the Sorbonne and is regarded as the first great scientist in the understanding of the effects of radiation.

There is a great distinction between Marie Curie and the MOD's superannuated official, Dr Braidwood. Professor Curie lived, worked and eventually died (from a form of blood cancer in 1934) seeking scientific truths of radiation, whereas Dr Braidwood, along with many others in government-appointed quangos, has devoted her working life to helping to conceal the truth of science; she and her like have created the schism existing in scientific consensus that we have inherited today.

Radium provides the first example of evidence that internal irradiation from radioactivity has a very serious impact on health if inhaled or ingested into the human body.

This knowledge evolved quickly from the dawn of the nuclear age. In 1895, Wilhelm Roentgen discovered X-rays whilst experimenting with the passage of electricity through an evacuated glass tube. He noticed that a phosphorescent screen elsewhere in the laboratory glowed because of some invisible energy that was created. He took X-ray pictures of his wife's hand, which showed her bones and wedding ring clearly. He had discovered gamma radiation.

A year later, in Paris, Henri Becquerel found that certain naturally occurring minerals gave off weak, but similar radiation.

In 1898, Mme Marie Curie coined the word 'radioactivity'. She began to look at materials that closely exhibited this effect and identified a new, novel, highly radioactive element besides uranium; she named it radium. Her epic work to chemically isolate radium, processing thousands of kilograms of radioactive ore found in Canada, resulted in the substance becoming commercially available.

The term 'radioactivity' is just one discovery in the Pandora's box of horror identified over a hundred years ago. Physics and physicists as a branch of science were greeted as harbingers of life enhancement. But what was the biological impact of this new scientific discovery? It did not take long for biology and biologists to find out.

By the 1920s, radium had become a sensation for industry. It was sold as part of a new and exciting age as an 'elixir of life'. The film industry took advantage of electric currents passing through the dead and bringing them back to life: Frankenstein's monster had been born.

In 2021, and with the benefit of hindsight, we know radioactivity is not the bringer of life; it is the direct opposite.

Radium was sold as an ingredient in toothpaste, hair restorer, tonic water and even as a cure for anything from arthritis to infertility. A popular and widely used brand in the US was Radium Water, often referred to in advertising as 'liquid sunshine'. One New York company claimed to have supplied more than 150,000 customers.

Another brand, Radithor, was so radioactive several users died from what became known as radium poisoning. The most published case of this was a Pittsburg industrialist, Eben Byers, who drank a two-ounce bottle daily for several years; he believed it made him fit and recommended it to friends. Mr Byers' fitness gradually deteriorated, and he died from a legacy of multiple decay of the jaw bone, anaemia and a brain abscess in 1932.

However, the radium poisoning deaths in the 1920s of nine young women employed by the US Radium Corporation was the first case of occupational radiation deaths. The women were employed between 1920 and 1924 to paint watch and clock dials with radium containing paint that gave luminosity. To keep their brushes pointed, the dial-painters licked the tips. Since the amount of radium in the paint was tiny, the employer assumed the procedure was safe.

This false perception of 'safety' has echoes today in the low dose, low level mantra of the MOD.

Just like the bomb test veterans, the dial-painters were told there was no danger at all in the work they had taken up. Nevertheless, just like the veterans, they began to suffer a range of serious health problems. Death certificates cited many different causes. (The same tactic was used in epidemiological studies of nuclear veterans' mortality in the 1980s and '90s.) The women were said to have died of stomach ulcers, trench mouth, phosphorous poisoning, anaemia, necrosis of the jaw and even syphilis.

You would have thought the women were veterans who had recently returned from the trenches of the First World War. Of course, medical practitioners in the 1920s knew nothing of the effects of radiation – just as today, the medical profession was kept completely in the dark on a need-to-know basis.

As with the Ministry of Defence in the claims of nuclear veterans, the US Radium Corporation of course denied liability. During a very long trial, Harrison Martland of the Harvard School of Public Health was able to do biopsies on the jaws of two of the dial-painters who were diagnosed as suffering from 'jaw necrosis and severe anaemia'. Both died shortly after Martland's biopsies. He confirmed the post-mortems showed high levels of radioactivity in the women's bones and organs.

Martland also tested 22 living employees of US Radium and everyone had blood counts that were unacceptably high. The writing was on the wall that workers were exposed to radiation, both externally and internally. Martland found that when the 22 living workers exhaled onto a fluorescent screen, the screen glowed. (Martland, 1929)

The US Radium Corporation, 'prompted only by humanitarian considerations', settled out of court for only half the amount claimed. But they still had not conceded that the ingested alpha radioactivity of radium was the prime causal link of the illnesses and premature deaths of their workers.

The dial-painters were early victims of the horrors released by the Pandora's box of ionising radiation. They were an early warning to society that the effects of radiation are toxic and deadly. In the 1920s, the cost in human lives was treated as a mere vexation by the US Radium Corporation: something to be ignored and covered up. Nothing has changed.

However, radium is just part of a huge mix of horrors of radiation that are a hazard to health. Radiation damage to nuclear test veterans is delivered primarily at the time of detonation in a massive burst and then in fallout of the bomb material. The fallout following a ground burst or detonation close to sea level is ionised rock, sand or water taken into the mushroom cloud and returning to earth as dust.

The nuclear test experimental programme was run on a strict need-to-know basis. The Atomic Weapon Research Establish (AWRE) scientists knew the truth. This is why they were the only ones with respirators. This is why they were the first to run for cover when it started to rain. The highest-ranking officers knew more than most but stayed silent. Other officers knew hardly anything at all about radiation. The lower ranks knew absolutely nothing.

New facts are added to the history archive of nuclear veterans all the time. Since the 1990s, the internet has been a great leveller in the quest for the truth. The main types of radiation at nuclear weapon tests, not listed in order of toxicity, are beta, gamma and alpha radiation.

Beta Radiation

Beta particles have high energy and can penetrate the skin. They can reach muscles, thyroid and many other glands, and lymph nodes. Because of the depths of the eyeball the particles can reach the entire lens of the eye but very few reach the retina. Lens cataracts in the eyes are due mostly to beta radiation.

This is of interest to me because after 11 months at a nuclear test location I was returned to a military hospital with acute recurring inflammation of the iris. (See Preface.) I'm pleased that beta particles very rarely reach the retina of the eye.

If receiving a high dose of this type of radiation, the early response is burning of the skin, like intense sunburn. Many veterans experienced this while wearing short-sleeved shirts and in shorts when lined up in the desert or on beaches as part of the 'indoctrination' process that formed part of the experiments; only a few wore all-body overalls as a means of protection.

A typical case of a nuclear veteran claiming skin cancer in the 1980s as attributed to radiation is the usual jumping through many hoops. A claim that the veteran was not present when a bomb was detonated leads to the veteran producing a photograph of himself and others with a mushroom cloud in the background. Then follows claims that the recorded dose of gamma radiation was not high enough to produce such an effect, the veteran was obviously spending too much time sunbathing etc.

Those who received very large beta doses had symptoms of trans-epidermal injury (dry and wet dermatitis, blisters and sore painful raw wounds) after a week or two. Unfortunately (or conveniently, for the MOD), medical doctors only had information on gamma doses (see below) and this is said to be too low to be the cause of such symptoms. For men who suffered these conditions it was put down to too much time in the sun or some other causation other than radiation.

Fallout beta (and alpha) radiation can also enter the bloodstream through wounds where the skin is broken or grazed, which happened often during work at nuclear weapon test locations. For the sufferers of trans-epidermal injury from large dose exposure to beta radiation, this would be another point of vulnerability in the already damaged environment of such locations.

Gamma Radiation

Gamma radiation is acute X-rays that penetrate all things. It is high dose, external and acute at the time of a nuclear detonation. It has almost exclusively been experienced by nuclear test veterans of all nuclear weapon powers.

To watch a nuclear bomb test detonation, a person should ideally be in a bunker with toughened, ideally tinted glass, to save the eyes from the blinding flash. For experimental purposes, the men were left in the open without any protective clothing or eyewear.

Gamma radiation and associated neutrons pass completely though the human body. As with all other forms of radiation effect, the damage can very often take 5, 10, 15 or even 30 years to become apparent. As with all radiation, even a low dosage is dangerous.

Using X-rays with pregnant mothers was banned only because of the pioneering work of Dr Alice Stewart in 1958. She showed that pre-birth X-rays involving only tiny amounts of gamma could cause leukaemia later on in childhood. However, she concluded that the huge increase in childhood leukaemia cases could not be explained solely by the low level of gamma radiation in X-rays; something else must be involved. Fallout from nuclear bomb tests was, she considered, a contributory environmental factor. She was vilified for even mentioning the possible connection – but X-ray of expectant mothers was stopped.

Alpha Radiation

Alpha radiation is extremely destructive but of limited range. Unlike beta and gamma radiation, the radioactive particles of alpha radiation cannot penetrate the skin. Alpha particles are difficult to detect and need special equipment and techniques to measure dose readings. The energy emitted is about 10 times greater than that of beta and gamma radiation. If ingested or inhaled into the body, alpha particles deliver more damage according to the time lodged in tissue, organs, bone and blood. For example, the residence time of an alpha particle of plutonium in the skeleton of a deceased individual is 200 years; that is, it would take 200 years for the body to remove half of it. Considering the life span of the average human, this type of radiation could be detected many years after death.

The assassination of the Russian dissident Alexander Litvinenko by ingestion of the alpha particle polonium-210 with a half-life of 138 days in 2006 is a recent and highly published account of the extreme toxicity of alpha radiation when inhaled or ingested into the body.

In an independent 2003 recommendation for radiation protection purposes regarding the health effects of radiation exposure, alpha and beta particles are regarded as chronic internal isotopic high risk radiation.

Dosimeters at nuclear weapon test locations only measured external gamma radiation. Veterans' agencies base all calculations on this dosage. They are then enabled to discount health damage to veterans because of the low recorded dose, as provided by the film badges worn by only about 1% of the participants. These badges did not record the external beta and neutron doses, gave no information on the internal alpha, beta and gamma dose and were only a poor estimate of the external gamma dose of the person wearing the badge. In many cases the badges were lost or the film ruined because of the high temperature and humidity.

In the American bomb test experiments, badges were worn by only 1 in 20 of the men dug into trenches close to ground zero. In the British experiments similar policy was adopted, and soldiers were ordered to crawl through the residual radioactive dust close to bomb detonation ground zeros.

The only personnel wearing respirators during the tests were government AWRE scientists. But then, they knew this was a priority. It is the only protection against alpha or beta particles being inhaled or ingested from the fallout or in any residual radiation.

A schism between physicists and biologists concerning the effects of radiation began in the 1920s. Through careful and profit-making lobbying of industrial corporations that radiation is harmless, the truth has been covered up for a hundred years.

The above need-to-know effects of radiation from the 1920s confirm that the UK Ministry of Defence has been aware of the effects of radiation for at least a century; to profess otherwise is a blatant lie.

Much of the need-to-know information in this book regarding the effects of radiation comes from the pen of Professor Karl Morgan (1907-1999), who worked with ionizing radiation for 56 years. In 1942 he was among the first scientists who worked on the Manhattan Project. His main expertise was as a nuclear health physicist. During his long career he was Professor of Health Physics at four leading universities in the USA. He is often referred to as 'the father of health physics' and noted as a gentleman of the old school and a man of quiet warmth.

At the end of his six-page essay 'Who is the Enemy?' in the book *In the Shadow of the Cloud* by Jim Lerager (Fulcrum books, 1988), Morgan said: "I have the horrible thought, what if some of the men not wearing a badge sat down on one of the 'hot' objects [i.e. objects emitting extremely high dose radiation] at five feet distance. The dose at contact could have been 100 times greater than recorded and there would be no record of the dose!"

Chapter 3: Opposition to Nuclear Tests

*"The nuclear establishment is conducting
a war against humanity."*
Dr John Gofman, former advisor to
the Atomic Energy Commission.

The advent of alpha radium's commercial use in the 1920s and the subsequent corporate cover-up of the biological health effects of this radiation had impact. It spawned a legacy of poor decision-making regarding public health that has persisted until today. It also opposed many scientists to radioactivity.

The ending of the Second World War by atomic bombs had made physicists the darlings of corporate business and governments. However, since 1945 many eminent biologists and others in academia, both in the UK and abroad, had noticed significant and unanswered confusion existed about the effects of radiation on long-term human health.

By the 1980s, the opposition to radioactivity had spread even wider. "A number of scientists have changed groups after becoming convinced that the risks are considerably greater than official estimates," wrote Dr Charles Sutcliffe, author of *The Dangers of Low Level Radiation* in 1985.

Dr Sutcliffe went on to say: "If a scientist joins the second group the consequences can be considerably to the disadvantage of his career. In order to carry out research into radiation risks a scientist needs access to the data, and also money and finances to study. Both of these essential factors can be removed or withheld from scientists who are known to think that radiation safety standards are too lax."

Yes, indeed. Nuclear veterans' archives have revealed a history strewn with the wreckage of careers of scientists and individuals who cherished scientific fact over corporate or political dogma.

In the months following the 1945 Hiroshima and Nagasaki atomic bombs, many scientists in Japan had doubts about the truth of the US scientists working with the US Army of occupation, who stated, "All deaths from the bombs have already occurred."

Any Japanese scientific papers expressing this view were impounded and US scientists took full control of the effects of radiation. The implication that 'all deaths from the bombing had already occurred' from the enormous heat of the fireball, the shockwave and the massive gamma radiation released at the time of detonation was undermined by the fact that residents of the two cities continued to die from a range of illnesses, in particular leukaemia, within seven years of the explosions. To prevent more genetically damaged children and stillbirths occurring, many Japanese women were forced to be sterilised.

Mixed message reports about the health effects of fallout from the bombing of Japan in 1945 was followed by excess leukaemia cases following atomic bomb tests in the Nevada Desert in the USA. Alarm bells had begun to ring again. The residual fallout of the bombing, which contained alpha and beta radiation, was being deliberately ignored.

In November 1951, just eleven months prior to the first British bomb test at Monte Bello, an eminent British biologist put pen to paper. Professor Alex Haddow (1907-1976), director of the Chester Beatty Research Institute, Royal Cancer Hospital from 1946-1969, noted that Sir John Cockcroft, director of the recently formed Atomic Energy Authority (AEA) supporting the nuclear industry, was being extremely evasive and unhelpful in answering many concerns regarding atmospheric nuclear bomb testing.

Professor Haddow wrote that questions asked by biologists of physicists had been met by what many believed was "a conspiracy of silence" enforced by "committees of stooges". Having read the report into the impact of the Nevada bomb tests and the number of leukaemia cases emerging from the bombing of Japan, he added at the end of his letter: "In the present case one realises that the risk to the population may be minimal, but one has in mind not the state of affairs today but what it may be in fifty years' time."

Cockcroft's response was a patronising put down. The die had been cast and a new nuclear power industry was planned – and nothing would be allowed to stand in its path. Britain was going to have its own nuclear deterrent and nuclear energy. The concerns of eminent biologists would not be allowed to stand in the way.

Science of any branch can only be trusted if it seeks the truth, is conducted with rigorous procedures and openness, and is guaranteed freedom from bias. Professor Haddow expressed fears that physicists would only provide the 'right' answers to concerns even though "all we require are the facts". The facts remained unanswered.

Professor Haddow's letter was written by him in his position as director of a prestigious institution researching cancer. He was an eminent physician and a pathologist. There is absolutely no possibility that he was not aware of the 1920s folly of the occupational exposure of humans to the effects of radiation when entering the body and the post-mortems indicating radiation ingestion. His letter was prompted by reports of huge numbers of leukaemia cases attributed to the bombing of Japan and nuclear bomb testing in the Nevada Desert.

Three score years and ten, traditionally noted as the lifespan of the human species in 1951, was being drastically shortened by the known man-made pathogens of physicists: radiation. In 2021, we can only guess the sense of frustration that Professor Haddow must have felt about radioactivity being deliberately released into the atmosphere. It takes little imagination to realise that Professor Haddow had very good reason for his concerns and fears for what physicists were unleashing upon humanity in the 1950s. The terrible cancer impact of global atmospheric nuclear bomb tests is still evident sixty years later.

William Shakespeare, as with much of his use of the English language, has the perfect words: "Time shall unfold what plaited cunning hides. Who cover faults, at last shame them derides."

The 'faults covered' is the schism of the 1950s between two main branches of science, biology and physics, with regard to covering up the effects of radiation on humanity. The 'derided shame', which still exists today, is the one so clearly and elegantly expressed in 1951 by Professor Alex Haddow: a shameful inability to tell the truth of science by the use of a "conspiracy of silence" and "committees of stooges" to give only the 'right' answers.

In 1962 Professor Haddow became president of the

Universal Union Against Cancer (now Union for International Cancer Control). By the mid-1960s he foresaw the extent to which bomb testing globally would escalate; the megaton hydrogen bomb yields that later forced an atmospheric bomb test ban signed by the three nuclear powers, the USA, USSR and Great Britain. He has been proved right in his concerns about atmospheric bomb testing. He lived to see all of this.

By this time many eminent physicists who had worked on the Manhattan Project had also become opposed to atmospheric nuclear bomb tests. However, a peer-reviewed scientific paper published in 2007 by an Emeritus Professor of Radiation Biology who had survived the atomic bombing of Japan as a 13-year-old explained how US scientists took control of the science of radiation damage to human health for radiological protection purposes.

In his paper *Cover-up of the effects of internal exposure by residual radiation from the atomic bombing of Hiroshima and Nagasaki,* Professor Shoji Sawada showed how atomic bomb fallout, the causation and prime source of legacy ill-heath of Japanese victims, was covered up by US scientists immediately they entered Japan.

Robert Holmes, Director of the Atomic Bomb Casualty Commission (ABCC), was tasked with portraying survivors of the Japanese bombing as 'the most important people in the world'. The 100,000 people killed at a stroke by the heat, gamma radiation and shockwave of the bombing were brushed aside through proclamations that the atomic bomb was the means by which to prevent all future wars. The physicists who had created the horror sought deliverance from their sins by claiming nuclear power could be safely harnessed for cheap energy and unlimited prosperity.

But however hard the ABCC tried to hide it – and every method was used – the fact was 'the most important people in the world' began, within seven years of Hiroshima and Nagasaki, to die or fall seriously ill in their thousands. Man-made radioactivity – even at low levels, as had been seen in the 1920s – could not by any stretch of the imagination be seen as anything other than harmful. Despite attempts to dub the afflicted survivors as suffering from 'an atomic plague', their illnesses – leukaemia, radiation sickness, illness and deformity passed on to unborn children, even to those yet to be conceived – was the true legacy of inhaled or ingested fallout.

This was extremely unhelpful news for the politicians, the military and nuclear industrialists, who realised the ABCC cover-up was not working. Something further had to be done because the truth of the effects of radiation would destroy all the plans they had for future prosperity.

Research funds for the ABCC were quickly switched to only treat survivors whilst avoiding at all costs exploring what had caused their illnesses and premature deaths.

The attempted cover-up by the ABCC led in the 1950s to the setting up of a radiation dose risk model based only on gamma radiation released at the time of a nuclear weapon detonation. This health risk model, eventually formulated by the International Commission for Radiological Protection (ICRP), totally ignores the acute long-term legacy health issues (for example, leukaemia and a wide range of other illnesses) induced by the inhalation, ingestion or possible entry into the bloodstream through cuts or abrasions to the skin of alpha and beta radioactive fallout particles.

The model formed the basis of policy to ensure that film badge dosimeters were only to be worn by about 1% of all armed forces personnel at nuclear weapon test locations. However, fallout particles do not register on film badges, therefore they were totally incapable of recording the dose of alpha and beta radioactivity. Only gamma radiation was recorded.

It is simple to describe the difference in comparable radiation risk between gamma radiation and fallout radiation. Imagine you are sitting by a red-hot coal fire. You can feel the heat radiating from the fire (i.e. gamma radiation) but it poses no long-term health risks to you. However, it would not be advisable to take a red-hot coal from the fire (alpha and beta fallout particle) and swallow it, as this would emit radiation internally and could damage or even destroy blood, tissue, organs or bone.

In the 1950s, the UK Government issued a flurry of top-secret archive documents confirming knowledge held by them that they wished to hide.

In 1956, the UK Medical Research Council (MRC) sent a secret report to the Government. It contained a warning that if nuclear testing continued, serious genetic damage could be caused to the population. The UK Prime Minister at the time, Sir Anthony Eden, responded in an internal memo: "It is a pity, but it cannot be helped."

Another widely circulated internal telex referring to the MRC report stated: "We do not want you to release any statement on the genetic effects of radiation. If you have to, a safer interpretation of the MRC report would be 'has not shown an increase' rather than 'shows an increase'."

As is always the case with the nuclear issue of power and prestige, this was not a time to listen to the voices of medical or other experts. The central decisions by this time were firmly being made by very few: the UK Ministry of Defence, Atomic Weapons Establishment and the Cabinet Office. The arms race was accelerating, and the UK desperately needed to work towards a thermo-nuclear megaton nuclear bomb to ensure its seat on the United Nations Security Council and to gain more information to assist a growing nuclear power industry.

A top-secret document entitled *Biological Investigations at Atomic Bomb Test Tests in Australia, 1956* [The National Archives DO 35/5493 251322], in its entirety, read as follows:

"The United Kingdom and Australian Governments have agreed that investigation of the biological effects of atomic weapons shall be carried out during trials at Maralinga in 1956. The possible effects of the ingestion of radioactive fallout (by men and animals – redacted) will be among the subjects studied. The work is sponsored by the Medical and Agricultural Research Councils Service Departments, and Home Office, and the Ministry of Agriculture, Fisheries, and Food of the United Kingdom, in close collaboration with Australian departments and agencies such as the Atomic Energy Commission, the Department of Health, the Commonwealth Scientific and Industrial Research Organisation, and Australian universities. The studies are being undertaken for the purpose of devising more effective methods for the protection of population, and agricultural production, in the event of a nuclear war.

The information obtained will be of considerable value in

relation to the peaceful use of nuclear energy. Effective precautions have already been developed to avoid hazards to the population from the use of nuclear reactors, nevertheless in view of the expected wide use of reactors it is prudent that every opportunity be taken to further our knowledge of the effects of radioactive contamination. Atomic bomb trials provide a unique opportunity for studying some aspects of this subject.

A few sheep and small animals will be used in part of the biological work at Maralinga. The conditions to which the animals are subjected will be similar to those which have applied for many years in medical, biological, and defence scientific establishments. Elaborate arrangements for the welfare of the animals are being made, and the scientists who will be in charge have wide experience of this type of work in the United Kingdom and in Australia."

In this document 'the conditions to which the animals are subjected' was noted. No mention was made regarding the conditions of the servicemen, who were ordered to crawl through the dust at short distance from bomb detonations.

It came as no surprise to nuclear veterans when this document turned up in the 1990s. Despite the effects of the ingestion of radioactive fallout already being well known from the dial-painters, the Manhattan Project, the bombing of Japan, the Nevada tests, and Monte Bello, none of the nuclear veterans at weapon test locations had any personal protection equipment or respirators.

By this time the men were used to a standard practice of 'indoctrination' of standing to face a bomb without any protective equipment. Men were also ordered to fly through the mushroom clouds. The above was all the fun of the fair, carried out allegedly to help develop safety equipment for nuclear industry workers. The intent was to enable the men, at the height of the Cold War, to return to their units and say: "I've stood close to a nuclear bomb detonation and it has done me no harm." This, of course, conveniently ignored the legacy of ill health and premature deaths that would not manifest for 5, 10 or even 30 more years.

However, the document DO 35/ 5493 251322, *Biological Investigations at Atomic Bomb Tests in Australia, 1956,* would prove to be an Achilles' heel to Australian Prime Minister Sir Robert Menzies' lie that 'no conceivable harm' would come to Australian servicemen and the population. It would expose the historic lack of integrity, ethics and morality used with regard to scientific data on fallout. Finally, it would lead Canberra to tell London that any proposed thermonuclear bomb tests of much higher yield would not be able to be carried out on the Australian continent, as Britain had hoped, but would have to go elsewhere.

Sir Ernest Titterton, a nuclear scientist who had helped fire the world's first atomic bomb – Trinity – in 1945 at Los Alamos, was head of the Atomic Safety Committee for the British nuclear weapon test series led by Sir William Penney. The power, prestige and profit mode of bomb testing was at full height with these two former members of the Manhattan Project, and their objective was to keep Australia fully in the dark regarding the science around the health effects of radiation.

By 1956, three atomic bombs had already been detonated in Australia. As a result of a change of wind direction, the first

British bomb in 1952 at Monte Bello, off the NW coast, had resulted in fallout recorded all the way across the Northern Territory to the east coast of Australia at Cairns, Townsville and Brisbane. The highest recordings were at Broome and Onslow. Thirty years later at the Royal Commission in London (see Chapter Five), it was admitted that the dose rates recorded by Titterton's safety committee were 10 times higher than had been made public.

Hedley Marston, who was oblivious to the full extent of fallout damage from the Monte Bello bomb, had, in 1956, established himself as a respected biochemist working for the newly established Commonwealth Scientific and Industrial Research Organisation (CSIRO). His speciality was agricultural science and when his expertise was called upon for the above biological investigations, in joint collaboration with Australia and the UK, he was naturally thrilled at the opportunity to make use of his scientific skills.

As the reckless impact of fallout from the Maralinga bomb testing became apparent to him, he became a 'whistle blower', standing up against the authorities of both governments over the lies told about the continental fallout over Australia.

It was a very brave decision to make because, as a newly appointed member of the Atomic Safety Committee (ASC), Dr Hedley Marston had signed the Official Secrets Act. His authority from ASC leader Sir Ernest Titterton was to investigate the impact of fallout within 100 miles of the Maralinga nuclear weapon test site, not the whole of Australia – and certainly not to go public with his findings.

It can be discerned from records held by nuclear veterans that the whole ethos of the Official Secrets Act during the Cold War was to ensure those working at the test locations were compartmentalised on a 'need to know' basis based on their own speciality. To go outside this remit and discuss with anyone else what they were doing would be a certain invitation to be prosecuted under the Official Secrets Act, which, for nuclear test veterans and others over the years, has become a *de facto* means of burying the truth.

I served at Maralinga for just under a year in 1965/6, by which time the whole area was contaminated with residual radiation. The message given to all servicemen was that the area was perfectly safe because major atmospheric bomb tests had finished seven years earlier; no mention was made of the 600 or so 'minor' atmospheric tests carried out between 1953 and 1963, which released quantities of highly toxic beryllium, plutonium and uranium into the atmosphere.

Although I was at Maralinga a decade after Hedley Marston started his monitoring of radioactive fallout there, I was oblivious to the extent of it until the mid-1990s when I read accounts of Marston's whistle blowing. I admire this man because he understood the importance of the facts of science over the false dogma of politicians and bureaucrats regarding the hazards of radioactivity to human health. He had the mindset of many biologists, such as Haddow in 1951, who had discovered the evasiveness of governments when it came to radiation risk; that is, he was interested in the impact of radiation on life, not death.

For years the Australian public had been repeatedly assured that no significant fallout had occurred during the nuclear tests. Whilst both the Australian and UK Governments continued to sing from the same devil's hymn sheet of deception regarding radioactive fallout, Hedley Marston, as an ethical scientist, set out to establish the truth.

During the 1956 biological investigations, Marston was chosen to conduct a survey to find how much beta iodine-131 from fallout was being absorbed into sheep's thyroids. He decided it was pointless to just check the fallout 100 miles from Maralinga, as was his remit from the Atomic Safety Committee. He was determined to go beyond the remit and find out just how far the radioactivity had spread.

Unbeknown to Titterton and Penney, he set up 34 monitoring stations across the northern part of Australia. Then Marston sat in his laboratory in Adelaide and waited for the arrival of the sheep thyroids. After completing his analysis, he was completely shocked. Thyroids from Alice Springs and Rockhampton showed radiation levels 400 times higher than expected.

Titterton's Atomic Safety Committee did not want to acknowledge this and put out press reports that levels were within safe limits; the message of Menzies' edict 'No danger' was fed to the Australian public.

As an avid devotee to the doctrine that the truth of science was of greater value than the wrecking ball of politics, Marston had no intention of bending his findings to suit protectionist dogma. He accused the Atomic Safety Committee of lying to the Australian people. He then wrote to a friend, nuclear physicist Mark Oliphant, director of the Research School of Physical Science and Engineering, who had been part of the Manhattan team that had built the first atomic bomb.

Oliphant had happily worked on the Manhattan Project in the belief that the awesome power of atomic weapons would never be used. He thought of the bomb as just a deterrent to end World War Two; when two were actually dropped on

Japan he said he was absolutely appalled at what it had done to human beings. This sentiment led to Oliphant being excluded from the joint Australian and UK team assembled for the Australian bomb tests approved by PM Sir Robert Menzies.

Marston stepped up his attack on the ethics of the Maralinga tests and the Atomic Safety Committee, which he publicly referred to as a "quasi-scientific pantomime under the cloak of secrecy and evasive lying by government authorities about the hazard of fallout; apparently the people of Whitehall and Canberra think the people of northern Australia are expendable."

So, after the Operation Buffalo series of four major atomic bomb tests at Maralinga ended on 22 Oct 1956, Marston secretly set up his own monitoring stations on the rooftops of Adelaide, close to his laboratory. He checked the measurements and was shocked to find radiation levels at 96,000, when 20,000 was normal. The thyroid results were higher than the readings from the north; they were 5,000 times higher than normal.

But Titterton's safety committee still assured the public that radiation had not spread outside of the Maralinga test site location, some 500 miles to the west. Marston was furious. His anger was not just about the betrayal of public trust but that fellow scientists could ignore scientific facts and involve themselves in a politically motivated cover-up.

Hanging over his head was the Official Secrets Act, used as a gagging order (as nuclear test veterans realised, decades later, when it was used as an excuse to stop their questions). Anyone who had signed the Act and then discussed radioactive fallout with anyone else was threatened with jail. But Marston continued to accuse the safety committee of lying and said that the Maralinga tests would increase thyroid cancer in humans.

He asserted that radioactive iodine would enter the food chain, and he also found, through analysis of milk, that fallout beta radiation strontium-90, with a half-life of 28 years, would bind to the bones in children. Marston explained: "There is a very serious likelihood that internal radiation from strontium-90 may, after a number of years, result in many painful deaths from cancer of the bone." His monitoring also showed that contaminated rain had fallen on areas 1,500 miles from Maralinga – including Adelaide in South Australia, and Brisbane in Queensland.

Titterton spun the story to the press that Australia had the lowest rates of strontium-90 in the world. He added that the British tests had not impacted on Australia. Behind closed doors, Sir William Penney said that Marston's report could be restricted circulation on 'political grounds'. It is almost certainly possible that Marston was only not formally arrested because this would have drawn attention to the 'problem' he, Titterton and the Australian politicians were facing.

Many years later, the Australian Minister Howard Beale, who Prime Minister Menzies had made responsible for the tests, wrote in his memoirs that Marston's revelations about fallout had created a massive problem for Canberra and could have cost him his job.

It's an interesting remark. Beale was more worried about his job than the health of the Australian population.

So, the political solution was that Hedley Marston was taken off the job for 'health reasons', he was smeared, irrespective of his political leanings, as a 'Red Commie', and his attempts to interfere with defence preparations were due to contact with 'left wing scientists'. It seemed the only way to discredit the work of an eminent scientist whose work could not possibly be factually discredited was to discredit or disgrace the man instead.

But Marston was not alone. Many leading scientists globally were waking up to the fact that atmospheric nuclear bomb testing was impacting on the human population and becoming a threat to the entire planet.

In Britain, Joseph Rotblat, who set up the Association of Atomic Scientists, was warning that even a small dose of radiation above normal background levels could increase legacy cancer in later years. Mark Oliphant, another member of the Manhattan Project team, attended a scientific conference opposing bomb testing in Pugwash, Canada, which concluded that strontium-90 from bomb fallout could universally harm the human race. And Nobel prize winner Linus Pauling calculated that each bomb detonation would result in at least 15,000 children being sacrificed – and the megaton arms race had barely begun.

In the schism between biologists – the science of the study of life forms – and physicists – the science that had created the wings of death at Los Alamos – eminent scientists from both branches were forming a consensus: radioactivity is extremely harmful.

Hedley Marston died in 1965. He lived to see the July 1963 atmospheric test ban treaty signed by the US, USSR and Great Britain; President John F Kennedy's speech (see Chapter Four) is ample explanation of the truth of Hedley Marston's monitoring of fallout. Two days before he died, Marston received academic accolades for his whistle blowing. As a testament to the efficacy of his findings, Sir Ernest Titterton confirmed the truth of the science by deciding Marston's warnings about strontium-90 in the bones of babies and young children was an excellent opportunity to actually find out what effect the use of nuclear bombs would have on a vast area of Australia.

In fact, an official record stored deep in the British National Archives confirmed Titterton's obsession with Marston's findings on strontium-90. Titled *Arrangements for the Determination of Strontium-90 Fallout in Australia,* DEFE 16/808, it included the following direction from Titterton: "Bring me the bones of Australian babies – the more the better."

When tasked with monitoring fallout in the biological investigations at Maralinga, Marston said he could do a better scientific job than the Pommies' so-called version of the truth – and he lived up to this assertion magnificently. Titterton was so impressed by Marston's monitoring he needed to know more.

Looking back, it is sad that Hedley Marston has not been formally recognised in his home nation for the stance he took. His concern was for the truth of science and for the health of the Australian people. But the collaboration between Australia and the United Kingdom runs far deeper than any consideration for such ethics and morality. Australia provided the uranium and Britain built the bombs. Both needed each other in the quest for power, prestige and profit. Sir Robert Menzies had sold the soul of his nation down the river to the underworld of Hades.

A treaty between the two nations in 1993 sealed a devil's pact to continue to collaborate together to avoid any compensation. This treaty appears to be the result of the failure of the Australian Royal Commission's attempt to land a blow for truth and justice; a political fudge, and a missed opportunity for accountability. (See Chapter Five.)

In 1958, a secret meeting took place on Christmas Island, attended by the Atomic Weapons Research Establishment (AWRE) scientists. The minutes reveal the presence of senior military officers. The AWRE scientists insisted their personnel be blood-tested for "medico-legal reasons"; that is, for the possibility of future legal claims for damage. This blood-testing request was referred to the Ministry of Defence and rejected. Many veterans believe this was the moment when the Ministry of Defence became the sole arbiter on radiation risk and damage to health. It was no longer a remit of the health and safety experts, or medical staff; it was placed entirely in the hands of the MOD and their contractual partner, the AWRE.

In 1959, when the International Commission on Radiological Protection (ICRP) and the World Health Organisation (WHO) met behind closed doors, they entered into an agreement that effectively 'gagged' the WHO from making any comment on radiation as a causal link to illness...

Chapter 4: Extent of UK Experimental Nuclear Tests

"There is nothing hid, which shall not be manifested.
Neither was anything kept secret,
but that it would come abroad."
Mark 4:22

By June 1956, the serious hazard of radioactivity to human health was already well known to the UK Government. Occupational deaths from ingested radium in the 1920s, the Manhattan Project and the Trinity bomb, the bombing of Japan, Nevada bomb tests, and the atmospheric nuclear tests at Monte Bello Island (three) and Emu Field (two), which averaged 23.6 kilotons each, had all exposed more and more scientific truths.

The stage was now set for seven final atmospheric nuclear bomb tests, to take place at Maralinga, South Australia between September 1956 and October 1957, in preparation for extending the UK's experimental nuclear tests to thermo-nuclear megaton yield at the Pacific atoll of Christmas Island.

These final tests were essential to further advance knowledge of the biological impact of the effects of ingested fallout on servicemen and animals. Running parallel to this blatant 'guinea pig' investigation were 600 or so minor trials to assist with development of the trigger mechanism for the Christmas Island test series. By now, Hedley Marston had exposed the lies of the Australian Prime Minister and the UK Atomic Safety Committee, led by Sir Ernest Titterton; it was known that radioactive fallout knew no boundaries, but the wheels of the band wagon of deception were coming off as it still rumbled along.

Debate of the accumulated scientific knowledge about nuclear weapons came to a head in the UK House of Commons in July 1956, a mere eleven years after the end of World War Two. This was a pivotal moment in history, when truth overtook the political lie that bomb testing could be done without any 'conceivable injury'.

On 16 July 1956, and 18 months from conception, the motion for the debate had been made, and the question was proposed: "That this House take note of the Report on the Hazards to Man of Nuclear and Allied Radiations." (Command order paper No. 9780 – Mr Turton.)

For a matter of such significant impact on human health and potential life – and death – changing impact globally, the debate took less than three hours. It was purely procedural; no vote of acceptance or otherwise was in the remit.

The Medical Research Council report of 1956 is a seven-part, 128-page document of scientific investigation by a nominated committee of 16 of the most eminent academics of the United Kingdom; that is, 11 professors and three Knights of the Realm, under the chairmanship of Sir Harold Himsworth, secretary of the Medical Research Council. Notable in the context of this book, Professor Alex Haddow was a member of the committee and also Sir John Cockcroft, director of the Atomic Energy Authority (AEA), so both sides of the biological and physicist schism of science were present. This was probably the debate that confirmed Professor Haddow's fears, expressed in 1951, that 'the possibility that purely military considerations will override any other advice'.

The report clearly indicated the efficacy of the serious

hazards of fallout and genetic damage, and yet the advice was politically ignored for military reasons.

Dr Edith Summerskill (1901-1980), MP for Warrington opened the debate. At the time this redoubtable lady was, at 55, a Member of Parliament, a Doctor of Medicine and a noted feminist. She was, therefore, not a push-over by any means. Far from it; she'd lived through two world wars and in 1949 had become a Privy Counsellor, having served as a minister in Clement Attlee's post war Labour Government.

During the middle years of WWII, at a time when women were not allowed to be members of the civilian Home Guard militia, she had formed the Woman's Home Defence, some of whose members went on to form their own groups, like the Amazon Defence Corps. During this time Dr Summerskill taught weapons training and basic military discipline. She was, therefore, a formidable and knowledgeable politician of a kind seldom seen in politics today, more's the pity.

Dr Summerskill opened the debate by saying: "I had the privilege of moving and urging the government to give further consideration to the long-term and remote effect of continuing nuclear explosions. Subsequently, the Prime Minister announced 'a representative conference would convene and consider the matter under the chairmanship of Sir Harold Himsworth'."

She continued: "Now that this report of the Medical Research Council is published, we must become, if we are to take our duty to humanity and posterity seriously, more alert to the appalling potential dangers of this new form of energy." She explained the knowledge already acquired: "Strontium in fallout can contaminate drinking water, crops or soil where it can be absorbed by the plants. Subsequently, man and animal will receive strontium both in their food and in their water." (This was almost a word by word reading of the intent of the top-secret biological investigations report in 1956 at Maralinga.)

"Strontium is easily absorbed and then stored for long periods in the bones of the body. Here it can give rise to bone tumours and, by irradiating the bone marrow, to aplastic anaemia or leukaemia. Most of the scientific bodies who have investigated this matter support the conclusions on the subject. The evidence that the young are more likely to develop these conditions is quite clear. One of the most revealing studies is the relationship between radiation dose and the incidence of leukaemia," Dr Summerskill continued. "The results, compared with those recorded of leukaemia among the populations of Hiroshima and Nagasaki exposed to radiation from atom bombs, provide clear evidence of the relationship between dose of radiation and the incidence of leukaemia. The findings of the United States report [the Nevada bomb tests] and the Medical Research Council committee are substantially the same about the danger of strontium in fallout."

This, of course, confirms the obsessive edict of the Maralinga Atomic Safety Committee's chairman Sir Ernest Titterton, at the end of the biological investigations of 1956 and Hedley Marston's findings on strontium-90 fallout, when Titterton stated: "Bring me the bones of Australian babies – the more the better."

In her opening address in the 16 July 1956 debate, Dr Summerskill brought the House of Commons' attention to page 80, para 4 (b) of the MRC report, which emphasized the effect of strontium in the bones. "Account must be taken, however, of the internal radiation from radioactive strontium which is beginning to accumulate in the bone. If the firing [of nuclear bombs] increases and in particular if greater number of thermonuclear weapons are used, we could within the lifetime of many now living be approaching levels at which ill effects might produce in a small number of the population. In my opinion, this constitutes a most serious warning." Dr Summerskill then added: "Following a report issued by the United States Atomic Energy Commission, particular importance was attached to the genetic changes likely to ensue from the exposure to radiation."

(The Combined History Archive of Nuclear Veterans (CHANV) shows that genetic damage increasingly became known to science. The Russians as well as the UK began cytogenetic blood testing in the 1960s. The Russians checked their own armed forces and industrial workers. In the UK, members of the armed forces have been denied such advanced investigative diagnosis since the testing ended in 1967. This diagnostic technology was solely controlled by, and use denied by, the UK Ministry of Defence until a study of nuclear test participants was published independently in New Zealand and double peer reviewed in 2009. See mention in Chapters Eight to Ten.)

Dr Summerskill's well-constructed address continued by saying that the MRC committee gave "careful consideration to the likely effects of genetic changes doubling the national rate of mutations and the amount of radiation likely to double the amount." And she added: "Sufficient knowledge is not yet available but a recent letter by Professor TBS Haldane in the *Lancet* suggested that in some respect there has been an underestimation of the dose required for possible genetic effects of exposure to ionising radiation."

(In the view of CHANV, any lack of knowledge is probably due to the ABCC's cover-up of fallout effects when entering Japan in 1945 and the 'conspiracy of silence' by the newly established UK Atomic Energy Authority, directed by Sir John Cockcroft. This was a cover-up and conspiracy that eminent biologists believed was being run by 'committees of stooges' of physicists who did not answer questions regarding the hazards of radiation.)

Mr Leslie Hale, MP for Oldham and a solicitor, interjected that, having spoken to a member of the MRC committee, apparently the committee was not called upon to consider all the genetic facts.

This comes as no surprise to nuclear veterans because, when assisting lawyers acting on behalf of the veterans in the 2000s (see Chapter Seven – Gathering the Evidence), we were told genetic effects and some other matters were not even considered within their remit of evidence required. Genetics has remained a sensitive area but is absolutely necessary when considering the overall betrayal that has taken place over many decades.

However, at the 1956 debate Dr Summerskill responded to Hale's interjection by saying that the MRC committee was of the opinion that "the level of radiation [required to produce a genetic effect] should not be more than twice the natural background level of radiation and it might be appreciably lower." She went further to say the biggest dose addition to natural background radiation in 1956 was 22%, from hospital diagnostic radiology, and that this must give us great concern when you consider radiological use in hospitals was now about five times higher than it was in 1952. (This was dealt with when X-ray was dropped for use on expectant mothers following the ground-breaking research of Dr Alice Stewart, who we discussed in Chapter Two. Dr Stewart also studied workers at the Hanford plutonium production plant in Washington USA and demonstrated that, even at low level doses, radiation is a substantial occupational health hazard.)

Dr Summerskill went on to say that X-ray used in 1956 for fitting shoes especially for school children, the luminous dials of watches, projection equipment and radiology department equipment in hospitals (the risk of all of which is now recognised) was increasing the radiation hazard by small degrees of danger annually.

The Minister for Health in the debate adopted an air of sophistry, as often used in politics; that is, seeming clever but being false and misleading, by taking the complacent attitude that he was not apparently aware of the most serious conclusions of the MRC report which he had appointed the committee to discuss. He was, in fact, making every effort to downplay the dangers of fallout and genetic damage and switch the debate to the less dangerous concern of X-ray being used to measure and fit children's shoes.

Dr Summerskill, however, quickly put the minister in the picture on more serious nuclear events relating to health. She quoted remarks made just 17 days earlier, before the Symington Senate Committee, by an outspoken Secretary of Defence in the USA, Mr Charles Wilson, which had been reported in the Manchester Guardian: "Our capability of inflicting devastation is not at stake. It is improving and will continue to improve."

She also quoted General James Gavin, Chief of Army Research and Development in the US, who, when asked 'If we had a nuclear war and our air force made a major assault against Russia with nuclear weapons so that the prevailing winds would carry the fallout over Russia, what would be the effect in the way of deaths?' replied with: "Current planning estimates run on the order of several million deaths, depending on which way the wind blew. If south east, they would mainly be in the USSR, although this fallout will extend to Japan and perhaps to the Philippines area. If the wind blew the other way, deaths would extend well back into Western Europe."

Dr Summerskill said this US report confirmed paragraph 290, page 69 of the MRC report: "Given sufficient number of bombs, no part of the world will escape exposure to biologically sufficient levels of radiation. To a greater or lesser degree, a legacy of genetic damage would be incurred and an increased incidence of delayed effects on individuals would be induced. Apparently only the wind will determine whether the same bomb will destroy an enemy or an ally or damage them genetically. As the wind is not confined to frontiers, the lethal fallout which is carried may affect both enemy and ally equally."

This Medical Research Council report made it blindingly obvious that increasing the weapon testing with higher nuclear yields was reckless. Whether or not the 1956 MRC report had been read and/or debated in Canberra, the report findings on genetic damage had historic impact. Australian Dr Hedley Marston's discovery (outside the Official Secrets Act remit) in 1956 that significant radioactive fallout covered all points of the compass of Australia was an alarm call to politicians. The maverick biochemist had found that, following the atmospheric bomb testing of kiloton yield atomic bombs, significant radioactive fallout was not just limited to a 100-mile radius of Maralinga and Monte Bello Island; it was found all over the continent.

Meanwhile, in Britain the Medical Research Council report on the hazards of radiation was critical of plans to expand testing to higher yields. That is, to atmospherically test megaton thermo-nuclear hydrogen bombs at megaton yield i.e. ten times greater than the yields of the kiloton atomic weapons so far tested.

This altered the minds of the Australian Government towards the atmospheric bomb testing weapon in Australia from 1957. The British venue for higher yield megaton bomb tests was shifted to Christmas Island in the Pacific Ocean and the possibility of any future detonations of large kiloton or other atmospheric nuclear bomb tests at Maralinga from was sent packing by the Australian government.

In the space of the next 40 years, Australia went from the compliant conspirators of Sir Robert Menzies to a realisation that they had been kept in the dark, to enragement enough to make a song and dance about it all in London to the Royal Commission of 1985 (see Chapter Five: Reckless Conduct), only then to finally return in 1993 to a mutual co-operation treaty with the UK to avoid responsibility or any possible compensation claims.

Five days before the 16 July debate in the House of Commons, the United States exploded its biggest yield nuclear weapon to date, a thermo-nuclear hydrogen bomb in excess of one megaton. Not that these facts were widely known at the time. The press were double-handcuffed by both the Official Secrets Act and 'D' notices to prevent publicity of anything remotely critical of government.

During the 1956 debate, Richard Fort, MP for Clitheroe commented: "When I saw on the Order Paper today that there was to be a debate on nuclear and allied radiations, I was struck by the fact that eighteen months ago when the Government set up the committee whose report we are now supposed to be discussing, the order had the more dramatic title 'Nuclear Explosions and the Genetic Effects'." He concluded: "It is obvious from the extraordinary clear summary in the Medical Research Council report that a great deal less is known than one would have thought when some of the generalisations were being made 18 months ago." Maybe the Health Minister who set up the MRC committee was as naïve as the public. From the perspective of 2021, here is a case of 'wake up, everyone and smell the coffee'. Nothing much appears to change in politics.

In the debate, Mr Fort expanded his thoughts. "An enormous amount of long-term research work, particularly in genetic effects of radiation, has to be carried out. It will go on for the rest of the century, and a good deal longer." (Just as Professor Haddow and other eminent biologists had feared in 1951.)

Mr Leslie Hale, a solicitor and MP for Oldham who had spoken to a member of the Medical Research Council, stated during the hearing that the MRC report committee was not called upon to consider all the genetic facts and, as the eminent biologist, Professor Alex Haddow had feared in 1951, research would carry on for 50 years to find out the real biological damage at a cellular level. This in fact has been the case and the results are now well known but still not talked about.

The forthright solicitor then asked: "Is the Hon. Member suggesting that we continue research work for a century, dropping bombs all the time to see what happens to three generations of the population?"

Well, that's not exactly what happened. But it's an accurate forecast of future events. In 1952, the 30,000-plus servicemen who would eventually attend nuclear weapon test locations had been recognised as the ideal experimental cohort: young, fit, vulnerable, politically neutered, naïve and therefore ideal to be abused and abandoned. The servicemen were considered perfect candidates for research that ended with three generations showing genetic damage by 2021. The causal link to teratogenic effect – that is, the occurrence of physical defects in the foetus, such as malformed limbs and stillbirths, in the offspring of a nuclear veteran – was admitted in 1956 by the government-appointed Medical Research Council committee composed of the UK's finest scientific brains. In 1996, a British Army Brigadier in a NATO directive confirmed it again as a potential hazard to the offspring of veterans who had handled depleted uranium tactical weapons. (See Chapter Seven: Gathering the Evidence.)

In the 1956 debate Mr Hale continued by saying that he agreed with Dr Summerskill's wide knowledge on the subject except for one point: "It is not the generals who are to blame. It is always the bishops and the politicians who plead for mass weapons and mass extermination – the politicians protect their dignity and the bishops protect their faith. This has gone on throughout the centuries, and now we have to face this issue at its most serious."

Regarding fallout, Mr Hale made note that: "Welsh sheep on the mountains are now showing signs of absorption of strontium far in excess of that at the time when the report was written." (A similar spike occurred in 1985 following fallout from Chernobyl in rain over the Welsh mountains.) "It is alright talking about 100 years," Mr Hale said, "but much of the world lives at heights above the Welsh mountains." Regarding genetic damage, he added: "The scientists knew the radiation is dangerous, it will damage bones, especially of the young but we do not believe it will produce a genetic effect, merely destroy life of the person exposed and is not transmitted genetically."

Of course, it's now self-evident in 2021 that scientists back then had not perhaps yet fully grasped the fact that fallout does not fall evenly and therefore thinly spread radiation over an area. The radiation is deposited in high density in rainfall and this is more likely over high ground. Also, unlike a biological virus, the genetic impact is transmitted to future generations through radiation-induced mutations in the genome, as indicated by chromosomal aberrations in the DNA of persons exposed to radiation.

The debate brought to notice that: "It is no use saying that gene-mutations can only affect one individual; they can soon affect the whole human race." Professor Haldane (mentioned earlier in the debate) had stated in the *Lancet* that the genetic damage question was seriously underestimated by the MRC report.

The efficacy of genetic mutation had in fact been confirmed much earlier in medical history. Mr Hale had spoken with Professor Haldane prior to the debate and was told that: "A spontaneous mutation of one spermatozoa in the testicle of the Duke of Kent in 1818 brought about the Russian Revolution because, as a result of that single mutation, Queen Victoria became a carrier of haemophilia, which did not affect her family, but she passed it on to the Royal Family dynasty of the Romanovs in Tsarist Russia." With the same black humour, the Professor also said, following a meeting with visiting scientists from Japan in 1954, "It was clear when we hear of births of two-headed children and so on, we know genetic damage is not one of the branches of science in which it can be said that 'two heads are better than one'."

For eminent scientists, the consensus opinion in 1956 was that the Pandora's box of horror mentioned at the end of Chapter One had not only been opened, but was now fully understood by both biologists and physicists on the Medical Research Council committee advising the United Kingdom's political leaders.

Mr Hale insisted during the debate that the Health Minister, Mr Turton, was wrong to be downplaying the findings of the report. Mr Hale said Turton was "as usual, completely wrong. The Medical Research Council's report dealt with the leukaemia produced by the genetic results. The MRC made it quite clear that it had considered the leukaemia results of the bombs at Hiroshima and Nagasaki – but had had no evidence upon genetic results other than leukaemia, some of which are manifesting themselves now."

(In 2021, this trait of ministers protecting government policy and backbench Members of Parliament being unconvinced by the ministers' sophistry is still a well-established strategy to avoid the truth.)

During the debate Mr Hale had to endure frequent interruptions and stated if anyone wished to interrupt again: "Let him give me some figures on the genetic effects, excluding leukaemia, of the bombs dropped on Hiroshima and Nagasaki. These are matters of great importance to the world. The whole question of genetic effects is one of supreme importance."

Mr Charles Orr-Ewing, MP for Hendon North, confirmed, in his words, that "the interjections were aimed to switch the debate away from the report and play down any hazards."

Dr Barnett Stross, MP for Stoke on Trent, said about the

report: "Can we imagine if we had given them different terms of reference, what they would have been saying to us about the danger of expansion of [nuclear] tests, and in particular, if we become so lunatic that we involve ourselves in a world war?" He added that they would say "we should not be concerned because, unlike other countries, we do not live out-of-doors and have very frail and unsubstantial houses that protect them."

The comment by Dr Stross that other countries had "unsubstantial houses" and lived "out-of-doors" and, therefore, if different terms of reference had been given to the Medical Research Council for their 1956 report this is what the Government would have said, is not an entirely incredible assumption.

During the Cold War the government had an underground facility equipped with water, electricity and air circulation, on hand for officials etc. to move into to continue government business in the event of a nuclear war. The civilian population, substantial housing or not, would have woken up to find their houses completely flattened and providing no protection from radioactive fallout.

Without being able to talk to Dr Barnett Stross today, it can only be assumed his remark during the debate was made tongue in cheek, perhaps to annoy the government. His comment did, however, raise a fine point of interest. Nuclear veterans also lived and worked mainly out-of-doors, without protective clothing, and slept in tents or flimsy huts, all in close proximity to thermo-nuclear hydrogen bombs or atomic bombs and the residual fallout thereof. It appears the Government now embarked on biological experiments at Maralinga and later at Christmas Island had another 'unique opportunity' not only to continue researching the possible effect of ingesting or inhaling fallout but also to investigate the genetic effects of persons exposed. The men were now admitted as expendable and within 50 years the Government got the answers they so desperately sought.

One fact is clear from the 1956 debate. Dr Edith Summerskill was not speaking in support of the government. From the full Hansard report, this applied also to others. In terms of reference, this short three-hour debate on a matter of health concerns was not binding on government. Decisions made as a result of the debate on whether or not the yield of bombs was to increase from 1957 onwards rested only in the hands of the Prime Minister, Sir Anthony Eden. Having read the MRC report and the warnings with regard to genetic damage, he decided: "It's a pity, but it cannot be helped."

By ignoring the scientific facts in the report, nuclear test veterans paid a heavy price to enable the United Kingdom to keep up with the USA and USSR nuclear arms race during the Cold War. The nuclear weapon tests by the US, USSR and UK now covered both hemispheres of our once pristine planet. The extent of UK testing now included the participation of young men from the UK, Australia, New Zealand and Fiji. The impact on the southern hemisphere, both outside of the weapon test locations as well as within, was huge.

It is tempting in 2021 to identify the heroes and villains of the whole scandal as it unfolds from the archives of history. However, the reader can decide for themselves. In 1956, UK nuclear weapon test experiments were still to run for another eleven years. As I write this, 69 years have passed since the first UK bomb test at Mont Bello in 1952. During this time the heroes and villains of this scandalous period of our history came as thick and as fast as the experiments became more reckless.

The report debated in the UK Parliament on 16 July 1956 is, however, of its time. The decision to ignore its recommendations can only be fully understood by anyone who actually lived during this era of history. In 1956, Britain had forces in the Western Allied occupation zones of Germany. Europe was threatened by an increasingly belligerent Soviet Union, which was nuclear-armed. Britain had recently fought and lost troops in the Korean War (1950-51). The British Empire was winding down and in the early stages of forming a British Commonwealth of Nations in its place. A crisis in the Middle East began on 13 June 1956 when British troops pulled out of the Suez Canal Zone and, ten days after the Medical Research Council debate, Colonel Nasser seized control of the Suez Canal for Egypt. If the UK had pulled out of future nuclear testing, it is probable it would have been seen as a humiliating climb down for those at the head of government – and possibly a suicide note for any aspirations to maintain the United Kingdom as a nation of some relevance in the world.

Nevertheless, this push for power and prestige sealed the fate of the 30,000-plus UK and Commonwealth forces used in the experiments which, in 1958, moved to the Pacific to test much larger nuclear weapons. In all of this, those who took part in the nuclear tests were the lowest denominator and were brutally betrayed. It is time for government to acknowledge mistakes of the past and not ignore science and history as if it did not happen.

Summary Appendix of Chapter Four

Some of the truths about the knowledge of radioactive fallout and genetic damage revealed in the 1956 Medical Research Council Report and ignored by government are listed in the following summary:

1. The original title of the study was 'Nuclear Explosions and Genetic Effect'. This was changed before publication to the more innocuous-sounding 'The Hazards to Man of Nuclear and Allied Radiation'.

2. The MRC Report revealed the following consensus opinions of Britain's finest experts in science in 1956:

   a. Fallout is an extremely grave concern. (Fallout was, in fact, regarded as the 'prime causal link' to ill health and premature deaths of nuclear veterans in the summary of the Limitation Trial of Nuclear Veterans in June 2009.)

   b. Furthermore, the MRC Report confirmed that, when inhaled or ingested, low dose, low level beta radiation strontium with a half-life of 28 years in nuclear fallout becomes 'internal emitting radiation'. This irradiates bones, giving rise to bone cancer and bone marrow and leading to leukaemia. The report also confirmed that young people and particularly children are more sensitive to strontium and are at greater risk of leukaemia.

   c. Fallout is indiscriminate because where it lands is entirely dependent upon wind direction. It knows no frontiers and kills both allies and the enemy. In addition...

   d. An absorbed dose of only 2 x natural background radiation is enough to produce genetic damage in an exposed person. Professor Haldane, in a letter to the *Lancet* a few days before the debate, wrote that this was possibly an underestimation. In the five years before 1951, background radiation had increased by 22% through radiology in hospitals, in shoe shops for sizing children's feet, in luminous watches etc.

e. In 1956, Radiological Protection Services worked under the Minister of Health. This quickly changed and it was moved to the control of the Ministry of Defence. This enabled the newly formed National Radiation Protection Board (NRPB) to control the references, protocols and methodology (heavily biased by epidemiologists) to produce, at great expense to tax payers, the significantly flawed mortality studies of the 1980s and 90s.

f. In 1956, the International Commission for Radiological Protection (ICRP) was working in close liaison with the World Health Organisation (WHO) and, in the debate, the need was expressed for this liaison to continue.

However, in 1959, behind closed doors, the WHO was excluded from making any comment on the health effects of radiation as this remit was only in the hands of the ICRP, which was controlled by the Atomic Energy Commission, an organisation intent on protecting the nuclear energy industry. (See comment by Dr John Gofman at the beginning of Chapter Three.)

3. On the danger of genetic damage, the report resulted in the following:

a. A review of the report's advice by the Prime Minister Sir Anthony Eden and his cabinet issued his edict regarding genetic damage: "It is a pity, but it cannot be helped." This has underpinned successive governments' policy to deny an honourable settlement of nuclear test veterans' claims.

b. During the debate, the Minister for Health sought to downplay the findings. The Deputy Speaker for the debate let it be known that the Foreign Office and the Ministry of Defence had sole control of policy in this matter.

c. Although the report clearly recommended 'not to increase the scale of nuclear bomb tests' the advice was ignored. The UK's participation in the nuclear arms race with the USA and the USSR had passed a point of no return.

d. Genetic damage is long term damage and it would take thirty years or more to assess. Research would be needed until at least the end of the century or even longer.

This confirmed Professor Haddow's fears expressed in 1951 of increasing cancer and other effects in 50 years' time.

4. The report confirmed that Members of Parliament did not blame the generals. They blamed the political leaders.

5. Servicemen who took part in the experimental nuclear testing were:
- lied to about the fallout hazard;
- had no meaningful military covenant for ensuring a duty of care;
- no protective clothing or respirators;
- were lied to about the genetic hazard they faced;
- knew nothing about the 1956 MRC Report until the 1990s;
- were under military orders;
- naively trusted those in charge;
- and were placed in a particularly vulnerable position.

Vulnerability sealed their fate. For the greater benefit to the nation, their health and premature deaths were considered expendable costs.

In the quest for power, prestige and profit from the nuclear weapons industry, the lowest denominator in the chain of cost analysis was the nuclear veterans. But this is not entirely true, as later decades show. The UK taxpayer has been equally treated with contempt. A bottomless pit of money has been taken from taxpayers' pockets to pay for the treachery and betrayal of the veterans by significantly biased studies plus huge legal costs etc. to prevent nuclear veterans and their widows seeking redress.

The devastated and blighted lives of nuclear test veterans and their families by a 'couldn't care less' policy of successive governments is a historic national scandal. Today the diminishing cohort of loyal servicemen who attended weapon test locations hold in their blood, tissue, organs and bone evidentiary proof of radioactive fallout-induced genetic damage leading to subsequent legacy ill-health.

The dead cannot speak. For those not cremated but buried, radiation will glow in their bones as evidentiary proof for many years.

The extended period of nuclear tests from 1958 brought more breaches of ethics and morality. The fact that the 1956 Medical Research Committee Report on the biological impact of fallout and genetic damage was ignored at UK Prime Ministerial level "as a pity, but it cannot be helped" set the UK, together with the USA and USSR, on a path of recklessness that wreaked enormous collateral damage on both global public health and the planet's once pristine environment.

Chapter 5: Reckless Conduct of Experimental Nuclear Tests

"There needs no ghost, my Lord,
to come from the grave to tell us this."
William Shakespeare

Leading academics who contributed to the 1956 UK Medical Research Council Report had unanimously agreed that all effects of radiation were bad and risked genetic consequences to the offspring. This is a consensus scientific truth ignored ever since by successive UK governments.

Further research was deemed necessary. This had already been triggered by the top-secret report 'Biological Investigations at Atomic Bomb Tests – Maralinga 1956' by whistle blower Hedley Marston. Through his 'off piste' monitoring of fallout (because he didn't trust the Atomic Safety Committee under Sir Ernest Titterton), the Australian biochemist had shown that fallout from bombs was not confined only to the nuclear test range. Directed by the changing winds, radioactivity had fallen on compass points 1,500 miles from the test range all over the Australian continent.

Australian Prime Minister Sir Robert Menzies had expediently lied that 'no conceivable injury' would result from the UK nuclear experimental bomb tests. The credibility of Menzies and the Atomic Safety Committee at Maralinga was now in absolute tatters. The MRC debate in London had confirmed and exposed the recklessness of the weapon test programme. However, this recklessness had earlier confirmed its genesis and had undermined the ethics and morality that underpinned the nuclear bomb test experiments.

In 1955, a top-secret internal communication stated: "We do not want you to release any documents on genetic effects of radiation." But this was too late. The false consensus of science was already being exposed by analysis of data from the bombing of Japan and the US Nevada bomb tests. The Medical Research Council just added confirmation of the emerging scientific truth.

At this time, at the height of Cold War paranoia, UK domestic law required that all persons potentially exposed to ionising radiation should be blood-tested for genetic susceptibility. By the 1960s, the UK was even using cytogenetic diagnostic blood-testing on nuclear workers to detect exposure to radiation. (See later chapters.)

In 1958, however, at a secret conference held on Christmas Island prior to the Grapple series of hydrogen bomb tests, the attention of those senior military officers present was drawn to the UK's domestic law on blood-test requirements. At this meeting scientists from the Atomic Weapons Research Establishment insisted their personnel be blood-tested for what they termed "medico-legal" reasons; that is, the possibility of future legal claims. They suggested all troops who participated in the nuclear programme should also be blood-tested for genetic susceptibility.

The discussion notes from the meeting show the senior military officers objected to the AWRE suggestions on the basis of knowledge that servicemen developed radiation-linked illnesses later in life and were not known to have genetic susceptibility (i.e. they had normal health compared to most civilians). Such blood tests, it was argued, could be used by the servicemen as evidence to show that their subsequent illness could only be due to the long-term effects of dangerous exposure to ionising radiation from experimental bombs. The Ministry of Defence was contacted in London to decide on the matter. They swiftly rejected the AWRE blood-test suggestion.

(The Combined History Archive of Nuclear Veterans and other archives have revealed over the decades that the MOD has always been against blood testing of any kind. They prefer other records that can be more easily manipulated by bias, doubt or bad faith, rather than real diagnostic evidence that shows radiation-induced damage.)

Many who have studied this period in nuclear history believe this is possibly the time when health and safety protection policy relating to radiation risk came under the control of the Ministry of Defence, who became the only arbiter of this matter. The Ministry of Health and the Ministry of the Environment no longer had any say in the matter.

That decision on Christmas Island to deny blood tests offers an explanation regarding the death of Royal Engineer Derek Redman mentioned in the Preface of this book. He died within hours of falling ill. Several times he had taken AWRE scientists (who all wore full PPE and respirators) to the ground zero of a bomb detonation without wearing any protective equipment himself. His swift death and burial at sea without a post-mortem was a means of throwing the matter 'under the bus' to avoid any future claims by his family.

Such nuances in the debate on blood-testing at Christmas Island in 1958 had not been given any prominence five years earlier. On 15 October 1953, an atomic bomb was dropped at

Emu Field on the Maralinga test range at 7 am in the morning. (Emu Field is a test site about 60 miles north of where the new atomic village of Maralinga was built prior to the bomb tests and minor-trial experiments there between 1956 and 1963.) Fired from a tower, the expected yield calculated by bomb test supremo William Penney was 5 kt. It left a deep crater and sucked up a lot of radioactive earth into a mushroom cloud. It was, in fact, a reckless 'dirty bomb' with huge capacity for toxic fallout. The fallout become known as the 'black mist', a notorious cloud that fell on indigenous nomadic Aboriginal people.

Over 30 years later, in 1984, and a year prior to the Royal Australian Commission travelling to London, Mr Justice McClelland and fellow commissioners met with elders of the Yankunytjatjara tribe to listen to their memories of the 'black mist'. An elder of the Aboriginal tribe said: "We heard the bang early in the morning. Before the sun had set, we saw the cloud coming. It was different from other clouds; it was black. By late evening it was above us. There was a sprinkling of rain."

One older Aboriginal "thought it was an evil spirit" so he told every one of the men present to shake their spears at the cloud to make it change direction. But it didn't. It brought instant vomiting and diarrhoea to all the men, women and children. The tribe's healer tried to make people better but then he died himself. Dogs that followed the nomads also fell dead. Aboriginals suffered a range of terrible effects. In 1984, blindness and partial blindness, plus many other eye diseases, were common in survivors. But the sparseness of medical records in the 1950s conveniently made it impossible to link any specific illness or premature death thirty years later to the 'black mist'.

But this in some ways is irrelevant because this incident had not been intended as a deliberate act of human experimentation. That was only arranged from 1956. The 'black mist' had been caused because the bomb should not have been fired at that time or at that height to the ground. This much was later admitted by the British meteorological forecaster Edward Siddons at Emu Field and by the test supremo Lord Penney in 1985 in London. They admitted calculations they had made on fallout probability were faulty. The weather was not suitable, and the bomb yield of 5 kt was underestimated – in fact, it was double that yield.

But the bomb test went ahead anyway because only 'a small number of people were considered likely to be affected'. That was a direct reference to the nomadic lifestyle of the Aboriginals. No consideration was made for their scant clothing and lack of PPE or respirators making them extremely vulnerable to fallout. Penney had taken account only that the nearest sheep farm from a small community was well over 100 miles away. Accidents happen. So what? The conclusion was that Aboriginals within the nuclear bomb test area were only a minor concern. Accident or no accident, it seemed the entrenched ethics of the day was that life is expendable.

This same negative objectivity also applied to the so-called 'minor trials' that took place on the Maralinga test range between 1953 and 1963. These trials released highly toxic and long-lasting beryllium, uranium and plutonium across the bushland and the radiation spread, depending on the vagaries of the wind. Frequent dust storms are well noted in this area of South Australia, with winds blowing potentially carcinogenic radiation hither and thither. Residual fallout radiation, the prime causal link to legacy ill health and premature deaths, has been left in this region ever since the Maralinga nuclear test range closed in 1967.

When I was at Maralinga in 1965-66 it was not unusual to find furniture and beds in accommodation covered with fine dust particles. When thermal air temperatures rise, dust particles become resuspended in the air and are blown by the wind in any direction to settle anywhere. This is a fact of nature – which, of course, is vehemently denied by desk-bound officials and politicians in the UK's Ministry of Defence.

These toxic dust particles carried on radioactive 'wings of death' would not register radiation, even if a rad-counter was waved only one or two inches above them. This is because man-made atomic fallout alpha and beta radiation is very difficult to measure. The emission tracks only carry to a distance of 1 mm or so. This type of radiation cannot penetrate the skin (as mentioned in Chapter Two) but if inhaled or ingested, landing in the eye or enabled to enter the blood via a cut or abrasion in the skin, it becomes a severe internal-emitting hazard, irradiating tissue, blood, organs and bone inside the body. This is an unseen and undetectable hazard and perfect for the 1956 Biological Investigations. Crawling through unmonitored radioactive dust and inhaling the particles may not produce an adverse impact for at least 5, 10 or possibly 30 years, allowing plenty of time for denial of any causal link to radiation.

However, the experimental use of men for investigating the effect of nuclear weapons of war has other military research precedents. Despite the abhorrence of chemical and biological weapons used in the First World War, it was a policy to test such lethal weapons on men in the 1950s. This reckless policy used young servicemen as 'guinea pigs' by deception. The experiments took place at the UK's Defence Science and Technology Laboratories, Porton Down, near Salisbury in Wiltshire.

In 1951, Porton Down scientists began testing nerve agents on young unsuspecting and trusting members of the armed forces. Those who took part were classed as 'volunteers'. The recruitment of the guinea pigs was done deceptively. Men believed they were assisting public health in trials to find a cure for the common cold.

This is a deception in clear breach of the Nuremburg Code, which states: "*The voluntary consent of the human subject is absolutely essential. This means that the person involved should have legal capacity to consent; should be so situated as to be able to exercise free power of choice, without the intervention of an element of force, fraud, deceit, duress, over-reaching, or other ulterior form of constraint or coercion, and should have sufficient knowledge and comprehension of the elements of the subject matter involved as to be able to make an understanding and enlightened decision. This latter element requires that before the acceptance of an affirmative decision by the experimental subject there should be made known to him the nature, duration, and purpose of the experiment; the method and means by which it is to be conducted; all inconveniences and hazards reasonable to be expected; and the effects upon his health or person which may possibly come from his participation in the experiment.*"

This is the code of ethics under which the Nazi doctors of 1939 to 1945's genocidal death camps were tried, convicted and hung. In 1946, the world was rightly appalled when the truth emerged of the experiments they carried out. Most shocking is the fact that both the UK and the US democracies actually adopted these practices on their own people during the 1950s and 1960s.

Britain and the USA never signed up to the Nuremburg Code, so technically, they could say they never broke it. But to ignore basic morality is just disingenuousness at its most despicable. As democracies said to only follow the rule of law, this oversight is inexcusable and morally bankrupt because it allowed democratic governments the freedom to use their own scientists, in the 'national interest', to abandon all ethics.

The 'volunteers' for Porton Down's chemical and biological weapon studies were therefore recruited by politically expedient deception. Many were mandatorily enlisted National Service conscripts at a difficult time in history – as were the nuclear test participants. As conscripts, some were even unwilling to be wearing uniform – but all were treated as human cannon fodder in the national interest. The Porton Down volunteers were offered an extra payment of £2 and three days' extra leave for volunteering, not to take part in biological and chemical weapon experiments, but for 'finding a cure for the common cold'.

Many years later I asked a good friend, Peter Ireneus, who had done his mandatory national service plus one year in the Grenadier Guards, if he had heard about the 'common cold research' at Porton Down while he was doing his national service. He said: "Yes, we all knew about it, but our Commanding Officer let it be known that no Grenadier Guardsmen should agree to go to Porton Down if invited."

This was excellent advice for Peter to heed. For a guardsman to go against the advice of anyone even just one rank above would be inadvisable, let alone ignoring the advice of the regiment's Commanding Officer. It shows perhaps that elite infantrymen were either lucky not to be used as guinea pigs at Porton Down or were regarded by the MOD as being more useful in the defence of the realm. Those in lesser military regiments or cohorts of Her Majesty's armed forces could be allowed to be experimented on – but not any members of the Grenadier Guards. Hats off and hip, hip, hurrah for common sense!

Records from 1951 to 1999 show a long history of volunteers being abused by Porton Down's sector for Chemical and Biological Defence. Besides sarin, a highly toxic nerve agent, other dangerous substances were tested on young servicemen. In a clear breach of the Nuremburg Code, none of these men were given information or had comprehension of the toxic elements they were subjected to. None had the opportunity to make a knowledgeable or enlightened decision.

They were assured by scientists and medical officers that there was 'no risk'. However, in a report by campaigning ex-Liberal Democrat MP Norman Baker published in the Daily Mail in 2021, one Porton Down scientist observed at the time: "If you advertise for people to suffer agony, you will not get volunteers." ('The day anthrax was released by Porton Down scientists in a tunnel on the Northern Line', *Daily Mail*, 7 February 2021.)

So lies and deception were the established ethics of the day. Experiments on servicemen of the nerve agent sarin were happening in Porton Down at the same time the 'black mist' fell on innocent Aboriginal nomads in the South Australian desert.

Because of some adverse reactions at Porton Down – one man had fallen into a coma – scientists were requested to reduce the maximum dosage given to volunteers from 300 mg to a lower safer range of 10 to 15 mg. A week later, six more volunteers were given doses of 200 mg. One of the young men was 20-year-old Leading Aircraftman Ronald Maddison, who, for his £2 bonus and three days' leave, was invited into a test chamber where 200 mg of sarin was applied to a cloth on the inside of his left forearm. Within half an hour he was on his way to hospital. The ambulance man who collected him from Porton Down was told: "Mention anything about this to anyone and you'll go to jail." Ronald Maddison died within three hours of arriving at hospital.

As with Lance Corporal Derek Redman on Christmas Island, Ronald Maddison was placed in a coffin with the lid firmly screwed down. Consequently, his parents were unable to view his body prior to burial and he was quickly buried without a post-mortem to confirm the cause of his death.

The Home Secretary at the time, David Maxwell Fyfe MP, put improper pressure on the coroner to ensure no mention of sarin poisoning was mentioned on the young man's death certificate. It took 50 years for the truth to emerge when, thanks to the Porton Down Veterans' Support Group, the inquest into Ronald Maddison's death was reopened in 2004. The verdict reached was that this young man had been 'unlawfully killed' by a chemical weapon. It was actually the unlawful killing of a young man duped by lies in breach of any ethical or moral standards expected in a democracy.

Members of the armed forces experimented on by the scientists at Porton Down as volunteers were nothing more than 'guinea pigs'. The government has been deceitful and has violated basic principles of ethics and morality. The disregard of government and authoritative institutions has been exposed in countless archive documents and press reports in the decades following the end of the Second World War. The health, wellbeing and even the lives of the public have also been disregarded when it suits government policy to do so in the name of what is termed 'the national interest'. This is a well-documented history that has hardly been spoken of.

It's not only servicemen who have been used as guinea pigs. During the 1950s and 60s, when the paranoia of the Cold War arms race was at its height, many clandestine experiments took place with regard to chemical and biological weapons and these impacted upon ordinary citizens going about their daily lives.

During World War Two, cadmium sulphate (an impurity of zinc) was recognised as a chemical weapon. People who worked with this chemical in industry, for example battery manufacture, had to wear personnel protection equipment, including respirators, to prevent inhalation of this chemical because it has been known to science as carcinogenic since the 1920s. Yet in the 1960s this chemical was dropped by aircraft over a 40-mile stretch of East Anglia, including Norwich. The government scientists' reasoning for this indiscriminate chemical weapon trial? To just see what would happen.

Former Liberal MP, Norman Baker recently spoke to a senior throat consultant, Dr Wyn Parry, about cadmium contamination in East Anglia. After relocating from Nottingham to Norwich in 1999, the doctor discovered that the incidence of oesophagus cancer was as high in Norwich as in Nottingham, a city with three times the population. Closer examination of the spike in cancer cases in the Norwich area corresponded with the flight path of the aircraft that dropped the chemicals more than thirty years earlier.

Some four and a half tons of this chemical has been released into the atmosphere by ship, aircraft and vehicle in the name of experimentation. In the 1960s, a machine towed behind a vehicle dispersed cadmium along a road near Frome in Somerset. In 1961, archive records show that a Land Rover driven by two scientists spewed cadmium onto roads between Ilchester and Bristol. The scientists driving the vehicle, who were wearing full protective clothing, were told to be careful of their own health; the public, in contrast, was left in ignorance. This experiment was also carried out in Cardington in Bedfordshire, and in Dorchester, Chippenham and several villages around Salisbury in Wiltshire.

Norman Baker's access to archive records also revealed that on July 26, 1963 a scented powder puff containing spores of freeze-dried anthrax was thrown out of the window of a London Underground tube train onto the tracks in the Northern Line tunnel between Colliers Wood and Tooting Broadway. The tunnel is seventeen miles long. Anthrax can cause eye infections, food poisoning and septicaemia, leading to life-threatening sepsis. The spores trapped in the tunnel took only 15 minutes to spread and contaminate every stop in the tunnel. There is no record of the impact on the public. But then, clearly the health of the London population was not a priority for scientists from the Defence Science and Technology Laboratories at Porton Down.

In 2016, the government issued a statement about the use of 'volunteers' at Porton Down. The statement simply said: "The volunteer programme has always been operated to the highest standards of the day." What the government spokesperson failed to say is that the ethical standards of the day totally ignored the Nuremburg Code and basic principles expected in a democracy; that is, the standards of the day have been extremely low or non-existent to the point of recklessness.

The above experimental abuse caused a wide range of illnesses and serves as a public warning that, without radical changes of ethics and morality, successive governments cannot be trusted as guardians of public health. We may believe we live in a democracy and we assume the government of the day has the best intentions regarding the health of the nation, but the facts of history speak for themselves. When governments control science, public health is often ignored.

Meanwhile, analysis of the bones of deceased babies and children by pathologists and coroners began in Australia in the 1950s. Britain and the USA followed this macabre research, which confirmed the conclusions of the 1956 UK Medical Research Council Report and the Biological Investigations undertaken at Maralinga. The false consensus of science had allowed the truth to be hidden by governments since the 1920s but now, faced with confirmation of the scientific fact that nuclear fallout was the prime causal link to ill health and genetic damage in persons exposed, the actions of governments show a complete abandonment of all ethics and morality.

In 1957, bones secretly taken from infants and some adults without family consent were sent to a laboratory in Melbourne for analysis. It was the start of one of the longest scientific experiments in history. Teams collected bones from all across those areas of Australia that experienced nuclear fallout and 22,000 bone samples, aged from new born to middle age, were sent for analysis. In this horror of human tragedy, to the scientists the most prized bones were those of babies and toddlers. The middle-aged and older bones were not wanted, so at least those people could go to their graves with their skeletons intact.

As people died, their bodies were taken from the mortuary with the co-operation of coroners and the required bones were secretly removed by pathologists. Parents and families had no idea what was going on 'in the national interest'. Archive records, which are a painful read even now in 2021, show this was all carried out with a perverse sense of duty.

Titterton, head of the Atomic Safety Committee at Maralinga, found it easy to get the exact bones he craved for analysis because the pathologists' minds were not set on ethics; they merely welcomed the extra dollars.

At the huge Australian Defence Base of Woomera, linked to Maralinga by landline telephone 300 miles to the west, the toll on young lives was catastrophic. The base had a rocket range used for testing early cruise missiles, and second only to Cape Canaveral at the time. The RAAF and RAF also flew aircraft from this base to enter the mushroom clouds for radiation readings. These often-radioactive aircraft had to be serviced and decontaminated, at great risk to the ground service crews. The total of personnel and families there at the time has been estimated at around 7,000 people.

Levels of strontium in babies born in Woomera were found to be five times higher than in adults, which themselves were higher than normal. In the small windswept Woomera Cemetery are the graves of 68 children, including 22 stillborn babies and 34 new-borns who lived just a few hours or days. The remaining twelve of these heart-breaking graves are of those who died between the ages of one and seven. It's obvious they were buried by military authorities because each grave is chillingly identical, as with mass war graves in military cemeteries globally. However, these children's graves are mostly stamped with just 'Baby', an identity number with the family name below, 'Died' followed by the date, and often one more word: 'Stillborn'. No words of comfort have been added, in what is an indictment of Australian government indifference. These babies and children all died during atmospheric nuclear testing at Maralinga in 1956-57 or within a few years.

These 68 innocent deaths are a testament to the callousness of governments because no admission has been made linking these deaths with fallout from Maralinga. No public investigation has been allowed and ever since, the grieving families have hit the brick wall of the Official Secrets Act; it's 'in the national interest', with access to government files being denied and hospital records unavailable.

With regard to the bone sample programme, the Melbourne laboratory found it difficult to cope with the numbers sent for analysis. The USA had started a similar programme globally with the cynically innocuous name Project Sunshine. Australian pathologists signed agreements with the US to ship body parts to the USA. This unethical and secret scientific research continued unabated until 1967, all funded by taxpayers' money.

Atmospheric bomb testing was ended by the US, USSR and UK in 1963 by a partial Test Ban Treaty, which allowed underground bomb testing to continue instead. Scientists globally had belatedly become worried that radioactive fallout from the increased number of atmospheric bomb tests had brought the health of the human race to a tipping point. In the US, scientists had confirmed that strontium in babies' teeth in

1962 was 50 times higher than in babies in 1950.

These scientific facts prompted US President John F Kennedy to say, in a speech announcing the partial Test Ban Treaty in 1963:

"Every inhabitant of this planet must consider the day when the planet may no longer be habitable. Weapons of war must be abolished before they abolish us. Continued unrestricted testing by nuclear powers, joined in time by other nations which may be less adept in limiting pollution, will increasingly contaminate the air that all of us must breathe.

"Even then the number of children and grandchildren with cancer in their bones, with leukaemia in their blood or poison in their lungs might seem statistically small to some in comparison with natural health hazards. But this is not a natural hazard and it is not a statistical issue.

"The loss of even one human life or the malformation of even one baby who may be born long after all of us are gone should be of concern to us all. Our children and grandchildren are not merely statistics towards which we can be indifferent.

"These tests befoul the air of all men."

These scientific truths, admitted almost sixty years ago by US President Kennedy, are the finest humanitarian truths regarding radiation damage to health ever spoken by any democratic leader, before or since. But, despite this truthful admission, the nuclear arms race rolled on. Bomb testing was banned in the atmosphere, but massive nuclear testing continued underground. China tested its first nuclear bomb in 1964, adding further to the massively accumulated build-up of long-lived residual radiation trapped within our delicate and formerly pristine biosphere.

The UK has a long record of removing body parts without family consent. On 16 November 2010, after three and half years of inquiry, a report of over 500 pages was published in the UK. This inquiry was into tissue and other body parts removed by pathologists in post-mortems of employees who had worked at nuclear installations.

The inquiry report, by Michael Redfern QC, attracted little media attention at the time because it was propitiously released on the same day as the announcement of the engagement of Prince William and Kate Middleton. This ploy is often used by government. That is, release any bad news that may embarrass the government on the same day any eagerly awaited good news of mass public interest is to be published.

Michael Redfern QC's report considered the families of the nuclear workers had been badly served. The motive given by the QC for the study and subsequent destruction of bones, organs, blood and tissue removed from hundreds of employees was to prevent any future compensation claims by the families. But this report was also of interest to nuclear veteran campaigners because, hidden in pages 89 and 90, was the admission that body parts of deceased nuclear veterans had also been removed, without family consent, during post-mortem analysis by pathologists.

Freedom of Information questions from independent nuclear test veteran campaigner David Whyte, who served with the Royal Engineers at Christmas Island in 1958 and is an associate of the Combined Veterans' Forum International (CVFI), found that nuclear test veterans in 2011 were still 'flagged' for post-mortem examination by pathologists without family consent, ostensibly for 'medical research'. However, removal, analysis and disposal of body parts also avoids any possible claims for compensation from the veterans' families.

The issue that set the Redfern Inquiry into action in 2007 came to light when a new Medical Officer at British Nuclear Fuels Limited (BNFL) was asked to re-examine data that had been obtained from organ analysis taken from former nuclear workers at the Sellafield nuclear complex in Cumbria over many years. The late Dr Geoffrey Schofield had held the data when he was BNFL's Medical Officer. Strangely, access to this data showed no evidence of the nuclear workers' deaths being related to radiation, nor had any family consent been obtained.

The new Medical Officer for BNFL had also found it odd that coroners appeared frequently to have notified Sellafield of former nuclear employees' deaths. The Redfern Inquiry found that an informal arrangement had existed between Dr Schofield, the driving force behind Sellafield's analytical work, and pathologists at West Cumberland Hospital, so that Schofield was informed when a post-mortem was to take place on any former Sellafield nuclear worker. If the name of the deceased was of particular interest to Schofield, it appears he had then taken somewhat unethical steps to obtain the organs.

The range of body parts removed and analysed in this clandestine and unethical matter included liver, ribs, kidney, testes, brain, heart and tongue. The Redfern Inquiry report concluded that although Dr Schofield and his colleagues had made no attempt to conceal their research and activity, they appear to have at least given some consideration to the ethical implications.

According to Martin Forward of the Cumbrian Opposition to a Radioactive Environment (CORE), and as reported in *Fissionline*, the International Bulletin of Nuclear Veterans and Families on the internet, the families involved have found no one has been held to account for this matter. The hardest part for them in this body-snatching scandal has been that, at different stages, each family member affected felt as if they had re-experienced bereavement as the true facts emerged.

One family, as was reported in the national press later, recalled that prior to burial the body of an uncle was found to have been fitted with a broomstick to replace the thighbone that had been removed from one leg.

The Redfern Inquiry team found that CORE's archive papers had given 'valuable lead into everything at an early stage'. CORE had also raised funds enabling Sellafield workers or their families to access advice and secure compensation for work-related cancers.

Another fact to come out of the Redfern Inquiry included the claim by the son of a Sellafield worker that his father's funeral had been halted so the company had more time to study organs removed from his body. This comes as no surprise to the Combined History Archive of Nuclear Veterans (CHANV) – not because nuclear test veterans have had body parts taken without family consent, but because it is well known as a standard practice with deceased coal miners prior to burial.

When my father-in-law Reginald Sladen, a former Forest of Dean coal miner, died in 2009, I had a phone call from the coroner's office just two days before the funeral. The reason for the call was to halt the funeral until a post-mortem could be carried out. This naturally caused distress, particularly for my mother-in-law, so I asked the coroner's office why this was necessary. The answer given was they needed to check the deceased's lungs to see if any residue of coal dust was present, in case the family decided to claim compensation from the National Coal Board in the future. I said my father-in-law had died from COPD – chronic pulmonary obstructive disease – for which he had already been through a long claims process resulting in compensation over three years ago. The phone call ended abruptly, and the family continued with the funeral arrangements.

The warning here is that we may all live in a democracy but where industrial and military liability for injury is concerned, the state stretches every sinew to avoid accountability and responsibility – even to the point of using taxpayers' money to assist in denial of an obligation to provide a duty of care, and even to the point of involving coroners, pathologists and other officials.

Over the decades, every nuclear veteran I've met or spoken to in the UK, Australia and New Zealand who participated in the UK nuclear weapon tests has expressed no extreme political views. All have sought only truth and justice – added to which, an apology would be appreciated. With a heritage of military service and duty I've found all veterans to be apolitical, yet any who actively campaign for the truth and for justice inevitably find themselves labelled a 'vexation' or 'anti-nuclear'.

The truth of the matter is all archive records and data collected show that nuclear weapons and the nuclear industry are inevitably entwined by a common denominator: denial of the hazards of radiation to health. All are subjected to a lack of ethics and morality. Nuclear veterans are regarded as a 'vexation' to government because they underpin the truth of radiation damage in their chromosomes and because they do not like being consistently lied to. Nuclear veterans are labelled 'anti-nuclear' because the denial of the truth of radiation hazard to man covers all frontiers and every aspect of the nuclear industry.

The Biological Investigations of 1956 specifically mentioned the link between nuclear bomb tests and the nuclear industry; that is, the bomb tests "would be of considerable value to the peaceful uses of nuclear energy" and for "devising more effective methods of protection."

The US inspired many of the experiments in this era. Officials in the USA even used innocent hospital patients as guinea pigs. Between 1953 and 1957, at least 11 terminally ill patients were injected with uranium to test the effects of radiation. Presidential apologies have been made since that date.

Following the 1956 Biological Investigations at Maralinga and the consensus of eminent biologists and physicists on the hazards of radiation in the UK Medical Research Council Report in the same year, it became inevitable that genetic damage, passed to the children and grandchildren, would become the next big embarrassment to be vehemently denied at all costs by government.

The post-war Japanese government had already embarked upon the forced sterilisation of female victims of child-bearing age at Hiroshima and Nagasaki because of the huge rise in stillbirths and genetically damaged children in addition to the childhood leukaemia epidemic. The fallout victims had manifested these radiation-induced effects within seven years of the atomic bombing.

Illnesses in those who participated in the UK nuclear tests followed a similar pattern to Japan's experience. Archive documents show that birth defects in the offspring of nuclear test veterans from Monte Bello, Maralinga and Christmas Island are ten times higher in the veterans' children and eight times higher in their grandchildren than in the general population.

This, like all other truths regarding radiation, has been fiercely denied by government. The maxim of Hitler – 'If you tell a lie, make it a big lie and repeat it often enough so that even government officials believe it' – had gone into overdrive by the end of the 1960s.

The government ignores genetic damage in nuclear veterans' offspring simply because admitting the truth means admitting the fathers were exposed to dangerous levels of radiation. The 1956 MRC Report agreed by a consensus of scientific opinion that genetic effects of radiation would pass to future generations. The 1951 fears of Professor Alex Haddow that continued nuclear weapon testing would have serious impact on human health had been confirmed as a scientific reality in only five years. But this is conveniently ignored. Denial of such facts has been followed by attempting to rewrite nuclear history in a sanitised version.

This negative-controlling doctrine is only fit for totalitarian states. It's worrying that a freedom-loving and law-abiding democracy such as the UK appears to have adopted this same totalitarian legacy regarding the nuclear bomb tests.

After thirty years of betrayal following the 1952 UK Monte Bello bomb tests, the fight for justice for the genetically damaged nuclear test veterans and their families began. Nuclear test veteran and Christmas Island Royal Engineer Ken McGinley, a charismatic natural born leader, founded the British Nuclear Test Veterans Association (BNTVA) in 1983. By this time the children and grandchildren of nuclear veterans had shown an excess of genetic legacy damage. This rang alarm bells throughout the United Kingdom.

Ken's battle for the 'All We Seek is Justice' campaign of the BNTVA would not be a fair and level contest. The Ministry of Defence would deny veterans and widows access to medical records, to individual dose and radiation levels at nuclear weapon test sites, to cytogenetic blood tests for diagnostic genetic damage, to any legal aid – and then set an agenda favourable to themselves for court proceedings that, inevitably, the veterans had no choice but to embark upon.

The bureaucrats of the huge Ministry of Defence department would then spend a bottomless pit of tax payers' money on significantly biased epidemiological studies to help shore up the shaky toxic foundations on which the recklessness of the weapon test programme rested.

Between 1952 and 1967, the government had produced a legacy of scandal for all future administrations to attempt to kick into the long grass. Successive UK governments have been unable to do so. This denial is an unnecessary legacy because all successive governments had to do was admit past failures, apologise and make amends for the ongoing suffering inflicted on loyal servicemen and their families.

Without a doubt, the 1956 MRC confirmation of the genetic hazard of radiation from nuclear weapon testing exposed a political problem. By the 1980s, the reckless conduct at UK experimental test locations had been further exposed to public view and had become the MOD's and the UK government's greatest fear.

Only one strategy has been offered by successive UK governments: to deny everything; close as many legal loopholes as possible; spend as much tax payers' money as needed to avoid accountability, responsibility and compensation; continue to ignore the truth in hope that all would be forgotten; and, finally, to bury all documents relating to the nuclear veterans in a new archive in the far northern tip of Scotland and make it inaccessible to nuclear historians and the general public for an unlimited number of decades.

Are these the actions of a mature democracy – or the actions of officials still locked into the Cold War policy of denial of the scientific consensus of the hazards of radiation?

Chapter 6: Legacy Illness in Nuclear Veterans and Offspring

"The loss of even one human life or the malformation of even one baby, who may be born long after all of us are gone, should be of concern to us all."
President John F Kennedy, 1963

In Chapter Three, reference was made to a November 1951 letter written by Professor Alex Haddow, eminent biologist, physician and director of the Chester Beatty Research Institute, Royal Cancer Hospital London. This letter, addressed to Sir John Cockcroft, director of the newly formed Atomic Energy Authority (AEA), expressed grave concerns about nuclear weapon testing. Haddow's concerns were because questions about radiation risk went unanswered by nuclear physicists. One question in particular in Haddow's list of concerns regarding nuclear bomb testing was his fear "not of the risk presently [in 1951] that may be minimal but what it may be in fifty years' time."

By the 1980s, research and knowledge of radiation damage had progressed, for example with diagnostic cytogenetic blood tests. The 1956 Medical Research Council Report regarding the health hazards of radiation had unanimously been agreed by eminent scientists from both branches of science. Biologists and physicists had agreed there was no safe dose of radiation exposure above two times the natural background radiation levels, and a low dose of absorbed alpha and beta radiation into the human genome would create genetic damage that would be passed on to future generations.

Fifty years after Haddow's letter, what had the research deemed necessary by the MRC Report revealed of the legacy impact of radiation on future generations? That is, would Haddow's fears "in fifty years' time" actually be confirmed? And, more importantly, in light of the accumulating knowledge about the risks of radiation, how was safety handled at bomb test locations?

When Ken McGinley founded the British Nuclear Test Veterans Association (BNTVA) in 1983, sixteen years had elapsed since the end of the UK nuclear weapon test experiments. In that period much had entered the press in the UK, Australia and New Zealand of the legacy health effects. The spread of radiation damage caused by nuclear bomb testing was not confined only to test locations, or by national frontiers; nor was it confined between either hemisphere of the planet. The weapon testing had left its genetic mark globally.

The impact of the reckless conduct of the atmospheric nuclear arms race and other weapon tests, the toxic effects of radiation on exposed persons from fallout and the genetic damage passed to future generations around the globe was common knowledge by the time the BNTVA was founded.

The victims of the 1945 bombing of Japan and from the 1950s US Nevada bomb tests had demonstrated two key facts, confirmed by experts in biology and physics in 1956: that there is no safe dose of radiation above natural background radiation, and that radioactive fallout is the prime causal link of genetic damage, and can also be passed to the offspring of persons exposed to ionising radiation.

Leukaemia cases were excessively high in Japanese atomic bomb fallout victims by 1952. Within six or seven years of exposure the Nevada test 'downwinder' victims and those who had participated at nuclear weapon test locations in 1950s USA also showed excess leukaemia. Fallout again, rather than gamma radiation, was the prime causal link. The 1952 to 1967 UK nuclear test participants joined the growing numbers of victims. It was a repetitive drip of toxic knowledge onto the ageless rock of biological life.

In 1983, alarm bells were ringing loudly with regard to a wide range of illnesses in nuclear veterans. Ken McGinley and the growing BNTVA membership were aware of one other fact: compared to the general public, the veterans' children and grandchildren had excessive cases of stillbirth or genetic defects from birth, with some surviving only a few hours or days and others having a lifetime of illness and disability.

All the above drew great attention from the press, not only in the UK but also among nuclear veterans in Australia and New Zealand. Added to this, on the near horizon, the Royal Australian Commission into the nuclear weapon tests held in Australia at Monte Bello, Emu Field and Maralinga would arrive in London on 7 January 1985.

However, as with criminal dramas often showed on television, very often attention needs to switch forwards or backwards in time to establish evidence. By 2001, numerous independent studies had been carried out on the health of nuclear test veterans' children – all of which have been ignored by the UK government because they quickly realised *control of science is more important politically than the actual truth of science.*

In 1999, for example, comprehensive research was carried

out on behalf of the BNTVA and the NZNTVA (New Zealand Nuclear Test Veterans Association) on the genetic impact among the families of both associations. The research, by Sue Rabbitt Roff of the University of Dundee, examined the available health records of 1,041 British, 238 New Zealand and 62 Fijian nuclear test veteran families.

This social scientist, with over 60 peer-reviewed papers to her name, grew up during the UK nuclear weapon tests in Melbourne, Australia. She taught at the University of Dundee for 20 years and her long-term health effects research of nuclear test veterans has supported more than 60 successful appeals against denial of pensions in Australia, UK and New Zealand.

Sue Rabbit Roff's research *Mortality and Morbidity of Members of the BNTVA and the NZ Nuclear Tests Veterans Association and Their Families* looked at the health records of 5,000 children and grandchildren of nuclear veterans, of whom 1,950 (39%) were found to have been born with serious medical conditions. By contrast, the national average is only 2.5%. There were found to be five times the usual rate of spina bifida cases. Half of the offspring had serious medical conditions, and many had the same skin, musculoskeletal and gastrointestinal conditions as found in their nuclear test veteran fathers.

Of the 2,261 offspring of the 1,041 British nuclear veterans, almost 10% had skeletal abnormalities, including over 30 of abnormally short stature, and 18 with spinal problems and scoliosis. More than 100 skin conditions were identified, and more than 50 children developed arthritis before the age of 30. Nineteen of the children had deformed hips and 14 had deformed kneecaps. More than 100 of the children of veterans had problems with sterility, and female offspring (24 in total) had problems with their ovaries. This pattern was shown to be continued with the grandchildren.

In a newspaper report dated 15 January 1999, 'The Dark Side of the Nuclear Family' in the *New Statesman*, Roff stated that the effects of radiation had been noted as early as 1947 in a UK Medical Research Council document. So by the 50s and 60s, UK scientists, military officers and politicians were well aware, as the MRC concluded, that "even the smallest doses of radiation produces a genetic effect, there being no threshold dose below which no genetic effect is induced."

These facts were also known to US scientists, military officers and politicians. In 1963, President John F Kennedy admitted that the death of even one child "should be a concern to us all". Yet in 1983, childhood deaths as a result of radiation exposure were not of concern to anyone in the UK government. It was just a political problem they wished to ignore.

During the 1983 to 2001 BNTVA chairmanship of Ken McGinley, his 'All We Seek is Justice' campaign revealed a vast amount of independent statistical academic evidence that the children and grandchildren of nuclear test veterans are indeed genetically damaged. This was also noted in the 1991 Northern Eye documentary, *Children of the Bomb*, for Tyne Tees Television, in which nuclear historian Dr Patrick Green interviewed nuclear test veterans' families who showed significant elevated genetic deformities.

The statistician John Urquhart had earlier confirmed genetic damage in the children of Sellafield nuclear workers' children. To avoid any bias, for the *Children of the Bomb* documentary John Urquhart's statistics were independently peer-reviewed by another scientist, Claire-Marie Fortin, who worked for the Centre for Industrial Safety and Health. Fortin concluded the figures on genetic damage were high enough "to set alarm bells ringing in government." The alarm was met with silence.

All the above begs the question, what prompted the Australian Royal Commission to travel to the UK in 1985 for any reason other than to vent anger over the conduct of the nuclear weapon test experiments in Australia between 1952 and 1967? Had their anger anything to do with nuclear veterans' ill health and premature deaths, or the safety of those who participated? Sadly not.

The UK left Maralinga in 1967 after carrying out a totally inadequate but extremely hazardous clean-up of the vast area given by Australia for nuclear bomb tests and biological investigation experiments. On leaving, the UK government announced the clean-up, code-named Operation Brumby, had been carried out meticulously and therefore "a full and final settlement of all obligation whatsoever of the British government arising out of the use of Maralinga and Emu including liability" was lethargically assumed in their report.

The UK professing at this stage no further 'obligation' or 'liability' was, however, very, very far from the truth. What really annoyed the Australian government was the huge cost needed to decontaminate the land of the mess left behind.

The fact of the matter is huge quantities of plutonium and other extremely radioactive contamination still remained at this nuclear bomb test location as a result of the 600-plus 'minor trials' carried out there between 1953 and 1963. After Operation Brumby a British nuclear scientist, Noah Pearce, wrote a sanitised report of the state of the test site, which became known as the Pearce Report. Plutonium was mentioned in this document; in fact, prior to Operation Brumby, containers of plutonium had been dumped into a large hole, and other holes dug into the ground close to Maralinga airfield and elsewhere were filled with a mass of radioactive Land Rovers, trucks and other contaminated equipment and just covered over with earth.

Eventually, due to pressure from Australia, the UK agreed, in strictest secrecy, to return to Maralinga and remove drums of plutonium and other toxic contamination from about 21 pits. However, it took almost to the end of the 1970s before anything happened. When I worked at the airfield in 1965-6 the area containing the most plutonium was known simply as 'the graveyard' and had just been fenced off with no significance attached except standard radiation warning notices.

In 1979, over 12,000 kilograms of extremely hazardous radioactive material was airlifted to RAAF Edinburgh Field, transferred to an RAF VC-10 and flown back to the UK. But the Australians had to go back to London again in 1985, and at other times, right until 2010.

The above only came to light because of a whistle blower who had served with the RAAF at Maralinga in 1960, who let Australians know about the plutonium buried there.

Operation Brumby, in 1967, was a shambles. The UK government's professed exclusion of any 'obligation' or 'liability' by completing this hazardous duty was found to be untrue. The shameful lack of accountability or responsibility towards the health of the men who took part in this hazardous operation is, however, a further indictment of recklessness at the time. The men working on Operation Brumby were treated with the same 'it is a pity, but it cannot be helped' attitude and the couldn't-care-less ethos of the 1951 British Prime Ministerial edict.

The totally inadequate clean-up of approximately 180 hectares of the most heavily contaminated part of the Maralinga nuclear weapon test site consisted of turning over, to a depth of just three or so inches, the desert topsoil using bulldozers. This created a huge amount of dust. To do this horrific task, the RAF provided a detachment of thirty-five young airmen, led by Flight Lieutenant Sam McGee, who was told absolutely nothing about the dangers he and his men faced, particularly the hazard of plutonium and other highly toxic radioactive materials left over from the 11 years of the 600-plus notorious minor trials.

In 2010, the now seriously ill retired RAF officer Sam McGee set out to trace all 35 of what he called the 'missing men of Maralinga' for a reunion. The men had all been ten to twenty years younger than him, but he could find only seven survivors. All the others had died prematurely of cancer.

As a detachment leader at Maralinga, McGee had been totally unaware of the hazards of the work. On leaving the RAF, the Official Secrets Act – referred to by veterans since the 1980s as a 'gagging order' to avoid accountability – guaranteed his silence and he felt terribly guilty about having unwittingly exposed his men to such dangers and for remaining silent for so long.

In 2011, former RAF Officer Flt Lt McGee also died of cancer. He was a bitterly disappointed man. But in all of history, truth cannot be hidden forever – not even for governments who try unsuccessfully to rewrite history.

In 1960, seven years before the closing of Maralinga and the

Operation Brumby clean-up, Avon Hudson, a 22-year-old RAAF Leading Aircraftsman, was posted to Maralinga during the minor trials. His insights have since confirmed the lack of safety already noted by many other nuclear test veterans at test locations from 1952 to 1967.

LAC Hudson was assigned to work with a British scientist, Ken Taylor. His duty was to drive Taylor to test trial locations and build platforms and pads on which monitoring equipment used by the scientist was placed. Hudson had been intensely interviewed and vetted before going to Maralinga and had agreed, by signing the Official Secrets Act, to never speak about anything he heard or saw.

During his time in Maralinga, the young airman noticed the difference between how the scientists carried out their work compared to the working procedures of manual military and civilian support staff. Awareness of the Official Secrets Act meant Hudson made sure not to write anything down but he meticulously remembered every detail.

This young airman was not happy with what he witnessed: everything to do with safety was full of contradictions. The British scientists wore full protective equipment in the experimental zones, including respirators, whilst military and civilian contract workers wore only shorts, shirt, socks and boots. Only the scientists and top brass were given any information about the hazards (issued in *Radiological Safety Regulations, Maralinga RSRM/56 (5)* – but not distributed; more on this later). Hudson was told nothing about the necessity to shower and scrub down meticulously after each visit to the test areas, but he, and other airmen, noted the scientists always, without fail, went to the shower cubicles and changed before leaving the test zones. Military and civilian contractors were kept absolutely in the dark about radiation and worked without any protective equipment, whilst the scientists stood back and used full protective gear while they took their measurements.

Hudson liked scientist Ken Taylor and got on with him very well. He enjoyed working with him and at times when he was not allocated to work, he took the scientist 'bush-bashing' by Land Rover around the Maralinga area and showed him some of the Australian wildlife present: birds, snakes, scorpions, spiders etc. In return, during some of these journeys Ken taught Hudson some of the scientific knowledge about which he had not been warned, such as the dangers of radiation contamination.

Hudson meticulously remembered everything he saw and heard, including the story of the burial of plutonium and, more importantly, where it was buried. For any reader of this book wishing to know more about this episode of Hudson's time at Maralinga, it was well covered by the Australian press in the 1970s. You can also read about it in chapters 9 and 10 of Frank Walker's investigative book, *Maralinga – The Chilling Account of Secret Nuclear Shame and Betrayal of our Troops and our Country* (Hatchett Australia, 2014).

What Hudson witnessed has been confirmed by every other veteran who attended the nuclear test locations. What happened at Maralinga was followed almost identically at Christmas Island from 1957. For example, LAC Hudson was one of approximately only 1% of military personnel issued with a personal dosimeter, calibrated to read from 0.1, 0.2, 0.3 etc., up to 1, 2, 3, 4 and 5. This standard issue dosimeter did not register anything above 5. When handing the dosimeter to a clerk to read after returning from a test zone, Hudson noted that the clerk often muttered to himself, "That can't be right, it's too high," and then wrote down a number observed by Hudson that was lower than the actual reading. He was also aware that the dosimeter was not capable of registering alpha particulates in fallout.

This recording of lower (false) radiation dosage is independently confirmed by nuclear veteran David Whyte, Royal Engineers, who also had a dosimeter given to him with a maximum reading of 5 whilst taking part in similar duties at Christmas Island in 1958. Likewise, Flt Lt Joe Pasquini, a navigator in an RAF Canberra who took radiation measurements at 46,000 feet above Christmas Island during hydrogen bomb tests in 1958. Both veterans found the same falsification of dose readings, as did Major Alan Batchelor, Royal Australian Engineers, who we will come to shortly.

Joe Pasquini kept a record in the aircraft's log book of the film badge recorded levels of gamma radiation the aircrew were exposed to. Years later, as reported in the UK *Independent* newspaper on 14 November 2011, he found archive official records of exposure were recorded as far lower, even though they used the same film badges.

An old phrase springs to mind with regards to the above: 'cooking the books'. In legal terms it would probably be noted simply as fraud. This deceit has been found to be prevalent in all of the so-called 'meticulous records' the Ministry of Defence has used to justify its policy of denial of radiation hazard since 1952. Added to which, figures in archive documents requested under the Freedom of Information Act or from other archives are often unavailable, incomplete or redacted with black ink before being released into the public domain.

LAC Avon Hudson was so dismayed by what he

witnessed that he did not sign up again to the RAAF when he left Maralinga, despite being promised promotion. Just as with biochemist Hedley Marston in 1956, he decided he would at some time in his civilian life live up to a promise he had made to himself and expose everything he had seen and heard whilst working at Maralinga.

As a nuclear veteran myself, I have a great deal of admiration for the bravery and humanity of both these whistleblowing Australians, and many others, who have shown that upholding the truth is preferable to standing aside and seeing the suffering of fellow nuclear test participants ignored – particularly having seen how badly the UK treats its veterans generally in comparison to other nuclear nations. Such things would not need to happen in any democracy if honesty and accountability prevailed.

Hudson confided his experience about the contamination at Maralinga, including the burial of plutonium, to the Australian Deputy Labour Party Leader, Lance Barnard. The fact that the UK had left plutonium behind after Operation Brumby rang alarm bells in the Australian establishment because the land was being handed back to the Aboriginal tribes from whom it had been taken. Now that Sir Robert Menzies, the former PM who had agreed (without consulting any other cabinet ministers) to allow Britain to explode nuclear weapons in Australia, had retired (in 1966), others of a younger generation soon grasped the dangers of the plutonium left behind.

This included Dr Helen Caldicott, an anti-nuclear activist and Dr John Coulter, a conservationist who later became an Australian Democrat senator for South Australia. It would be hard to invoke the Official Secrets Act against Mr Hudson now because so many others were aware of and had spoken to the press about the hazard the UK had left buried at Maralinga. If any move had been made against Hudson with regard to breaching the Official Secrets Act then others, including academics and senior politicians, would also have had to face the same nonsense.

Given that the UK government had stated in 1979 that all the plutonium had been removed, all was set for the Australian Royal Commission to descend upon London. Maybe it was memories of the 'body-line' bowling in the 1930s cricket tests that sparked a sense of being cheated by the Pommies yet again? Who knows – but feelings in Australia were running high and a strong show would probably go down well with the public, who felt betrayed with regards to fallout and much else. The strontium-90 fallout and the bone sample scientific research programme must have played their part. The Australian public were not impressed – and neither were many in government.

In the 1990s, an interesting archive document came to light. It was issued by the Department of the Atomic Weapons Research Establishment (DAWRE), the RAF/AWRE, the Test Range Health Physics Adviser and the Trials Superintendent, known as the Range Commander in 1956. With over 60 pages, it contained information that LAC Avon Hudson had not been told in 1960; information I had not been told or given the opportunity to read in 1965/6. I've no doubt it is also information that the RAF detachment on the horrific Operation Brumby clean-up were deliberately kept unaware of.

Radiological Safety Regulations – Maralinga RSRM/56 (5)

The introduction to this 1956 document stated that these regulations were "to ensure protection of all personnel at Maralinga and the general public whilst imposing minimum restrictions on work." The document was said to apply to all concerned with the Maralinga trials, whether at Maralinga or "its outstations of RAAF Edinburgh Field near Adelaide, at Emu, or anywhere else in Australia."

The document's introduction admits key facts had to be kept hidden from all who served at nuclear weapon test locations.

1.1: "The danger is particularly insidious because the effects are not immediately felt and damage may only become apparent after a period of years... Damage may arise not only from external exposure but from the irradiation of internal organs as a result of ingestion, inhalation, injection into the bloodstream through a cut or abrasion, or even by absorption through intact skin."

9.2: "Personnel monitoring must primarily be the individual's responsibility. Gamma ray dosage will be measured by film badges and portable dosimeters will be available to all personnel working in active areas or buildings."

11.2: An explanation is given on what to do if an individual is in a test area and suffers a cut or abrasion to the skin. "If possible, the cut should be held under running water within 15 seconds and held there while the whole wound area is scrubbed with a soaped brush for at least five minutes. The flow of blood should be encouraged by mild pressure on the wound. The surrounding skin should be monitored and washing continued until all this is inactive."

The fear of alpha and beta particles entering the body were well known and obviously feared.

"A sterile dressing, not a strip of the Elastoplast type, may be used as a temporary cover until qualified medical attention has been received. The object causing the wound will be kept and tested for contamination."

Interesting. It shows the depth of knowledge held by officials of the serious hazard of low dose, low level alpha and beta particles and the urgent measures needed to prevent such alpha and beta radiation from gaining access to the inside of the body.

All the above information was kept from men, and not applied – possibly because of the 'imposing minimum restrictions on work' caveat. However, it is more likely that, because of the secret Biological Investigations at Atomic Bomb Tests (see Chapter Three) – initiated in response to the wide-ranging fallout over the Australian continent – it was a necessity to allow individuals to become contaminated. After all, the Atomic Safety Committee's insatiable need under Titterton to 'investigate radioactive fallout by men and animals', allow 'the unique opportunity for bomb trials to further knowledge of the contamination' and comply with Titterton's 'Bring me the bones of Australian babies' had all set scientific investigation and experimentation as a greater priority than the safety and health of individuals.

In 1957, Australia took over as Health Physics Safety Monitor at Maralinga as a result of the demise of any trust in Titterton's Atomic Safety Committee following Australian biochemist Hedley Marston's whistle blowing about the far-ranging fallout contamination in the country.

This should have resulted in better safety for the servicemen and civilian contractors. But, according to former

Australian Royal Engineer, Major Alan Batchelor (*Fissionline Report* 28, 2013), who I came into regular email contact with from 2002 when he was Vice President of the Australian Nuclear Veterans Association (ANVA), and who I met in Sydney when visiting relatives in 2006, nothing changed at all.

Alan wrote that when he served at Maralinga during the 1957 Operation Antler bomb tests, 76 members of the Australian Royal Engineers troop signed for film badge work without any protective clothing in what was called the 'Blue' bomb test area. Whether or not a dose was recorded, all troops should have been included in the official Australian dosage records – but only 7 of the 76 are recorded. The regulations on safety, now under Australian control, were said to be strict: "The removal or non-entry of dosage information confined to selected groups engaged in high risk operations can only be deliberate and should be regarded as a criminal act, denying access to information in compensation claims."

Fiddling the figures is a 'criminal act' indeed.

It's apparent the Australian authorities had inherited the same mindset as the disgraced British Atomic Safety Committee under Titterton. The film badges would have only recorded gamma radiation. The more toxic alpha particles in fallout can only be recorded by placing dust on a scintillator plate monitor, a sophisticated and delicate monitoring device able to trace the emission of 1mm short tracks of ionising alpha radiation.

Former Major, Alan Batchelor wrote: "The occurrence of radiation sickness and potential for other long-term effects was ignored. Gamma dosage readings for some servicemen were removed from official listings without explanation and no account was taken of ingested or inhaled radioactive substances or other metallic poisons.

"The absence of any alpha dosage in the official documentation provides sufficient evidence that this was never recorded for participants. Also, when a person processed through the Health Physics facility, there is no evidence that the radioactive material or other poison was measured or estimated."

In 1957 the Royal Australian Engineers on Operation Antler worked under safety regulations that were still unchanged by a government led by Prime Minister Sir Robert Menzies. Power, prestige and profit, which had led to allowing Britain to use Australia for nuclear testing, was still very much in play under Menzies' edict of 'no conceivable injury'. Control of safety may have shifted from Titterton's discredited Atomic Safety Committee but obviously nothing had changed.

The hazards of radiation were scientific facts known in 1957, as shown in RSRM/56 (5) above, and by many in politics (for example, the MRC Report of 1956) but by the time the Australian Royal Commission descended on London in 1985, and indeed up until 2012, most lawyers had little idea of the prime causal links of radiation with legacy ill health (as later chapters will show).

The International Commission of Radiological Protection (ICRP) sets radiation risk levels. The safety levels of dosage for nuclear workers are significantly biased to favour the nuclear industry. Acceptable dose levels are based only on gamma radiation and totally ignore the effects of inhaled and/or ingested alpha and beta fallout particles. Once inside the body, alpha and beta particles act as 'internal emitters'. Lodged in tissue, blood, organs or bone, this type of radiation is a very serious (but deliberately unrecorded) hazard.

For example, alpha energy in fallout is about 10 times the average of beta or gamma radiation and has a longer residence time than gamma, which passes straight through the body. An alpha particle of plutonium in the human skeleton has a 200-year risk factor, i.e. it would take 200 years for the body to remove half of it. (Dr Karl Z Morgan, *In the Shadow of the Bomb*, 1988.)

Between 1983 and 1985, BNTVA membership increased significantly under Ken McGinley's chairmanship. I became a paid-up but non-active member in 1985, the same year I had an enlarged thyroid gland partially removed by surgery.

Three years earlier, I had travelled with members of the family back to Australia for the first time since leaving in 1966. This trip was to visit relatives in Brisbane and Sydney. Australia had changed a great deal economically and socially since the 'six o'clock swill' I remembered from Adelaide in 1965. But one thing had not changed: the sheer positivity, the 'get up and go' attitude and good-natured character of the people. Because of this, my optimism for the forthcoming Australian Royal Commission visit to London was as high as that of the BNTVA membership and the British press.

So what happened when they visited? It was basically a political fudge.

History and news articles from the time show that Lord William Penney and his long-time associate from his Manhattan Project days, Sir Ernest Titterton, came under fierce pressure from the Commission's Australian lawyers later in the hearings, but initially things were very quiet. In the early months the Australian lawyers listened to countless witnesses without having access to any of the documents that had been promised to them by the UK government.

The British Prime Minister, Margaret Thatcher had given promises of co-operation but no files or documents were forthcoming. But then things changed dramatically. Australia's counsel, Peter McClellan, ripped into the British government's reluctance to release documents when he said: "Secrecy in the national interest has always been a convenient alibi for failure of disclosure. But today it is hard to believe that Britain is in possession of any atomic secrets unknown to the great nuclear powers. We're not here to poke our noses into British technical secrets, but there is a certain minimum of information to which, as a host nation to the nuclear tests, we feel entitled to have access to."

This challenge to the British government produced an explosion of headlines within the British media; it was covered by the BBC and ITN and was on the front pages of all the newspapers. Ken McGinley, in just two years, had established himself and the BNTVA with the media and the public, who had all become aware of the suffering caused to nuclear test veterans and their families. The political acrimony between the Australian and British lawyers had kicked off. It was as if it was a replay of the 1930s' Ashes body-line bowling controversy.

Prime Minister Margaret Thatcher's reaction, prompted by officials, was to let the Australians have the documents they craved. Give it to 'em with both barrels. As a result, almost 40 tons of paper was delivered to the Commission's office in London over a period of two weeks. The ploy was obvious and devious: if you can't get rid of the Australians and their complaints, let them drown in the volume of information provided.

Some of the information among this mountain of documents was reported as useful but what jumped out clearly from the pages was the total subservience and complicity of the Australian Prime Minister, Sir Robert Menzies. In all that had occurred during the nuclear weapon test experiments on the Australian continent, Menzies had virtually given the UK a blank cheque to do whatever they liked with the land – and also with the Australian people.

The *bête noire* of the 1952-67 debacle of poor planning, poor safety and bad faith that impacted upon Australia was clearly and inevitably identified as Sir Ernest Titterton. He came under severe pressure from the Australian Commission lawyers for working for the UK rather than the Australian government as head of the Maralinga Atomic Safety Committee. This is rather unfair, because he was working for both the UK and the Menzies government. But someone had to take the blame and divert Australian public attention away from Australia's political complicity.

As mentioned, Lord Penney was also put under pressure. Ken McGinley made sure the media were aware of Penney's failings. It got to Penney and it was noted he was being deeply affected by the many allegations levelled against him by the press, such as using the men as human guinea pigs. Penney was forced to respond to the latter by writing to the press about having concerns about the 'dreadful problem' of the many stories of nuclear veterans' children being born genetically damaged.

With the benefit of hindsight, I really wish I'd paid more attention to the significance of all of this at the time. Thank goodness other sources recorded it.

Lord William Penney died six years later at the age of 82.

When campaigning for nuclear test veteran recognition, the UK *Daily Mirror* had let it be known that, at the time of the Australian Royal Commission visit, Penney was battling with the liver cancer that eventually killed him.

Ken McGinley did not know this when he shadowed Lord Penney at the Commission hearings. When interviewed on TV in 1985, the BNTVA chairman accused Penney and his political masters of 'crimes against humanity'. Later, McGinley confided with investigative journalist Alan Rimmer, author of the book *Between Heaven and Hell* published in 2012, that as leader of the BNTVA and a nuclear test veteran himself, he had great difficulty having any sympathy with Penney. His only comment was: "The fact is that people like Penney and his ilk destroyed thousands of lives, and I can't really forgive him for that."

During and after the Australian Royal Commission hearing in 1985 many in the public and press came to understand the damage done by radioactive fallout and poor safety – but this soon faded from the headlines.

Lord Penney, and others in senior positions, did very well from the nuclear bomb test programme. The bomb tests confirmed the thoughts of US General Smedley D Butler, who wrote in his 1930 book, *War is a Racket*: "War is the only thing that is international in scope and in which profit is measured in dollars and the losses in lives."

Penney was showered with honours, elevated to the House of Lords and took up several academic positions in retirement. He lived out his life in rural splendour, twenty miles from Oxford in a substantial 17th century cottage with huge gardens and manicured lawns. His reputation as the 'smiling killer' of the Manhattan Project sat easily alongside his natural sunny disposition, despite his part in opening the Pandora's box of manmade radioactive horrors and the misery it wrought upon the nuclear test veterans, their families and others.

Before he died, Penney burnt all his private papers (as one would expect from a loyal servant of embarrassing policy) and left a substantial sum of money to build a play park for local children in the village where he saw out his life. It's a gesture seemingly at odds with the man in 1958, at the height of his fame, who, when invited to a drinks party by British Prime Minister Harold Macmillan and asked how many hydrogen bombs it would it take to destroy Britain, replied: "Five or six will knock us out, or to be on the safe side seven or eight," before adding, with his characteristic smile: "I'll 'ave another gin and tonic, if you'd be so kind."

As Britain's nuclear bomb supremo, Lord Penney secured our nation's leaders with prestige and power but also left a legacy of shame and scandal that will stain our history until it is admitted.

The Australian Royal Commission returned to Australia in November 1985 with a two volume, 615-page report with 201 conclusions and 7 recommendations. The parting shot from the senior British QC, Robin Auld, in his final report dismissed the Commission by suggesting it was 'a fuss about nothing of any interest'. In other words, it was a political 'fudge' that continued to deny the hazards of radiation.

What stunned the population of Australia most was reading about the betrayal of the nation by Sir Robert Menzies, who had retired in 1966 just before the clean-up of Operation Brumby.

The Commission recommended compensation to be paid to military staff, civilian contractors and Aboriginals who were exposed to radiation, and for the Aboriginal people whose land had been seized for bomb testing. It also recommended Maralinga and Emu Field should be decontaminated to a standard that allowed the Aboriginals to return to the land. This took years, and it was not until 2010 that some areas were habitable, but there are still some areas excluded from habitation.

However, meaningful just and honourable compensation for the military and civilian contractors has never been enacted. Those who served and suffered would have to spend the rest of their lives fighting for justice.

In 1993, Australia and the UK signed a treaty that ensured continued exchange of information between the two nations in order to avoid any future compensation. This treaty ended a 41-year history of Australia being fully complicit with the UK test programme, a policy decided by Sir Robert Menzies in 1952 without consulting his cabinet. The two countries fell out in 1967 over Australia's anger about the contamination of a once pristine continent, but reunited in 1993 to avoid any joint accountability and responsibility towards the legacy ill heath, premature deaths and genetically damaged offspring of servicemen involved. It was a sordid see-saw of political convenience without any shame.

Since then, several actions of the UK and Australian governments have been enacted into policy in tandem: that is, the refusal to cytogenetically blood-test nuclear veterans, the heavy reliance on easily biased epidemiological studies, the creation of Ministers of Veterans to ensure enforcement of policy against the interests of nuclear veterans and their families is maintained, plus other agreements to deny justice.

Many independent studies have been carried out since the 1980s regarding the ill health of nuclear veterans' children. All have shown a significant excess of stillbirths, new-born babies living only a few hours to a few days, deaths in toddlers, deformed bodies and young lives ruined. All have been callously ignored.

The latest research in the UK, in December 2020, was a Global Health Survey (GHS-2020) by LABRATS International. LABRATS (Legacy of Atomic Bombs – Atomic Test Survivors) is an NGO founded by Alan Owen FBCS CITP, a former chairman of the BNTVA and son of a nuclear test veteran. Alan was seen as 'a breath of fresh air' compared with what the very few remaining members of the BNTVA had experienced since 2002. However, he left the BNTVA in 2020 because of intimidation from trustees, who pressured him to cease challenging UK government policy denying nuclear veterans and families an honourable and just settlement for their many grievances, and set up LABRATS.

LABRATS' GHS-2020 research provides a snapshot of the worldwide atomic survivors community's health problems. Offspring of nuclear veterans have shown high levels of physical health conditions and mental problems, which confirm many earlier studies. The percentage of miscarriages within the community is found to be 29.2% for those who are offspring of nuclear test veterans, and an extremely wide range of medical conditions have been listed. Overall this survey revealed that the descendants of nuclear test veterans continue to struggle on a daily basis.

For full details, visit www.labrats.international.

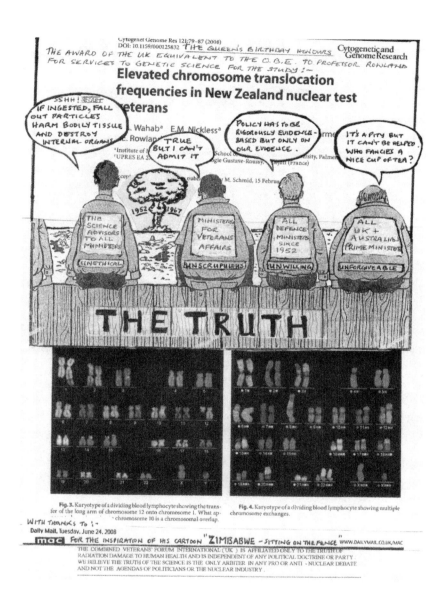

The Truth

The political reaction to the 300% increased genetic damage in nuclear veterans shown by the Rowland cytogenetic blood test study of nuclear veterans, which was peer-reviewed in 2009.

(Inspired by a MAC Daily Mail cartoon published a year earlier.)

Chapter 7: Gathering the Evidence

"Everyone has a right to freedom of opinion and expression. This right includes freedom to hold opinions without interference and seek, receive and impart information and ideas through any media and regardless of frontiers."
Universal Declaration of Human Rights, Article 19

Gathering the evidence of nuclear damage to health has taken many decades. In 1951, the eminent biologist and director of the Chester Beatty Research Institute, Royal Cancer Hospital, Professor Alex Haddow had expressed concerns that the impact of nuclear bomb tests would not be fully known until 50 years had elapsed. The 1956 UK Medical Research Council report confirmed research was needed to fully understand the consensus of both biologists and physicists that exposure to low dose radiation is harmful and a causal link to genetic damage passed to the children and grandchildren.

The evidence has been confirmed. And yet, in an age where understanding of all new discoveries, from the internal combustion engine to computer technology, has advanced year by year, the causal link of the hazards of radiation to man has been denied, with both occupational industrial and military dogma pronouncing it as being perfectly safe. Nuclear hazards have been lied about politically as being of 'no conceivable injury' and callously dismissed as "it is a pity, but it cannot be helped" at the highest level in two major democracies. These are both politically motivated assumptions that are patently untrue and callously dismissive of science.

Knowledge of the causal link of radiation exposure to legacy ill health continued to emerge, confirming Haddow's fears. During the 1980s and 90s, nuclear veterans and their widows began to realise their many grievances about a lack of duty of care for the health conditions they suffered were being politically excluded from accountability and responsibility. During this period, and earlier, pre-emptive political measures were put into place by those with vested interests in industry, the military and government to help enforce denial of any obligation to provide a duty of care.

In 1959, a little-published event took place behind closed doors. Representatives of the International Commission on Radiological Protection (ICRP) and the World Health Organisation (WHO) met and entered into an agreement which effectively 'gagged' the WHO from making any comment on radiation-linked illness. This administrative arrangement only favoured the growth and expansion of nuclear industry. But at what cost?

Within a decade or so, Dr John Gofman MD PHD, former Director of Health Research at the Lawrence Livermore Laboratory, USA and a former advisor to the Atomic Energy Commission, stated: "The nuclear establishment is conducting a war against humanity." Dr Gofman's statement is a sober and knowledgeable comment from someone with a long connection to the nuclear establishment and it reflected the growing unease amongst many eminent scientists.

Not all the facts in this book came into the hands of nuclear test veterans as dated. But, year by year, decade by decade, evidence came to light from the darkness of archives, the press and other sources. All are facts entered into the public domain. Between the 1980s and 2000, the causal link between radiation exposure and genetic damage passing to future generations emerged. The consensus view of both biologists and physicists, agreed unanimously in the 1956 UK Medical Research Council report, is therefore confirmed.

Since the 1960s it has been possible to confirm, by cytogenetic blood analysis (a new diagnostic technology), whether persons exposed to ionising radiation have chromosomal abnormalities (genetic damage) even if the damage occurred decades earlier. The USSR used this advanced diagnostic technology as early as the 1960s on nuclear industry workers and on their nuclear test veterans. It did not take long for the UK to use this new diagnostic – but only behind closed doors.

In 1968, Rosyth Naval Dockyard in Scotland started servicing and refuelling nuclear powered submarines. Dr H John Evans of the Medical Research Council Unit, Western General Hospital, Edinburgh began taking blood samples annually from 197 men occupationally employed in this nuclear work. The radiation dose estimates were taken from readings provided by the Admiralty Radiation Records Centre. The annual blood tests continued for 10 years.

When Dr Evans' 10-year study *Radiation Induced Chromosome Aberrations in Nuclear Dockyard Workers* was published on 15 February 1979, it showed that, whilst radiation exposure was below the internationally accepted maximum permissible level for workers of 50 mSv per year, there was a significant increase in chromosomal damage in the men's blood. This chromosome damage was found to increase as the dose increased. That is, Dr Evans found that low dose radiation was a causal link to genetic damage in persons exposed.

Four years later, Dr Evans found significant genetic damage in a nuclear test veteran. On 24 January 1984 he wrote a letter headed 'Christmas Island Atomic Bomb Tests' to Dr David James of the UK Medical Research Council, London, asking for permission to carry out cytogenetic blood tests on other Christmas Island nuclear veterans. Dr Evans' letter said that the nuclear veteran tested "has a not inconsiderable amount of chromosome damage in his blood cells which would not be inconsistent with having received radiation exposure 20 or more years ago."

Details of this did not come into the hands of nuclear test veterans until the mid-2000s, despite the information being in the public domain since 1985. The power of the internet is a very helpful leveller in the gaining of knowledge.

This was a case of a dedicated scientist expressing a wish to use new diagnostic technology to assist in helping people potentially exposed to ionising radiation in the past, to identify the damage to their DNA and possibly enable them to receive earlier remedies to assist them in life. A perfectly reasonable human right – except for the fact it is related to exposure to radioactivity.

Not surprisingly, Dr Evans' request was turned down by the Ministry of Defence. This case, and other facts, confirmed nuclear test veterans are being deliberately excluded from cytogenetic blood analysis. Advanced diagnostic technology is ignored by MOD policy in favour of epidemiological statistical studies that are incapable of showing damage at a cellular level but are dependent only on cause of death on certificates. Which, of course, never give radiation as a causal link. The medical profession is in the dark regarding the health hazards of radiation as a result of the ICRP/WHO agreement of 1959.

In 1984, the Black Report suggested that epidemiology in radiation-linked deaths was a methodology of bias just used to reassure public opinion. This report was triggered by the excessive death rate of children from leukaemia in the village of Seascale, close to the Windscale (Sellafield) nuclear energy complex. The childhood death rate was statistically shown to be a shocking ten times (i.e. 1000%) more than the national average.

The controversial Black Report set out to show, by a very strange application of epidemiology, that childhood leukaemia cases in Cumbria had nothing to do with radiation but were due only to chance. When it was published, it stated that "the increase in leukaemia is so huge it cannot be due to radiation; some other factor may be the cause."

Sir Douglas Black, who led the Inquiry, admitted to Peter Wilkinson, Director of Greenpeace, that the primary function of the Inquiry was to 'reassure the Cumbrian public'. But a former Prime Minister of Ireland, Charles Haughey, who had seen a rise in cancer cases on Ireland's east coast and campaigned against nuclear waste being discharged into the Irish sea by pipeline from Sellafield, described the report's conclusions as a "dreadful piece of whitewash" and added: "If there is a high incidence of leukaemia in any area where a nuclear plant is situated, surely to God the obvious interpretation is that the plant is responsible for it. These figures alone would, in my view, justify closing the plant immediately for further investigation and certainly putting a lot of people in prison who have been telling lies over the past four or five years about this matter."

The 'any cause other than radiation' conclusion of the Black Report is an example of the *modus operandi* used for decades by epidemiologists to deny radiation is a causal link to ill health, premature deaths and genetic damage passed to children of persons occupationally or otherwise exposed to ionising radiation in the past.

Therefore the 'right' answer, according to this discredited branch of science, is to seize upon any cause: smoking, drinking, population mixing, the death rates are impossibly too high, the emissions of radiation are too low, poor diet, illness by radiation phobia, or excessive leukaemia death rates of 1000% in children is 'just a chance occurrence' .

Twenty-one years after President Kennedy's declaration that 'even one human life should be a concern to us all', it appears, from the 1984 Black Report, that nuclear policy was to deny all and admit nothing. This is the tragic morality and ethics of nuclear industrial advanced knowledge when compared to alternative industries or inventions.

By 1985, Ken McGinley had proved to the BNTVA membership, the press and many politicians that, under his chairmanship, the pursuit of 'All We Seek is Justice' was based on the reality of what was happening and what had happened in real time to nuclear test veterans and their families. The Australian Royal Commission had been a charade, but the message in numerous press reports and documentaries had kept the hazardous effects of radiation in the UK press. But for political leaders, badly advised by officials, it was just water off a duck's back.

Then, on 26 April 1986, a serious nuclear accident and tragedy occurred in Chernobyl, in the Soviet Union. Chernobyl is the most serious nuclear accident of many that have happened to an industry professing safety and reliability. The fallout from Chernobyl covered most of Europe and parts of the UK. Many deaths were admitted but thousands of deaths have been denied.

Reports in the UK press mentioned that Chernobyl town's fire section, by their sacrifice in the first hours, and without any protective clothing, had prevented Reactor 3 from going the same way as Reactor 4, which had released 4,000 times more radioactivity than the accident at the Windscale (Sellafield) nuclear plant in 1957.

The Windscale (Sellafield) nuclear reactor accident involved the reactor core overheating and catching fire. Before it was extinguished, this spread with changes in wind a plume of radioactive fallout over a large area of the British Isles. The accident came about due to the pressure of obtaining the weapon-grade nuclear materials urgently needed, in a very short space of time, for the Operation Grapple series of thermo-nuclear megaton hydrogen bomb tests at Christmas Island.

The accident caused thousands of gallons of contaminated milk to be poured down the drains across Britain. In the UK at that time, children received free milk at school and the government did not want to risk them drinking milk contaminated by strontium-90 and other radioactive fallout from the accident. Because of changes in wind direction, some of the radioactive plume crossed the Irish Sea from Cumbria and fell over the east coast of Ireland. This resulted a few years later in a spike in cancer rates and deaths. Any causal link to the cancers resulting from the accident was denied by the UK Government.

Dr Chris Busby, Britain's leading independent expert on

low dose, low level radiation, gained access to meteorological charts at the time of the Windscale accident and found the charts had been changed on the days following the accident to indicate none of the fallout went in direction of the east coast of Ireland. Anything published by the press or other media liable to embarrass the government during this period was gagged by 'D' notices and the Official Secrets Act.

However, Ministry of Defence officials over many years, and with what many nuclear veterans regarded as a perverse sense of dark humour, issued statements to the effect that the hazards of the nuclear weapon tests at Christmas Island in 1957/8 were no different to the natural background radiation levels found in the United Kingdom during these years.

For once, some element of truth could be attached to this statement. The background level of radiation in the UK had risen as a result of the fallout from the Windscale accident and this suited officials with regard to the view that no perceivable hazard existed at Christmas Island.

Such, it appears, is the way information is obfuscated when deemed by officials to be in the national interest.

The Windscale accident is another example of deception in nuclear history. It is like peeling a very large onion without protective eye goggles and revealing successive never-ending layers of deception enough to make any person weep.

Six of the Chernobyl firemen died of acute radiation poisoning within weeks of the accident, and many died later. This was just one cohort of the many who assisted in the horrendous clean-up – and then there were the deaths and serious ill health of the civilian population exposed to fallout.

The newspapers in Scotland mentioned that the Soviet

firemen were great fans of British football. Many offers of help were made to the Soviet people. McGinley decided this was a case that deserved recognition by the BNTVA.

McGinley's reaction was both altruistic and humanitarian, and stated irrespective of the ideology of the country where fellow humans had suffered badly from radiation exposure. These ordinary citizens were regarded as 'brothers in arms' doing a hazardous job for their nation. McGinley asked the Renfrewshire Fire Department to strike two plaques in honour of the Soviet firefighting heroes who, by their selfless action, had prevented the disaster from being any worse.

Instead of this symbol of solidarity being sent to Chernobyl in a diplomatic bag, the BNTVA chairman decided he would deliver it himself. This was not an easy task. The Soviet Union was known to be a very difficult place to visit without political sanction from Soviet leadership. But this was the era of 'Glasnost' with a new Soviet leader, President Gorbachev, who wished the old USSR to open its doors to the outside world. So, after contacting the Soviet Embassy, two weeks later Ken McGinley received, to his surprise, an invitation to travel to Chernobyl as an 'honoured guest' of the Soviet people.

Before travelling to the Soviet Union McGinley was given two footballs, signed by all the players of Celtic and Rangers, to hand to the Chernobyl firemen. This of course was of great interest to the British press – and publicity for the BNTVA. Yet it did not stop the questions about how many years McGinley had been a member of the Communist Party. His bemused answer to conspiracy theorists was: "I was a Catholic." McGinley later told *Fissionline* editor Alan Rimmer this seemed to satisfy them.

A recently published book *Manual for Survival – a*

Chernobyl Guide to the Future gives another perspective to the anti-nuclear labels attached to campaigning nuclear test veterans and others. After ten years' field research into Ukrainian archives, author Kate Brown, award-winning US Professor of Nuclear History and an environmental teacher at the Massachusetts Institute of Technology, found that: "Soviet scientists, bureaucrats and civilians documented staggering increases in cases of birth defects, child mortality, cancers and a multitude of life-altering diseases years after the disaster. Worried that this evidence would blow the lid on the effects of massive radiation from weapon-testing during the Cold War, scientists and diplomats from international organisations, including the UN, tried to bury or discredit it."

Ken McGinley's reference to the heroic firefighters of Chernobyl as 'brothers in arms' is relevant when comparing two groups of service people exposed to the hazards of radiation in the national interest. As mentioned earlier, false accusations of being communist or anti-nuclear is a tactic often used by an industry whose lobbyists and apologists abhor any mention of the words 'humanity', 'solidarity' or 'altruism' when challenging the failure to control the hazards of radiation that impact on the lives of persons exposed.

Similarly, academics, nuclear test veterans and others campaigning for the truth find the words 'ethos' and 'morality' are words not recognised by the nuclear establishment – nor is the word 'principle' ever to be found in their nihilistic vocabulary.

In mid-1993, with regards to 'principle' of policy relating to radiation-linked illnesses and disabilities, I wrote to John Smith MP, then Labour Party leader in opposition to John Major's

Conservative-led government.

On 24 August 1993, I received a response from Dr John Reid MP, Armed Forces Spokesman for the Labour Party, to whom John Smith had passed my letter. Dr Reid wrote: "You will be pleased to know I specifically raised this point in a defence debate just prior to the parliamentary recess. It is our firm view that the nuclear test veterans should be regarded in the same way as any other serviceman or woman who was injured in the service of their country and we have constantly asked the government to take this approach. Unfortunately, the government still refuses to concede the principle involved but you will be sure that we will maintain our pressure upon them to do so since it is only in the fashion we can reasonably expect that justice will be done, even after all this time."

However, on becoming Secretary of State for Defence in Tony Blair's 1997 Labour government, Dr John Reid reneged upon the above firmly held principle.

This is a common trend of bad faith repeated for decades by successive UK governments. When asked why a 'firm view of principle' to settle nuclear veterans' claims is reneged upon when gaining office, the answer given by any newly appointed minister from any political party – if any is given – is that, on becoming a minister, they have been made 'privy to information formerly not known to them' with regards to this matter.

When asked what 'new information' they have become 'privy' to they do not respond and remain silent. The circle of unprincipled deception is complete, underpinned by policy and treaty obligations.

In fact, UK nuclear test veterans did not discover the reason for the Blair government's backward somersault on 'principle' until 18 February 2008, when an associate of the Combined Veterans' Forum International (CVFI), Major Alan Batchelor, Vice President of the ANVA, sent a copy of the Australian Treaty Series 1993 No 40 signed between the British and Australian governments on 10 December 1993 which explains the bi-lateral situation of joint policy in detail.

Australian Treaty Series 1993 No 40 10 December 1993

Presumably as a result of the 1985 Australian Royal Commission conclusions to decontaminate the test sites and allow the Aboriginal people to re-inhabit lands taken from them in the 1950s, this treaty between Australia and the UK agreed that:

1 & 2. The UK agrees to pay Australia as full and final settlement an ex gratia sum of £20 million in five parts between 1994 and 1998 in relation to the decontamination and clearance of the test site.

The Treaty then agreed:

3 & 4. To indemnify each nation against any loss, costs, damages or expenses each may incur or be called upon to pay as a result of any such claims by any person, natural or legal.

5. To consult, at the request of either, on the conduct of the legal proceedings arising out of a claim and on the manner in which any claim may be settled.

6. Any member of HM Forces or a person employed by the UK Government shall not be included in any claim. (However, this paragraph was said to have no application to members of the Commonwealth of Australia.

Prior to this treaty, for a short period in 1991-92 the BNTVA obtained a window of opportunity allowing nuclear veterans to apply for disability pensions from the UK Department of

Health and Social Security (DHSS). Several members did so, including me, and, after submitting claims plus enduring a medical examination by DHSS doctors, some obtained various percentage disability war pensions according to their rank at time of service.

But this DHSS loophole undermined the agreements made in the treaty and as a result had to be closed. Henceforth, claims were now handled by a newly formed Veterans Agency and placed under the political control of the UK Ministry of Defence. The UK government and MOD bureaucrats took very little time use the bi-lateral treaty to prevent any claims being granted.

This was also replicated in Australia. Nuclear veterans and their widows now found the shutters on claims were firmly slammed shut. Before a veteran or a widow entered an appeal court the decision had already been made to reject the claim. This information came from an associate of the CVFI, nuclear test veteran Archie Ross, who often attended such hearings with veterans or widows. Appeal hearings became known to nuclear veterans as 'kangaroo courts', used against a section of the electorate now effectively disenfranchised as *personae non gratae.*

It appears no such treaty of co-operation to undermine nuclear veterans' claims has existed between the United Kingdom and New Zealand. This was demonstrated in 1999, when the leader of the New Zealand Nuclear Test Veterans Association, Roy Sefton QSM, began his attempt to have 50 survivors of the 551-strong cohort of New Zealand nuclear veterans from the UK's Christmas Island tests cytogenetically blood-tested for radiation-induced genetic damage. It was the first such study to be free from UK government or MOD interference.

Sefton asked a New Zealand party leader, Winston Peters for help. This resulted in a meeting between Peters and the UK High Commissioner to New Zealand, where Peters was warned that any help offered to nuclear test veterans would be regarded as "an unfriendly act by the United Kingdom government." Not quite the reaction one would expect from one sovereign independent state to another. According to Sefton, Winston Peters was not impressed.

This was a desperate and unsuccessful attempt by the UK to prevent advanced diagnostic technology being used on nuclear test veterans able to show evidence of radiation damage. However, the New Zealand government did not bow to UK pressure. Instead, they said to the NZNTVA: "If you raise half the money for the study, we will pay the rest." The study began in 2001 and was peer reviewed in 2009.

The Australian Treaty Series No 40 of mutual co-operation between the UK and Australia accounts for the difficulties experienced by the Australian Nuclear Veterans Association (ANVA) from 1993 to use similar cytogenetic blood-testing studies on their own veterans from the UK bomb tests.

In 2001, cytogenetic blood testing of Australian nuclear veterans was being strongly advocated by Democrat Senator Lyn Allison. However, as the with UK nuclear test veterans in the 1980s and 90s, the Australian veterans were only given the option of taking part in a blind, biased epidemiological study of death certificates, without blood tests, to 'assist' their case. Conducted by Adelaide University and with epidemiological methodology and protocols set by the Australian government, the ANVA were cynically betrayed.

In a media release on 13 July 2001, Democrat Senator

Allison said: "I challenge the Veterans Minister to stop stalling and hiding behind epidemiological tests. Epidemiological studies can't compare to state-of-the-art blood tests, which can tell us if a person was irradiated and what impact there has been on their chromosomes."

Later, the enlightened senator said: "It is tragic and heartless that Australian governments have knocked back 96% of compensation claims by servicemen and civilians." (Report by Colin James for *The Advertiser,* 25 August 2001.)

As predicted, the epidemiological study in Australia, published in 2006, was as politically biased and as significantly flawed as the UK NRPB studies of the 1980s and 90s. All had epidemiological conclusions of insufficient dosage of radiation exposure to allow for claims for a wide range of legacy ill health and genetic damage. The bi-lateral treaty between Australia and the UK gave a big impetus to denying Australian veterans a duty of care, just as it had done for the claims of the United Kingdom's veterans throughout the previous two decades.

Australia was obviously still locked into Sir Robert Menzies' false politically expedient lie that 'no conceivable injury would arise from nuclear bomb testing' and the UK still followed its callous "It's a pity, but it cannot be helped" edict, which ignored the consensus view of the 1956 Medical Research Council report that radiation is a causal link to legacy ill health and genetic damage.

For two governments who often pride themselves as being guided by science, it's clear that they only let science guide them when it suits them.

Therefore, it's fair to say the only positive to come from the 1993 Treaty of co-operation between the UK and Australia to deny nuclear veterans' claims is that it gave full justification to nuclear veterans from those countries to do the same. That is, to co-operate in collecting and exchanging evidence to assist with legal action that Rosenblatts of London were due to commence, on nuclear veterans' behalf, and without any legal aid, in 2005.

Since two democratic governments could conspire with each other to deny compensation, then, in the interests of the truth of science, the veterans believed they had a democratic right to seek archive documents deliberately withheld to avoid responsibility and accountability. After all, the use of the Official Secrets Act had, by this time, become acknowledged by nuclear veterans as a discredited and one-sided gagging order to prevent access to information that the nuclear families needed to use as evidence in claims being made without legal aid.

A 'confidential' document written in 1996 confirmed that denials of the truth about low dose radiation were not supported by the knowledge held by the government at the time.

NATO Field Commanders (ACE Directive 86.63), written by Brigadier J.T. Holmes, UK Army Director of Staff Operations, gave advice to field commanders about the use of tactical depleted uranium field weapons. It stated that, if inhaled or ingested: "Low level radiation (LLR) exposure produces a risk to soldiers of long-term health consequences. Additional health risks that may occur are teratogenesis [genetic damage passed to children] and mutagenesis [the origin and development of mutations] and associated psychological and social consequences. The hazard from LLR may be alpha, beta or gamma radiation."

This document did not get into the hands of nuclear test veterans until the mid-2000s but it gives some insight into the knowledge held by Government and denied since the first atomic bomb test of 1952. Low level radiation, particularly fallout alpha and beta (deliberately unrecorded on dosimeters), which could be lethal or cause legacy ill health etc. if inhaled or ingested, continued to be ignored, except in archive documents for use by ministers and the highest ranks of the military.

In fact, archive records held by the Combined History Archive of Nuclear Veterans (CHANV) in the UK, Australia and New Zealand show the brigadier was only acting on information available back in 1979 via a UK Medical Research Council report 'for government eyes only' following 10 years of annual cytogenetic blood testing of 197 occupational nuclear workers. That is, that low dose radiation 'even below the maximum permissible annual dose of 50 mSv showed significant genetic damage and this genetic damage increased as dose increased.' This officer was only quoting known science. His directive also refers to the psychological and social consequences of low dose, low level exposure.

However, the conspiracy of silence and duplicity over the matter has continued unabated.

By 2000, every nuclear test veteran and widow attempting to gain justice had become increasingly aware of the mixed messaging on radiation damage to health from press reports compared to government policy. In a society where government often falsely states they are 'only following the science', they have been seen as totally disingenuous when it comes to nuclear risk. In direct contrast to the continued denials of government, press reports and documentaries on the subject that show the reality of what nuclear families experience on a daily basis give absolutely no credibility to the policy used against nuclear veterans.

In 2001, following Ken McGinley's years of running the 'All We Seek is Justice' campaign, the BNTVA ceased to be a campaigning association. His leadership had been brought to an end by fractious infighting amongst the committee and most members, myself included, left within a few years of witnessing the abject surrender by the next chairman.

However, the ever eloquent Ken McGinley was not finished campaigning yet. He was quickly brought back by the nuclear veterans' *pro bono* legal counsel, led by Rosenblatt Solicitors of London, for the Nuclear Veterans Limitation Trial, which ended in 2009.

In Australia, the ANVA, also hampered by a totally contrived and biased epidemiological study, was ably led by the campaigning Vice President, Major Alan Batchelor, and fighting against all odds.

Only in New Zealand did the NZNTVA, led by Roy Sefton QSM and beyond the interference and prejudice of the UK government and Ministry of Defence, have any freedom of movement.

In London the MOD, as always, had access to a bottomless pit of tax payers' money to block nuclear veterans from finding justice through well-funded legal counsel and many barristers to muddy the future waters. Even Canberra could be relied upon to give expert witness support from epidemiologists. It was a power struggle of truth against unlimited capital.

In the post-millennial years the fight for a just and honourable settlement of claims was to become a struggle heavily weighted against nuclear veterans and their families, who were denied legal aid and access to information and regarded as a vexation by ministers and officials in what was 'undoubtedly a political problem' rather than one of scientific denial inherited by successive UK governments.

One fact is clear in the true history of the UK nuclear weapon test experiments. Despite the sanitised history portrayed by successive governments, the veterans who were actually at the bomb test locations have evidence of radiation-induced genetic damage in their DNA and they have consistently been lied to. Today's bureaucrats and politicians weren't there, and their recollections may vary because the records of radiation doses at those locations is an inheritance to which they also have been denied access.

The archive records held by nuclear test veterans show the advice of the consensus view of the UK Medical Research Council Report of 1956 has been ignored by both the Australian and UK governments. Instead, both nations have embarked on a vindictive political agenda to work together to deny legacy ill health, premature deaths and genetic damage passed to the children and grandchildren of veterans.

Their sole political objective has been to save money and deflect embarrassment. The legal fight that followed had its ups and downs, but despite the odds it did not end with the complete victory that the government desperately strove for, at great taxpayers' expense.

The nuclear veterans may have lost by an inconclusively narrow 4:3 verdict, which many consider unsafe, at the Supreme Court in 2012, but they went on to win a moral and ethical victory, a huge achievement against a war of attrition fought with unlimited public funds by government lawyers using every means possible to deny justice.

Without legal aid, with constant appeals by the MOD using legal technicalities against any successful stages of trial verdict, and with the withholding of and/or denial of crucial and pivotal evidence from being heard, the issue is far from being resolved – as the following chapters will reveal.

In 2021, nuclear veterans and their families have every reason to feel proud. Truth and history is on our side, and that is the final arbiter.

Chapter 8: The Violation of Nuclear Veterans' Access to Personal Information

*"It is a human right for individuals to know the level of
radiation to which they have been exposed...."*
Article 7 of the Lesvos Declaration, signed by 17 eminent
scientists from 10 nations, 2009. (This human right is ignored
by the United Kingdom Government.)

As nuclear test veterans and their families in the UK, Australia
and New Zealand entered the new millennium they were all in
a very vulnerable position. The BNTVA chairman and founder
Ken McGinley had been replaced by a new chairman, John
Lowe; the association began to lose membership and apathy
plus defeatism quickly set in. At the time the general
impression was that the new chairman and committee leaders
of the BNTVA had begun looking at members' futures only
through the bottom of empty rose-tinted beer glasses.

October 3rd, 2002 marked the 50th anniversary of the UK's
first atomic bomb at Monte Bello Island. The BNTVA arranged
a protest to be held in London and letters were sent out to the
membership and others. As a member since 1985, I was invited.
It was an opportunity to judge for myself the current state of
the association, about which I and many others had become
increasingly concerned. So my wife Dawn and I travelled from
Gloucestershire to see for ourselves. I was only two years off
retirement and I did not know that this invitation would result
in many visits to London over the next decade.

We arrived in London on a beautiful sunny autumn day. The main cohort of the BNTVA, resplendent in association badges and blazers, were massed on a deep grass verge opposite Downing Street with their backs to the huge Ministry of Defence complex. A large number of people of all ages assembled on the pavement between the green verge and the broad main road: teenagers (veterans' grandchildren), older adults (veterans' children) and the more elderly – veterans themselves, plus wives and widows of veterans – and others showing support.

Suddenly a detachment of police officers arrived and began erecting steel waist-high barriers through which those assembled on the pavement, including my wife and I, were corralled, tightly-packed like sheep, onto the main road.

Dawn and I stood next to an elegantly-dressed elderly lady and gentleman; I later found out they were siblings. The lady remarked to her brother: "If they had their way," she nodded in the direction of police, "we'd all be in the Tower of London." When I asked her why she had travelled to the protest, she said: "My husband sailed to Monte Bello with the task force as a scientist. After the bomb test he was asked to urgently take a box of radioactive materials on his lap by passenger plane back to London. After returning home, he died quite young from cancer."

On the other side of me in the tightly-packed corral the daughter of a nuclear veteran held a protest placard on which was pinned a drawing of a man in uniform placing a bundle of clothes into a washing machine. I asked her what the meaning was behind her picture. She replied: "I drew it for my dad when I was a little girl after he'd written a letter to say 'Don't worry about me, I'm looked after very well at Maralinga; I've even got my own washing machine to decontaminate my overalls when I get back from the bomb test sites.'" I then asked this lady if her dad was here today. "No, he died from cancer a few years after he came home," she replied.

Shortly after these two brief conversations, the new BNTVA chairman came across from the grass verge and addressed us all. "You are not allowed to cross the road to Downing Street to deliver your petition," he said. That was the intention of the veterans' children and grandchildren. "You are to stay here," he continued (corralled like sheep), "but you may hand out leaflets to any passing pedestrians. However, do not block the pavement."

This was a huge disappointment, particularly for the banner-carrying children and grandchildren.

At this moment, because it had recently been in the news, I had a vision of a young man looking up the gun barrel of a tank in Beijing's Tiananmen Square. Events in history teach many lessons. But one stands out. When bureaucrats and politicians determine their 'own truth' rather than deny the reality of events, democracy quickly dies. This day confirmed to me that, with litigation fast approaching, the newly formed Combined Veterans' Forum International would be needed to exchange and pass to lawyers information deliberately withheld for decades to assist in achieving justice.

It was a few years later that we discovered that the elderly widow I'd spoken to had attempted to gain a widow's pension from the Ministry of Defence. Her application had been refused because the Ministry told her that her husband had not been a member of the armed forces on the Monte Bello taskforce. She told them her husband had travelled with the taskforce after being given honorary Royal Navy officer rank and naval uniform to sail with the flotilla, therefore he was entitled to share the same conditions on board as the service officers.

In any event, it mattered not. If her young scientist husband had been a member of the armed forces her application for a widow's pension would still have been denied as 'a pity, but it cannot be helped.' Without knowledge of the radiation levels at bomb locations, the non-recording of alpha and beta fallout radiation, the denial of blood-testing, it's become almost impossible to gain justice.

In 1985 I had founded the Combined Veterans' Forum (CVF) with Australia and New Zealand nuclear veterans and other campaigners, initially with a Post Office box number, and later with computer email contact. Among its members were Australian nuclear test veteran leaders, the New Zealand Nuclear Test Veteran Association chairman and others such as the leading British independent radiation expert Dr Chris Busby who, with Richard Bramhall, had set up the Low Level Radiation Campaign (LLRC).

In 2002 we were joined by Shirley Denson, the widow of RAF Canberra pilot, Sqdn Ldr Eric Denson who had flown twice through nuclear mushroom clouds to collect radiation samples at Christmas Island in 1958. Already a redoubtable and courageous campaigner, she had four daughters and a number of grandchildren, many of whom had suffered genetic damage since birth. Her husband Eric committed suicide 17 years after the bomb tests, at the age of 44.

Shirley, a strong, charismatic and independent character, had operated her own individual campaign from her London home by phone and post before she contacted me in 2001. As a consequence, when Shirley joined the CVF in 2002 it was renamed the Combined Veterans' Forum International and Shirley was listed on the letterheads of newsletters as CVFI co-founder. This helped with the many letters she posted to those she lobbied over the years.

Shirley was an excellent networker and built up a great rapport over the phone with Roy Sefton, the NZNTVA chairman, who by 2007 had joined the CVFI Action Executive. I did likewise with the Australian Association leaders, Ric Johnson and Alan Batchelor of the ANVA. Being within easy travel of central London, Shirley had made many useful contacts over the years. This was the initial concept of both the CVF and CVFI: nuclear veterans working together with other campaigners for justice and recognition for all who had participated in the UK nuclear weapon test experiments.

This worked very well within the CVFI for ten years until late 2012, when Shirley and Roy Sefton objected to my interest in CVFI associate David Whyte's use of Freedom of Information Act questions in attempts to gain evidence of certain key factors to assist nuclear veterans' and widows' claims.

In my view, it did not make any sense to object to using FOIA because the AVGL legal team, led by Rosenblatts, and expert witnesses in the litigation were also aware that hidden evidence was difficult to access without Freedom of Information questions or, at the very least, by invoking a court order to obtain them. As a result of this 'storm in a teacup', Shirley and Roy both wrote letters disassociating themselves from the activity of the CVFI.

By 2013, legal action had ended in the stalemate of the Supreme Court split 4:3 verdict blocking compensation claims of the Atomic Veterans Group Litigation.

From its inception the CVFI was deliberately not run along the lines of an association but only as a forum. We only wanted self-funded active campaigners to be associated. There was, therefore, no committee to fall out with each other, no membership fees etc. Even in 2002 we knew we had to be independent of all this because we had seen with the BNTVA that it had led to inertia, apathy and surrender. As it happened, that was only a utopian dream in a time of nuclear test veteran discord.

The sole focus of the CVFI was to exchange information between the UK, Australia and New Zealand in support of all who had participated in the UK nuclear weapon test experiments, and, of course, to gather information for use by Rosenblatts of London in their case for the Atomic Veterans Group Litigation (AVGL). Beginning from a zero start point of knowledge, particularly in how government policy to exclude justice had impacted upon any progress, it was a legal mountain to climb for any law firm. Added to this was the need to grasp and understand the complexity of the science underpinning the whole legal quest for justice.

With the benefit of hindsight, expecting professional lawyers to take any notice of what nuclear test veterans had to say about the science of nuclear detonations fifty years after the event was a pretty forlorn hope. However, by the end of the litigation process they showed they had grasped and belatedly used the evidence we had sent them, all of which was fully supported by referenced data. (My own view is that any one who can read the conclusions of a scientific report is capable of seeing where the truth exists.)

At the time I failed to realise just how threatened the Nuclear Veteran Associations felt about our independent CVFI activity. The were fearful perhaps because they did not understand the concept of individual thought at play not being run by committees funded by members. The BNTVA were very unhappy and parochial about the CVFI from the very start. The ANVA, particularly under the vice presidency of Alan Batchelor, who was the driving force behind the association, were very cooperative and supportive, as were the New Zealanders, led by Roy Sefton. But, under the surface, many association-minded veterans viewed those involved with the CVFI as anti-nuclear and disloyal to the government, or worse. Many could not understand the concept of working together.

Within three years or so the CVFI Action Executive had increased to four with Ken McGinley, the former BNTVA chairman and Roy Sefton QSM, the chairman of the NZNTVA. We were supported by four independent campaigning nuclear veterans as CVFI associates: Barry Smith (ex-RAF), Archie Ross (ex-RAF) and David Whyte (ex-Royal Engineers) – all Christmas Island veterans – and, from 2006, Alan Batchelor (ex-major, Royal Australian Engineers and vice president of the ANVA), who served at Maralinga.

Dai Williams, a business executive, also became an associate and, from the very beginning, we were lucky to have as a legal adviser Ian Anderson, a Scottish international advocate and attorney at law based in New York, whose legal expertise included radiation cases and other toxic torts. Ian has been involved in cases at the United Nations and also in the European Union at Strasbourg.

Sadly, during the writing of this book in 2021, three key members of the CVFI have died: Roy Sefton, Alan Batchelor and the redoubtable Shirley Denson.

In 2002, the internet proved a quick and convenient means of communication, particularly for accessing international press reports and the wealth of information accrued by investigative journalists in press reports and books about the nuclear bomb tests increased exponentially, year by year. The information gained is all widely available and archive documents, even those marked classified or secret, emerged from national archives in London, Australia or New Zealand.

All that was needed, I naively thought, would be a level playing field on which legal process could proceed with the knowledge gained.

We found science regarding radiation as a causal link to ill health strictly controlled. As with much else, in particular access to radiation levels, hospital records and blood tests are missing, redacted or simply lost. The main blocking mechanism is the political imposition of the 1993 treaty series between the UK and Australia to avoid compensation, and the 1999 associated caveat, mentioned in Chapter Seven, regarding independent cytogenetic blood-testing that led to the political warning that "any help to nuclear veterans is regarded as an unfriendly act by the UK government."

The first decade of the new millennium had shown the nuclear veterans to be in a vulnerable position. However, with regard to the understanding of science on radiation hazard to health and genetic damage agreed by unanimous consensus of the UK's most eminent biologists and physicists (the UK Medical Research Council's 1956 report) and the callous prime ministerial edict that "it is a pity, but it cannot be helped," these facts were being steadily overtaken by an ever growing consensus truth: low dose, low level radioactive fallout is the prime causal link of ill health and premature deaths and this hazard is passed to future generations.

Since the 1990s, one eminent scientist and radiation expert (particularly with regard to low dose, low level radiation) stepped up magnificently, at great expense to his own career, to assist nuclear veterans in achieving justice. The government and the MOD may uphold the dogma that any help to nuclear veterans is an 'unfriendly act', but Devonshire-born Prof Dr Chris Busby has an ethos that any help he could give these men was an act of necessity based on scientific truth.

In fact, in late 2002 Busby had already broken the biased and malign grip on causation of ill health etc., which the Ministry of Defence mistakenly believed they had firmly under their control. Dr Busby is the UK's leading independent expert on low dose radiation. This is important because being independent ensures he is free from bias and the manipulation of government-funded studies and committees with protocols to provide only the 'right' answers to frame policy.

Added to this independence, he has many other scientific credentials. His books *Wings of Death: Nuclear Pollution and Human Health* (1995) and *Wolves of Water: A study constructed from atomic morality, epidemiology, science, bias, philosophy and death* (2006) and his role as scientific secretary to the new European Committee on Radiation Risk (ECRR) enabled him to be a direct, enlightened and extremely credible challenge to the outdated and significantly biased consensus of the hazards of radiation, particularly related to alpha and beta fallout, which had been ignored for decades.

Another advantage is that in his books, Dr Busby writes in a way that means anyone who can read is able to understand the complexity of exposure to radiation hazards. The information enables anyone, even without any knowledge of science, to draw their own conclusions with regards to the truth.

For example, the fact that radiation dose records of nuclear veterans had been found since the 1950s to be institutionally manipulated to a bias by recording primarily only gamma (x-ray) radiation and ignoring alpha and beta fallout is at the heart of Dr Busby's success. He showed this, as an expert witness, in the case of the death of Maralinga nuclear test veteran Gerald Adshead, winning his wife Eva a widow's pension appeal hearing in late 2002.

Gerald Adshead died in 1999 from a malignant brain tumour. Following the guidance of the SPVA's *Statement on Radiation Policy* advice to Defence Ministers and Pension Appeal Tribunals (see Chapter Two), Eva's widow's pension was originally refused on the basis that it was deemed unlikely that exposure at Maralinga – which did not register on Adshead's external gamma-dose film badge dosimeter – could have been sufficient, by epidemiology, to bias the result of any cancer. This deception is now widely acknowledged as the 'red herring' used by epidemiologists, dependent on the inaccurate 1950s ICRP risk model to bias judgements.

"It is of interest," wrote Dr Busby in his second book, *Wolves of Water,* "that the US test veterans with cancer are automatically given pensions on the basis that the cancer may have been caused by fallout." (Pages 317-8)

"I have always argued that for the veterans, film badges are irrelevant as the badges only register external radiation. The hazard for Gerald Adshead was the internal dose from fallout material. Maralinga is an extraordinarily contaminated place where uranium bombs were exploded."

The extent of contamination at Maralinga had been exposed by the whistle blowing of former RAAF LAC Avon Hudson in 1972 (Chapter Six). A mass of plutonium and other toxic material left buried and scattered across the desert by the 600 plus 'minor trials' was abandoned when the UK left Maralinga. Such was the nature of the London–Canberra collaboration between 1952 and 1967 that the Australian federal government no doubt hoped that the truth of the contamination at Maralinga would remain safely fenced off and in pits, hidden in UK classified documents. But politicians of the State of South Australia thought otherwise.

I only suspected the above when, in September 1992, I wrote to the Ministry of Defence about the extent of residual radiation many had witnessed at Maralinga during the 11 months that I was there in 1965-6. For example, close by the air terminal, where I often worked, a large area referred to as 'the cemetery' was fenced off with 'keep out' radiation notices.

The response I received, dated 28 October 1992 and from Dr C J Morgan of Sc (Nuc) 2a MOD, stated the aim of the comprehensive clean-up carried out was to "reduce the radioactive contamination to a level to which risk to personnel would be so low that the presence of Health Physics staff would no longer be required." The MOD's scientist stated in his letter that this was the aim the Pearce Report of '1964'. But this report was not written until 1967.

1964 was one year before I arrived at Maralinga and three years before the extremely hazardous and unfinished Operation Brumby clean-up, during which the lives of Flt Lt Sam McGee and his decontamination team of 35 young RAF airmen were decimated by cancers from the radioactive dust they inhaled or ingested.

The scientific assessment by AWE scientist Noah Pearce of the clean-up of Maralinga was not written in 1964, but in 1967. When it was studied in Canberra, the report shocked politicians as it was a sanitised version of events that made no mention of the deadly plutonium, uranium, cobalt-60, beryllium and other toxins buried in pits close to the surface, or of the 'minor trial' shots of assorted radioactive material scattered across the desert. Dr Morgan's letter to me is just another example of the 'need to know' mentality that encourages hapless bureaucrats to deliberately release false information intended to deceive.

My belief that in 1965-6 Maralinga was fizzing with residual fallout is an established fact. It took until 2010 to decontaminate this nuclear test site of the toxic radioactive poison – and some areas are still not habitable, even today.

The 2002 widow's appeal which Dr Busby won for Eva Adshead were told her husband Gerald was an army lorry driver ferrying equipment back and forth from the bomb test area at Maralinga. Dust is a prime hazard at Maralinga and Gerald suffered a red rash on his neck.

Eva won the case. It helped that, in late 2002, Dr Busby had used as evidence an advance copy of the first report from the European Committee on Radiation Risk, due to be published in the new year. (*The ECRR Regulators' Edition: Brussels 2003, Health Effects of Ionising Radiation Exposure at Low Dose for Radiation Protection Purposes*). The tribunal appeal judge was referred to page 12 fig. 3.1., showing that external gamma radiation is a low risk radiation compared to (unrecorded) internal, chronic, isotopic alpha and beta particles from fallout, inhaled or ingested into the body, which, as internal emitters, irradiate blood, tissue, organs and bone at a cellular level, resulting in a cumulative high risk in comparison to gamma radiation.

Interestingly, Dr Busby noted in his book *Wolves of Water* that, after the case was won, Eva gave him Gerald's old army dosimeter as a memento. Dr Busby remarked that he keeps it on a shelf to remind him of all the poor servicemen, technicians and national service recruits defending their country, standing out in their khaki shorts in the desert with their backs to the flash and hands over their eyes – all of whom were betrayed by the MOD, the scientists and the health establishment.

We thought this widow's hearing could be used as a precedent in future litigation and we passed information about it to Rosenblatt solicitors, along with much else of similar relevance over the next decade. But it wasn't until the end of litigation in 2012-13 that, frustratingly to campaigning nuclear veterans providing evidence, the evidence was used by Rosenblatt's lead counsel Neil Sampson, who dramatically demolished the MOD's so-called expert witness Dr Anne Braidwood. (This is covered in later chapters.)

It's possible Dr Busby's expertise regarding the prime causal link to ill health was side-lined by veterans' lawyers for so long because of the MOD's huge smear campaign against him on the basis of being considered anti-nuclear. This ploy had already been cynically used in the 1950s when Australian bio-chemist Hedley Marston exposed the fact that strontium-90 fallout covered the whole continent of Australia. For this Marston was called a 'Red Commie'. Such tactics to avoid accountability are ultimately the only option available to those who have nothing credible to say about science. It appears to be the last refuge of an industry and culture with nowhere left to hide, without credible answers that can stand up to an open and unbiased courtroom cross-examination. The truth feared most by the MOD is that radiation is indeed the toxic hazard to health and causation of genetic damage unanimously agreed by the consensus view of the Medical Research Council Report of 1956.

The long-running policy to deny access rights to personal information to assist nuclear veterans and support their claims has a very long history. Before leaving office as Prime Minister, Tony Blair had put into law the Freedom of Information Act. He later admitted to the press that this was possibly his biggest mistake.

One nuclear veteran, however, has tested the Freedom of Information Act to breaking point. David Whyte, who served at Christmas Island with the Royal Engineers, was one of only approximately 1% of nuclear veterans who carried a dosimeter or wore a radiation film badge during these experiments. He quickly realised the readings being recorded were false, manipulated to be lower than the actual dose he was exposed to whilst working in forward areas close to nuclear detonations. Mr Whyte's conclusions are similar to the accounts given by the Australian former LAC Avon Hudson and Major Alan Batchelor, who both served at Maralinga, as well as others, such as Joe Pasquini, an RAF observer officer flying at 46,000 feet above Christmas Island.

In 2006, Mr Whyte started asking the MOD searching questions about the radiation levels whilst he was at Christmas Island; he found, as with many before him, he was given no proper or credible answers. Eventually, in March 2008 and using the Freedom of Information Act (FOIA), the MOD released to him a document GZ/12/RM taken from ES1/602, an interim report document for Operation Grapple bomb tests at Christmas Island.

This document made no mention of the actual level of radiation; it only showed the rate at which radiation depreciated over a 150-hour period. So Mr Whyte persisted, again using the FOIA to request access to the *actual levels* of radiation. Finally, on 11 January 2012, he received a letter from a Mr Andrew Tranham to say that the questions he was asking on the subject of film badges were a 'vexation', and that the graph ES1/602 was now being placed under Section 14 (1) to deny any further information being given. (Section 14 (1) is in fact the gagging order under which any FOIA requests can be responded to with: "It is not in the national interest for you (or anyone else) to know these facts," i.e. the government has the right to violate your access to personal information about the level of radiation you have been exposed to, and neither you nor anyone else has any rights at all in this matter.)

A following report of Mr Whyte's FOIA First Tier hearing shows quite clearly, even with dogged persistence over six years, that access to records of personal information is too difficult for any nuclear veteran or widow to pursue. Most nuclear veterans and widows would not have reached this stage but would have given up after a year or so. The same is also applied to lawyers or experts acting on behalf of nuclear veterans. Those who persist, if not labelled anti-nuclear, are told that asking questions is a vexation and, by inference, those asking questions officials refuse to answer are labelled a vexatious person.

The only rational conclusion is that the Ministry of Defence and the government are afraid of the truth. Nuclear veterans are in a unique position. They are treated with contempt by a democracy that, by its actions against them, appears to be becoming a quasi-totalitarian state. It's an ironic situation considering these veterans sacrificed their health and their lives to protect the nation from communist ideology during the Cold War.

Mr Whyte was therefore left with no other option but to write to the FOIA Commissioner expressing the difficulty he was having in obtaining the information he sought, and questioning the unsatisfactory graph ES1/602 he had been sent in 2008. His questions needed answering; it's a basic human right that any person potentially exposed to radiation needs to know how much radiation he or she has been exposed to. It's ultimately a question any nuclear veteran, veteran's widow or legal counsel acting on their behalf needs answered in order to proceed with litigation. It appears that refusal to grant this access is a sign that levels of radiation at weapon test locations were higher than professed and are therefore a significant embarrassment to the government.

So, David Whyte was granted a First Tier FOIA hearing. He was the first nuclear veteran to ever get this far through the barriers erected to prevent all nuclear veterans and their families from accessing their personal records.

Mr Whyte promptly booked two nights' accommodation in London and travelled down from Edinburgh by train for a First Tier FOIA Tribunal, set for 16 February 2012.

This hearing was to be a modern-day David and Goliath success for the nuclear test veterans' campaign for justice. It revealed much about the inner workings of the UK government and the dark attempts to deny evidence requested by nuclear test veterans and their families. And information came to light that would never have been known if David's questions had been answered back in 2006.

Unusually for a pension appeal/tribunal hearing of a nuclear veteran or their widow, four supporters attended Mr Whyte's hearing, including a journalist, Susie Boniface. Unusual, of course, because journalists are not sent invitations to attend such hearings. The less the public know about them the happier the MOD remains. The Ministry of Defence was represented by a female barrister and sent four suited government officials to face Mr Whyte, who was acting as his own counsel.

The following is taken from a report by the Combined Veterans' Forum International, written the day after the hearing. The CVFI noted, and circulated, the report as worthy of close press, media and public examination with regard to the reasons given for non-disclosure of personal information required by nuclear veterans and their families. A copy was also sent to other interested parties and to the nuclear veterans' legal team, Rosenblatts of London.

In additional to the withholding of evidence regarding Mr Whyte's radiation dose levels and general dose levels at Christmas Island (as shown on graph ES1/602), the following factors records relating to his FOI case also apply:

1. His blood count, taken after the tests, was missing.

2. The result of a lymph node removed for analysis was also missing.

3. Other hospital records were missing.

4. He had offered to pay the NHS for a cytogenetic blood test but was refused.

In line with other surviving nuclear test veterans, Mr Whyte's submission at the hearing was that a conspiracy of silence was being conducted against all nuclear test veterans and the UK's Commonwealth allies who attended the nuclear weapon test experiments.

The spokesman for the MOD was observed to open his submission lackadaisically by affirming that: "The Ministry of Defence will not allow any information that is incorrect to be made public." This caused amused incredulity amongst Mr Whyte's four supporters, who must have thought to themselves, "This is going to be fun!" because the raw data on radiation levels at Christmas Island shown on the graph released to Mr Whyte in answer to his questions was not incorrect but incomplete. The graph did not include any figures at all.

The MOD spokesman, under cross-examination by the tribunal panel, admitted the raw data for the graph existed but a search had found that this data was not held by the MOD but by a 'contractual partner', the Atomic Weapons Establishment (AWE). Under further cross-examination it transpired that the AWE holds two databases relevant to the questions asked under the FOI by Mr Whyte. One is a database named 'Merlin'; the MOD spokesman said he did not know the name of the other because he did not have "high enough security clearance".

The MOD spokesman then added that the working relationship between the MOD and AWE was "contractual for appropriate information" and he added that the answers he had given were ones he was therefore "comfortable with". Yet, at this early stage, he was looking very uncomfortable.

The thankfully unbiased chairman of the tribunal then stated that indeed it was established, therefore, that not all the archive records relating to radiation levels were held by the Ministry of Defence, but by their contractual partner, the AWE.

The MOD spokesman then admitted that a conference had been held with the AWE and a named official of the Section

Team for Freedom of Information from the MOD's Strategic Weapons Department regarding Mr Whyte's FOI questions.

The chairman of the tribunal made the point that none of the internal emails between the MOD and AWE had been made available to the tribunal and he further commented that the involvement of the MOD's Strategic Weapons FOI team raised "the need to do independent research before this type of tribunal."

Throughout the cross-examination, both the MOD spokesman, in his role as 'expert witness' at the hearing, and the MOD's appointed barrister were exposed as being totally out of their depth. The MOD spokesman was lacklustre throughout and clearly uncomfortable and well out of his comfort zone. Both he and the barrister appeared to have expected this to be yet another expenses-paid away day where they easily dismissed another nuclear veteran or widow as a 'vexation' for the temerity of merely seeking the truth.

The MOD barrister rose in brief summary and, in the opinion of the four tribunal observers – two members of the CVFI Action Executive, Shirley Denson and me; a business executive, Dai Williams; and Susie Boniface, a well-known award-winning freelance journalist – opened her summary with a very bizarre statement: "The Ministry of Defence has not helped itself by bending over backwards to be helpful." She then conceded the information sought by Mr Whyte was not considered classified and added: "It should be in the National Archives."

But of course this information is *not* in the National Archives. This personal data is still being deliberately withheld, despite Mr Whyte's many years of attempting to access it. If it truly is "not considered classified", as the MOD's barrister conceded, a great deal of time, effort and taxpayers' money has been expended on violating the rights of nuclear veterans to access it.

Sensing that the MOD barrister appeared unfamiliar with the actuality of the evolving situation, due perhaps to her ignorance of past precedents in legal extracts from earlier cases, Mr Whyte stood up and presented her with a copy of *Roche v the United Kingdom* (2005), referring to breaches in human rights under Article 8 of the European Convention of Human Rights (ECHR) and highlighting references to the *McGinley and Egan* (1998) nuclear veterans case at Strasbourg, in which the UK Ministry of Defence lawyer had concluded by reasoning from evidence: "The government has asserted there was no pressing security reason for retaining information relating to radiation following the tests … Where a government engages in hazardous activities, such as those in the present case, which might have hidden adverse consequences on health of those involved in such activities, respect for private and family life under Article 8 requires that an effective and accessible procedure be established which enables such persons to seek all relevant and appropriate information."

As with much else, the above two assertions by the MOD have been ignored for decades while they have continued to lie about and conceal access to information sought by nuclear test veterans and their families.

Susie Boniface passed a scribbled note to me which simply read: "They are stuffed."

Mr Whyte won his appeal hearing. Shortly after the hearing, he received an apology from the Ministry of Defence, a refund of his rail fare from Edinburgh and, only after a dispute, the MOD also paid for his two nights' accommodation in London because, they must have conceded, even for David beating Goliath it would have been impossible for him to have travelled to London and back from Edinburgh in just one day to attend the hearing.

But since that day any further progress in legal procedures for Mr Whyte has been 'stayed' by the cowards at the MOD ('stayed' is a legal term for the delay in any future course of litigation). This appears to be the only possible defence the MOD has left to avoid accountability. Common sense and a pragmatic analysis of Mr Whyte's appeal hearing tells us that when inveterate liars are given enough scope to be cross-examined in front of impartial judgement, they inevitably condemn themselves.

The 'conspiracy of silence' first identified by Professor Alex Haddow in 1951 still applied over sixty years later to Mr Whyte's hearing. It appears his victory in exposing the withholding of radiation levels and blood tests and interdepartmental collusion by government officials ensures that, duplicitously, he and other people with such credentials are kept out of all future legal process.

Overall, through analysis of the combined history archive of nuclear veterans, it is hard not to conclude there is a strong element of criminality in all of this. Otherwise, the only answer is that supine and cowardly political leaders are persisting in anti-democratic deception worthy only of a totalitarian state towards those who have loyally served the nation.

It's worth adding that Dr Busby's successful 2002 appeal for nuclear widow Eva Adshead and Mr Whyte's FOIA First Tier Tribunal success have one thing common: both Dr Busby and Mr Whyte have been 'stayed'. Dr Busby has been prevented from giving expert witness support in nuclear veterans' cases and Mr Whyte is excluded from court for exposing how radiation levels are withheld from any person potentially exposed to ionising radiation – even though this is "not considered classified".

But this paranoid control of science and manipulation of data regarding the impact of the hazards of radiation exposure goes much wider. Even senior politicians who search for the truth are 'stayed'.

The first report from the European Committee on Radiation Risk (ECRR), used as evidence by Dr Busby in the Adshead pension appeal, was published in 2003. The content of this report gave an updated risk model for calculating the health risks of exposure to ionising radiation. Unlike the post-war 1950s ICRP risk model (or the MOD'S *SPVA Radiation Advice to Ministers*, analysed in 2010), the ECRR radiation risk model uses evidence from the most modern research, from new discoveries in radiation biology and from human epidemiology to create a system of calculation that gives results which are at the level of the living cell and based on observation of disease in exposed persons. In other words, it takes into account 'internal emitting' radiation inhaled or ingested into the body (previously ignored by the ICRP), which is an unrecorded dose from radioactive fallout.

The ECRR risk model is not recognised by the UK MOD. This department clings to the outdated and significantly flawed ICRP risk model of the 1950s; that is, a risk model that protects the nuclear industry rather than the health of persons potentially exposed to radiation.

In 2001, under Tony Blair's Labour Government, UK Environment Minister Michael Meacher MP set up a Committee to Examine Radiation Risk from Internal Emitters (CERRIE) and announced that there would be "a review of models used to estimate health risks from radioactive emitters taken into the body." The new committee's remit would be "to consider present risk models for radiation from internal radionuclides in the light of recent studies and identify any further research that may be needed." The minister added: "The committee's review takes account of the views of all parties in the debate on the risks of radiation. It aims to reach a consensus where possible. On topics where differences of view remain after all deliberations, it will explain the reasons for these and recommend research to try to resolve them."

A report by Mark Gould and Jonathan Leake in the *Sunday Times* on 1 August 2004, 'Government gags experts over nuclear plant risks', reported that just before the committee issued its final report after three years of investigations, all twelve members of the committee were sent letters by government lawyers warning them they could be sued for defamation if they included the views of Dr Chris Busby, the UK's leading independent expert on low dose, low level fallout radiation, and Richard Bramhall of the Low Level Radiation Campaign (LLRC). The final report that was published excluded the views of Busby and Bramhall.

Michael Meacher, the MP responsible for setting up the committee, was quoted in the *Sunday Times* article to be "furious that not all the experts' views will be represented." He was sacked from his ministerial post in 2003 but still contributed a foreword to the CERRIE Minority Report, which came out in 2004: "Science can be only trusted if it is pursued with the most rigorous procedures that guarantee freedom from bias. For this reason, I deliberately set up the committee on a balanced basis with all opposing views fully represented – the first such science committee that I am aware of.

"Unfortunately, it seems that the procedures which prevailed in the committee, while they have allowed discussion of a wide range of topics, have produced a Final Report which does not accommodate a full and fair representation of all views.

"Why does the Final Report present only one side? This is very worrying for it is hard to conjecture that, if the leukaemia peak was real following the Chernobyl disaster, anything other than the radiation from Chernobyl could have caused it. If that were indeed the case then the estimates of radiation risk which currently are used to set policy would fall to the ground and many other health phenomena, including the notorious cluster of childhood leukaemias near Sellafield, might find an explanation." (The Black Inquiry of 1985 had attributed a ten-fold increase in childhood leukaemias as 'just a chance occurrence' – see Chapter Seven.)

Meacher also noted in his foreword to the CERRIE Minority Report that: "Preliminary discussions with scientists from both sides of the divide persuaded me that the current model of radiation hazard, based as it is almost exclusively on the consequences of gamma irradiation delivered from outside the body in a single massive dose from an exploding atom bomb, was very unlikely to be a reliable indicator of the cumulative impact of chronic inhalation and ingestion of radiation. As Environment Minister I was required to take responsibility for policy in many relevant areas."

The two independent CERRIE members barred from

having their views included in the Final Report, Dr Busby and Richard Bramhall, said that after Mr Meacher was sacked the committee was taken over by people with pro-nuclear views who did their best to suppress opposing opinions.

Fears the committee was being gagged were echoed by Marion Hill, a member of the Secretariat who resigned from CERRIE. In 2004, Hill was a senior scientist with 30 years' expertise in radiation safety. In her resignation letter she stressed she was not a member of the Green Party and signed her letter as Technical Director of Enviros Consulting. She accused the CERRIE chairman and another committee member of biasing the report so the views of Dr Busby and Richard Bramhall were marginalised.

Combined armed forces nuclear test veterans from the UK, Australia, New Zealand and Fiji have been, to varying degrees, politically excluded from obtaining a duty of care, recognition, accountability and compensation for their test participation.

The 1993 bi-lateral treaty between the UK and Australia to co-operate together to avoid potential compensation claims from nuclear veterans confirms that violations of veterans' access rights to personal information etc. would form a major part in turning a level playing field, needed for justice in the Limitation Trial due to start in 2006, into an unequal upward quagmire of hardship.

Non-disclosure of evidence would make it extremely difficult for the nuclear test veterans, without any legal aid, and their legal representative, Rosenblatts of London, to compete against the bottomless pit of tax payers' funding possessed by the government's Treasury Solicitors Office (TSol).

Despite this unfair disadvantage, the truth about nuclear

veterans and their families' claims would not disappear. It is a truth of history that is self-evident: even low dose radiation is a hazard to health when inhaled or ingested.

Chapter 9: The Nuclear Veterans' Limitation Trial

"Fallout is the prime causal link to veterans' ill health and the Rowland study is crucial and pivotal evidence."
Mr Justice Foskett, the High Court, London, June 2009

Following the 50th anniversary of the Monte Bello nuclear bomb test, nuclear veterans continued to be treated as second class citizens. They had endured this treatment and denial since returning from nuclear test locations in the 1950s and 60s. Their legacy health and genetic damage passed to their children and grandchildren had been ignored as if it hadn't happened.

To avoid any duty of care or payment towards pensions and compensation for years prior to the Limitation Trial of 2005, the Ministry of Defence and the government repeatedly used the mantra: "The standard practice of government is to settle these matters by litigation."

Officials and senior politicians knew of course how difficult it would be for nuclear veterans and widows to engage in litigation. This is because documents giving evidence of radiation dose levels at test locations, personal dose records and hospital records etc. had been deliberately lost, deleted, redacted or withheld. Added to this, the government's use of the 'national interest' and the Official Secrets Act had become recognised as nothing more than a cynical ploy to avoid access to evidence needed by the veterans, their widows and their lawyers.

Nuclear test veterans gave loyal service to the nation yet

since returning from the test locations they had been used as political footballs by successive administrations when it came to any obligation for their health concerns. They were left with no other option but litigation to achieve a settlement of claims. Legal aid, available to criminals, terrorists and any number of other people who have broken the law, is callously denied to veterans.

For decades this policy has helped governments to ignore the obligation to provide the principle of a duty of care for those injured, disabled or killed in service to the nation. In the jaded eyes of desk-bound officials, the lack of any meaningful military covenant enshrined into law ensures no liability – and they were determined to keep it that way. It's also a policy that appears to have provided officials with annual bonus payments over the decades, as often reported in national newspapers.

Therefore, the need to collect, collate and pass to the nuclear veterans' lawyers scientific and other evidence necessary to assist a favourable outcome of claims had become an inevitable priority. In 2002, the veterans' lawyers had a very difficult task because they were starting virtually from scratch with very little knowledge. Studies of veterans' mortality had been shown to have been manipulated. The science of causation of radiation damage at a cellular level was strictly controlled by government, who had the advantage of taxpayers' money to block a just and honourable settlement of claims.

However, the veterans had no qualms about what the MOD and government intended to continue to deny. Information kept flooding in, all adding to a growing combined nuclear veterans' archive of data collated to expose the MOD's decades of irresponsibility and unaccountability as employer of those who serve the nation.

Concealment, cover-up, denial, lies and obfuscation, undermining of scientific committees and truth, deliberate covert experimentation in the name of medical research, secret and unethical removal of body parts without family consent – all clearly have no moral or ethical justification in a democracy. This is the justification known by nuclear veterans and to be proved by Rosenblatts in litigation against the UK Ministry of Defence.

In 2005, the Atomic Veterans Group Litigation (AVGL), led by Rosenblatts Solicitors of London, commenced legal action, which ended in 2013. The first and longest phase of AVGL was the Nuclear Veterans Limitation Trial, which took place between 2005 and June 2009.

Throughout this period new and often highly relevant information continued to emerge from archive records, and also from events in real time, and this impacted upon evidence already acquired and also affected the ultimate outcome. New documents were passed to Rosenblatts with comments, but the importance we placed upon certain factors was rarely acknowledged. But then, we had no idea how the legal process was being shaped or of the enormous pressure the veterans' lawyers were under. This wasn't a factor at the time, but by 2012 the NZNTVA's Roy Sefton and CVFI jointly had to comment on imperative points needed to be focused upon in order to attain a just and honourable settlement of claims.

The Limitation Trial focused on a legal technicality (the statute of limitations) with which the MOD intended to deliver a knockout blow to the 1,011 claimants registered as cases in the AVGL's class action. A single blow by this method would end continuation of the claims. There was absolutely no level playing field. Rosenblatts had virtually started from scratch in 2004, whereas the MOD had the undoubted advantage of planning for this litigation since at least 1993. The statute of limitations was therefore a cunning and considered means by which the government's Treasury Solicitors (TSol) meant to quickly quash the litigation.

The date 1993 refers to the December 1993 bilateral Treaty Series between the UK and Australia, who had agreed to work together to avoid any claims of any sort with regard to pensions and compensation. Litigation as the only means of settling claims was in fact confirmed through the MOD's messaging via officials and ministers over the previous two decades; that is, 'The standard practice of government is to settle these matters by litigation.'

Similar to their attitude towards the Australian Royal Commission of 1985, the government almost certainly felt the AVGL claims would not prove challenging for the Treasury Solicitors. The MOD legal team had numerous highly paid barristers to call upon and a huge financial advantage. On the other hand, Rosenblatts, working without legal aid, had to take on many part-time staff to help sift through a mass of information.

Email exchanges between the UK, Australian and New Zealand veterans via the Combined Veterans' Forum International (CVFI) from the turn of the millennium were probably seen as no concern compared to the decade-long preparatory head start the MOD had. Of course, we veterans had no knowledge of the 1993 treaty until around 2007 and, presumably, neither did Rosenblatts know about this clandestine collaboration between two democratic states when they prepared for legal action in 2004. In any event, Rosenblatts were focused upon evidence and may not have had any interest in the politics underpinning everything nuclear.

The Limitation Trial depended upon 10 nuclear veterans' or widows' cases, selected from the AVGL's 1,011 claimants, being tested in court to decide whether they qualified within the statute of limitations. Of the 1,011 claimants, only 268 were members of the BNTVA. This was a clear indication that the BNTVA, now a charity, was representing the interests of only a minority of claimants seeking compensation and an admission of liability. It was not known at the time, but it rapidly became apparent that as a charity, the BNTVA had no interest in holding the government to account.

Of the ten test cases, five were BNTVA members and the other five were taken from the 70% of AVGL claimants who were either former members who had resigned their membership, or veterans who had never been members, plus a few Australians. Founder and former chairman of the BNTVA Ken McGinley was one of the test cases chosen.

Ken's 'All We Seek is Justice' campaign had died in 2002 when he was deposed as chairman and the new BNTVA leadership had in fact barred attempts by many campaigning nuclear veterans for Mr McGinley's membership to be restored. Disrespectful and unacceptable conditions were placed on his reinstatement which no person could possibly accept. But Mr McGinley's appearances both inside and outside court during the trial period, which involved frequent trips to London, helped keep hopes alive.

The statute of limitations in the Limitation Act 1980 required each claimant to have registered with the AVGL within three years of having *evidence and proof* of being irradiated to be accepted as a claimant and entitled to go forward for compensation. The use of this legal technicality was considered unreasonable not only by veterans but also by many scientists, backbench MPs and others outside the Westminster bubble determined to deny any settlement of claims.

The Limitation Trial was a nonsense, not just because for years the Official Secrets Act prevented nuclear veterans and their widows from speaking out about the nuclear weapon tests, but also because of other factors, such as missing medical records and biased access to evidence. The actual time scale of acquiring evidence or proof for all claimants went through three stages spanning decades; that is, from *suspicion* to *belief* before it could be said a veteran or widow claimant finally knew they had *evidence* or *proof*.

The Atomic Veterans Group Litigation was fundamentally a case of loyal members of the armed forces and their families who, because of their vulnerability under military law, (i.e. no meaningful military covenant enshrined into law for a duty of care) had been betrayed and abused by the MOD and let down by the political cowardice of successive governments for decades. It would have been much fairer and more reasonable if the statute of limitations had been applied the other way around. That is, at what date, under their duty of accountability, did the MOD have the knowledge and evidence that the men had been exposed to ionising radiation?

As usual, the MOD had set the parameters and methodology for the legal case, just as they had done in the past for the manipulated and biased mortality studies etc. Most of the 10 test cases of AVGL claimants, for example, were only able to *suspect* illness or death was linked to exposure to radiation, perhaps in the 1970s (as was true for the remaining 1,001 claimants in the AVGL class action). By the 1980s and 90s, due to press reports and many documentaries on the excessive statistics of legacy ill health and premature deaths, many then began to *believe* radiation exposure was the causation of their illnesses, early death and excess genetic damage in their children and grandchildren. But it wasn't until 2007 at the earliest, but 2009 for sure, that any claimant could say they knew they had *evidence and proof* to support their claims.

The crucial evidence and proof is shown by science in the blood. It is not shown by statistical epidemiology manipulated from death certificates and then regarded as 'just a chance occurrence'. This 'crucial and pivotal evidence' came from the peer-reviewed cytogenetic blood analysis by world-renowned cytogeneticist Professor Rowland in New Zealand. This analysis showed men who had attended a nuclear test location had 300% more chromosomal translocations (genetic damage) than servicemen who had not attended such a hazardous location.

Of course, the Limitation Trial was a nonsensical legal delaying tactic and widely acknowledged as such. I wasn't one of the 10 test cases selected for the Limitation Trial but, like all the others, I went through a similar thought process that took me from suspicion to belief – and then I gained unequivocal evidence and proof from the Rowland study.

Perhaps the reason I was not one of the 10 test cases was because I had not attended a nuclear bomb test location at a time when major nuclear weapons were detonated in the atmosphere. Perhaps the legal team was not confident enough to include a case at that time that did not rely on exposure to gamma radiation dose released at the time a nuclear bomb exploded. Maybe it was because the whole defence case for the

MOD was heavily reliant on the gamma dose recorded and epidemiological interpretation of what ill health, if any, could be causally linked to this type of radiation exposure only.

Perhaps it was because my own AVGL case notes included the fact I'd been awarded a disability war pension in 1992, and that the disability began at a nuclear weapon test site in 1965 and I was flown back as an evacuee to a military hospital?

A disability that began at a nuclear test location was an advantage most other claimants did not have. My claim was settled in May 1992 by the Department of Health and Social Security (DHSS) War Pensions Directorate, following a full medical examination by a DHSS doctor and submission of service records etc., plus a written assertion I made that my disability began at, stemmed from and was directly attributable to my service at Maralinga.

In 1992 I stressed the causal link as residual radiation at Maralinga in 1965, where 7 major bomb tests and 600-plus 'minor trials' over the period 1953 to 1963 had left the location contaminated by accumulated ionising radioactivity. With hindsight, I was lucky. If the disability I claimed had started a year, 5, 10, 15 or even 30 years later, the MOD would, by epidemiology if needed, say it was 'just a chance' occurrence. Nevertheless, it exposed a loop hole that needed closing.

By 1994 the War Pensions Directorate had been taken out of the DHSS and placed under the control of the Ministry of Defence's newly established Veterans Agency. A Minister for Veterans was created to enforce policy, undoubtedly to comply with the 1993 bilateral UK–Australian treaty of collusion and connivance. Prior to the MOD Veterans Agency taking over, claims applications had been handled by a Parliamentary Under Secretary of State (PSoS) in the MOD.

I remember receiving a letter from a member of this old boys' club back in the 1980s. The letter came from a PSoS Lord something-or-other but even today I still have the impression, from the letter's content and after seeing many official letters of similar mixed-messaging, of him spending a morning declining pension claims from widows of irradiated husbands before spending the rest of the day perhaps at some London club or other.

The 1993 bilateral treaty, which veterans knew nothing about until around 2007, is almost certainly the prime contributory factor for having no option but litigation to obtain accountability. Just as the UK Government was creating a Veterans Agency under political control of the Minister for Veterans, so too was the government in Australia (the Department of Veterans Affairs, DVA). The replicated complicit co-operation from bomb testing in Australia still continued unabated.

At the time, creation of a Minister for Veterans probably sounded to the public and press like a helpful move by both governments. But creation of this post was just a cynical public relations exercise, not a caring or helpful act towards nuclear test veterans. The word 'spin' had crept into the dictionary and this was a classic example.

In both Australia and the UK, the post quickly proved the direct opposite to the spin: the Minister for Veterans was a political gatekeeper to provide only misinformation to support government policy regarding nuclear weapon tests and subsequent denial of liability. It took very little time to work out that the Minister for Veterans was actually a minister enforcing policy *against* the interests of nuclear veterans and their families.

It's a post with a fast-revolving door. Any politician venturing into this post with ideas of actually helping nuclear veterans does not last long. Those who survive in the post are the ones who remorselessly keep to the 1950s edict of "It is a pity, but it cannot be helped." And after all, they may have learned from New Zealand that 'any help to nuclear veterans is regarded as an unfriendly act.' Not exactly motivational for a career-minded politician seeking advancement and an enhanced salary with ministerial status.

There was positive news, however, when, independent of government control, Dr Chris Busby won a widow's pension appeal for nuclear widow Eva Adshead. Her husband's brain tumour was shown, by the shifting consensus of scientific understanding of radiation risk, to be causally linked to inhaled and/or ingested radioactive fallout particles accumulated in the dust at Maralinga. Gamma radiation dosage on Gerald Adshead's film badge was irrelevant. It actually took until 2009 for the legal firm Rosenblatts to firmly grasp and begin to understand this truth of nuclear science. When they did, and the AVGL's appointed QC Benjamin Browne and Rosenblatts lead counsel Neil Sampson used it in court, it delivered a devastating blow to the MOD's expert witnesses.

I emailed Ian Anderson, the CVFI's legal advisor in New York, early in the litigation to say that being a claimant on the AVGL was like being a passenger on a runaway train, without brakes, without an emergency cord, hurtling down a steep mountain track and not knowing who was in the driver's cab. All we veterans could do was sit and wait for the outcome.

Fellow CVFI Action Executive member and co-founder

Shirley Denson lived within easy commuter distance of the City of London and did her best to keep us informed, but she had no computer or any desire to use one, so it was either long phone calls or letters in the post. Ken McGinley was also not on email. Those in regular computer contact were Roy Sefton in New Zealand, Alan Batchelor in Australia, Barry Smith, David Whyte and Dai Williams in the UK, and a few others. But it's surprising how many contacts we were able to make through cyberspace with only six or so computers, and how much information came our way.

There was good reason to be optimistic: the Dr Busby/ Adshead Pension Appeal Tribunal of 2002 and David Whyte's FOIA Tribunal of 2012 showed the outcome of any verdict would depend on whether the evidence could be fully examined in court, without any outside interference, and whether it would be heard by an unbiased and impartial judge. Other factors, both negative and positive, were also at play.

As the Limitation Trial progressed, more evidence emerged. In fact, more confirmation of the causal link to ill health regarding the hazards of radiation came into the public domain.

In November 2006, the Russian dissident Alexander Litvinenko was assassinated by agents of the Russian State at a hotel in London. This event was immediately considered vital evidence by the CVFI Action Executive, to be passed to Rosenblatts Solicitors and any other contact on our growing list of international addressees. This is because during the tragic meeting with his assassins, Litvinenko drank from a teapot that contained a minute, invisible to the eye quantity of the alpha radioisotope polonium-210. This is a low dose alpha radioactive isotope amongst a myriad of the Pandora's box of the same type of alpha and beta present in radioactive fallout. Tragically, he died within a few days, and photos of him in a hospital bed filled the UK's national newspapers for several days.

On 26 November 2006, a newsletter written on behalf of the Combined Veterans' Forum International's Action Executive was circulated to a list of contacts internationally, including the AVGL's solicitors, Rosenblatts.

Headed 'The Genie is Now Out of the Bottle – Exposed: The Hypocrisy and Deception of UK Government's Radiation Risk Scientists', the CVFI newsletter contained the following extracts:

"The recent shocking death of Alexander Litvinenko by ingested polonium-210 resulted in the UK Government's sponsored radiation risk scientists falling over themselves to reassure a worried British public not to panic.

"The scientists confirmed there is no risk from this type of radiation – unless eaten, inhaled or entering the blood stream by a wound. Pat Troop, a scientist at the UK's Health Protection Agency, Professor Dudley Goodhead, the former chairman of the Committee Examining Radiation Risk from Internal Emitters (CERRIE), and other government-sponsored scientists issued press and television news statements that 'no risk arises from this type of radiation unless it gains access to inside the body'."

The CVFI newsletter then stated the fact that, "Whilst chairman of CERRIE in 2003, Professor Goodhead, along with a member of the Committee Secretariat, Dr Ian Fairlea, biased the Final Report on radiation risk from inhaled or ingested alpha and beta radiation, to exclude the independent views of Dr Chris Busby and Richard Bramhall.

"Another member of the Secretariat, scientist Marion Hill, in her letter of resignation in 2003 over the sabotage of the committee, told the Sunday Times: 'It's a complete failure when you have a committee that is not allowed to write anything about disagreements in science.'"

The CVFI newsletter then went on to say the admission by HPA, now Public Health England (formerly NRPB) scientists and the chairman of CERRIE, Professor Goodhead, that ingested radiation is a severe toxic hazard when gaining access to the inside of the body, after decades of denial that such radiation is a prime causal link to the ill health and premature deaths of nuclear test veterans, exposed both men as being hypocritical and fraudulent.

The nuclear test veterans were exposed to such radiation, including polonium-210, inhaled and ingested into the body, at the nuclear test sites of Australia and the Pacific. Polonium-210 was used in the trigger mechanisms of nuclear bombs and was just one of many alpha and beta particles in the fallout.

The CVFI's newsletter summed it up by stating that the genie of radiation risk, bunged up by decades of deception, had now been released, and UK-sponsored scientific experts had been hoisted by their own petard.

We hoped the importance of this event in 2006 had registered with Rosenblatts. But we had no idea whether it had until 2012, because information sent by combined veterans' efforts in the UK, Australia and New Zealand was almost completely one-way traffic. This is accepted because, as with the situation in 1985 when the Australian Royal Commission had 40 tons of documents dumped in their London office in two weeks, Rosenblatts had limited resources and manpower to deal with the pressure of the mass of data sent to them.

The circumstances of Litvinenko's high profile and tragic death by radiation poisoning did, however, give some explanation to one pivotal question. That is, the high-level role Professor Goodhead appears to have played in the sacking of Environment Minister Michael Meacher, who initiated the CERRIE committee. The CVFI had believed since at least 1992 that accumulated residual fallout is as great a hazard as whole-body dose gamma radiation and that the nuclear veterans were highly vulnerable to abuse with regard to this issue. The Busby/Adshead widow appeal case, plus the ECRR 2003 recommendations on the health effects of ionising radiation exposure at low dose for radiation protection purposes, i.e. that fallout is a considerably higher risk to health by about a factor of 20 when gaining access inside exposed persons than the risk of gamma radiation, is now self-evident – but denied by the MOD.

Earlier in 2005, a CVFI newsletter had been circulated to Rosenblatts and also to the Australian Nuclear Veterans Association on the subject of the CERRIE report and Environment Minister Michael Meacher's 2003 sacking.

A copy was also forwarded to the CVFI's legal advisor Ian Anderson, international advocate and attorney at law in New York, asking for his comments. Ian's email of 14 August 2006 (below) gave the wider picture as seen by an international legal expert of toxic torts, nuclear accidents and other cases of persons potentially exposed to hazardous radiation and other poisons. Mr Anderson has worked on radiation and other cases at the United Nations and in Europe. His response was more detailed and concise than I ever expected.

"You are quite correct about government suppression of

information and manipulation of reports. In many ways, the tactics of the UK Government are no different from those of corporations sued for product liability. Meacher obviously did not understand the rules of the game and probably thought it was the government's duty to protect the British public. The rules of the military–industrial game are international. From the beginning of the nuclear age, governments quickly realised there would be a high risk of accidents, both in the manufacture of nuclear weapons and the use of nuclear power. So, during the Cold War and to date, no government of a nuclear state, friendly or otherwise, will reveal a nuclear accident in another nuclear country for fear its own accidents would be revealed in retaliation. Thus, the UK remained silent on nuclear accidents in the Soviet Union and the latter kept quiet about the 1957 Windscale disaster and the effects of the US Nevada Tests. (Chernobyl was too big to cover up, though official attempts are periodically made to minimise it.) The manipulation of the NRPB reports is just part of the ongoing policy to suppress and withhold information on the actual dangers of nuclear radiation from civil society, who would otherwise be in a panic and force cessation of all nuclear activity throughout the world. Military power and profits are of course at stake here. Genetic testing for stable chromosome damage, if done properly and honestly, is a formidable weapon to wield against this policy. It is clearly the means by which the UK Government can be defeated in court, if Rosenblatts decide to use it."

In just 12 sentences, Anderson had provided a full explanation of why so much effort and public money has been put into denying the irradiation of nuclear test veterans. The whole debate between anti-nuclear 'ban the bomb' or pro-nuclear protectionist lobbies evolved from this international

Cold War consensus between nuclear powers. The nuclear veterans and their families belong to neither lobby; they are just victims seeking the truth of their irradiation.

In London, Shirley Denson had a close friend who I met on several occasions. Sue Davis was an amazing and likeable character and could have gone in any direction during her life. She was very good at summing up a person on first acquaintance, so it was always interesting to seek her opinion after meeting anyone on either side of the nuclear divide. But her direction in life had undoubtedly been decided for her by the atomic bomb.

Sue's brother, older than her by a decade or more, had served during the Second World War as an RAF pilot, and survived. In 1958 he went to the Christmas Island bomb tests and flew propeller transport aircraft; not the Canberra jets with 'Top Gun' younger pilots, who flew through the mushroom clouds at 46,000 feet to collect radiation samples (like Shirley's husband, Eric, who committed suicide 17 years later), but at a lower altitude, where he also flew through radioactive fallout. He died from a very rare type of leukaemia six years after returning from Christmas Island. The consultant who diagnosed his illness was absolutely sure excessive exposure to radiation was the causal link of his death.

Sue spent three years with solicitors in the 1960s trying to get recognition for her brother's death from the Air Ministry, before the formation of the MOD. She was informed by senior officers that no recognition could be made for his service at the nuclear tests because nuclear bomb testing was not regarded as active service. It would have been different, she was told, if her brother had been injured or killed in combat with an enemy.

So, that's it: have a leg blown off stepping on a land mine, get shot by a sniper or have an enemy mortar shell dropped on to you and it is recognised as entitlement to a duty of care. However, if you're irradiated by an invisible, unseen enemy and commit suicide 17 years later after suffering years of pain, or you die of legacy radiation-induced leukaemia after exposure to radiation in hazardous service to the nation, this means nothing to the bureaucrats and politicians.

The last time I saw Sue was in June 2009, shortly before her death and after the successful verdict of the Limitation Trial. She was in very frail health but delighted with the outcome, but she said: "I do wish all the veterans weren't walking around with nuclear mushroom cloud badges on their blazers. But the MOD will, in any case, appeal against this verdict."

Since her brother's death she had spent her whole life campaigning against nuclear weapons. But who could possibly condemn her? Shortly before her death, Sue Davis passed all her solicitor's notes from the 1960s regarding her brother's death to the CVFI.

Before Ian Anderson's email in August 2006, many veterans had already begun to believe the denial of a duty of care for nuclear veterans was undoubtedly a political decision. But none of us had believed it was international. At the time, this knowledge brought home to me the huge task faced by Rosenblatts. Ian's email answered many questions about why compensation or recognition for nuclear veterans is vehemently denied.

Of the four major states involved in Cold War nuclear bomb testing who had provided armed forces personnel during the experiments, i.e. the USA, UK, Australia and USSR, only one of the three democracies ignored the rules of pro-nuclear protectionism with regard to compensation: the United States of America. Perhaps this is due to President John F Kennedy's 1963 speech, or perhaps it was the earlier statement by the first President of the US following the American War of Independence, George Washington: "You can judge a nation by the way it treats its veterans."

(The USSR has also recognised the service given by their nuclear test veterans. They often led military parades before becoming too aged; they also have free access to military hospitals for life, to cytogenetic blood tests and remedial medical treatment, subsidised housing and other pragmatic help.)

But the motivation for compensation by the USA is more likely because of the economic strength of the US in the 1990s. However, the expert evidence of Professor Rosalie Bertell to the US Senate Commission on Nuclear Veterans' Welfare brought compensation to the men. Professor Bertell, a world-renowned biochemist and PhD researcher in cancer and the health effects of low level radiation, simply explained to the US senators the prime source of hazard: "Although it is true that alpha radiation, the primary radiation in early fallout, can be stopped by a sheet of paper, when this same radioactivity is released inside the body it does about 20 times the cellular damage as the equivalent dose of gamma radiation."

Unlike many others in the world of science paid handsomely to lie or become merchants of doubt about the real hazards of radiation, Professor Rosalie Bertell's evidence could be trusted because of her innate care, honesty and ethics as a member of the Order of Grey Nuns. The senators agreed any US veteran who had attended a nuclear weapon test location was entitled to compensation of $75,000. They did not have to prove the dose they were potentially exposed to; they only had to provide evidence they had served at a nuclear test site.

The Australian veterans were also seriously considering legal action for compensation. In January 2007, whilst visiting relatives in Sydney, I met ANVA leaders Ric Johnson and Major Alan Batchelor, with solicitors from Stacks Goudkamp present. I was unable to tell them anything about the progress of the AVGL Limitation Trial despite being in almost daily contact with Rosenblatts' office by email because the CVFI were completely in the dark. All I could say was that the UK veterans had been left with no other option except litigation to achieve a just and honourable settlement of claims.

However, the Sydney legal firm Stacks Goudkamp found they could not litigate in the Australian courts anyway because the Australian Federal Government in Canberra was using the same legal technicality in defence as the UK and the statute of limitations in Australia had long since passed. The 1993 treaty was evidently being followed meticulously every step of the way by both nations.

A few Australian nuclear test veterans and widows began to apply to Rosenblatts to join the AVGL litigation.

After the Supreme Court verdict of 2012 (see Chapter Ten), while on a visit to Australia I saw it reported in the Australian press that the lawyer leading the AVGL litigation, Neil Sampson, "was mystified why the government was so determined to fight the nuclear veterans to the bitter end. At some point they would be spending more on lawyers defending the case than it would cost to grant compensation to the veterans. The political benefit government could have achieved by settling this vastly outweighs the cost of defending it. We are talking peanuts in terms of how much the court cases cost them." (This was also mentioned in the book *Maralinga* by Frank Walker, published in 2014.)

The email from Ian Anderson in August 2006 about the international protective consensus of nuclear powers explains why Neil Sampson 'was mystified'. I can, however, understand why Mr Sampson did not make public reference to it. At the start of litigation, I had hoped Rosenblatts would have engaged Mr Anderson as a consultant; he had experience in dealing with governments in matters of radiation damage to health and therefore they would have had someone at hand who could have explained the many traps set by governments to avoid accountability. But it wasn't to be, perhaps because Ian is based in New York and email is not regarded as an absolutely 'secure' method of communication.

In the circumstances, Rosenblatts did magnificently to get the AVGL claimants all the way to the Supreme Court, to a narrow 4:3 inconclusive verdict, in March 2012 – but that was only a pyrrhic victory, achieved without all the veterans' expert witness evidence being heard.

Later, through pension appeal processes in 2012-13, Neil Sampson is reported to have managed to get 250,000 pages of documents released to him that were not made available to the Australian Royal Commission lawyers in 1985, despite 40 tons of documents being dumped in their London office. He believes there is a similar amount still locked away in MOD archives. The possible whereabouts of these were indicated in the First Tier FOIA appeal hearing won by nuclear veteran David Whyte in February 2012.

During the AVGL Limitation Trial process the New

Zealand nuclear veterans, under Roy Sefton's chairmanship, were waiting for the results of the Rowland study to be announced sometime in 2007. The tempo had begun to quicken and this led to activity to derail the runaway AVGL train, which was already hurtling down the mountain railway track.

The Litvinenko admission by government-sponsored scientists that alpha particles inside the body are a serious hazard to health was also admitted by a Shadow Minister for Veterans. I'd written to my MP, Mark Harper, on 26 November 2006, not long after he was appointed Shadow Minister for Veterans by the Conservative Party, to congratulate him on his appointment and also ask him a few questions, including some on the death of Alexander Litvinenko by radiation poisoning.

Like many MPs of all divides of ideology, when elevated to a ministerial position the answers they give are inevitably given on advice of officials. It is said that the safest way to ensure promotion from the back benches and to stay off them as a minister is to only ever give the 'right' answers, the answers that agree with departmental policy. Since he had been elected MP for the Forest of Dean constituency I had found Mr Harper always willing to answer questions and I expected he would respond to my question about the tragic death of Alexander Litvinenko in words that reflected the understanding and policy of his new MOD post regarding radiation risk from alpha radiation poisoning.

After three months, on 1st March 2007 I finally received a reply. Mr Harper wrote: "Although it is true that polonium-210 is very dangerous when ingested it cannot be inferred that all radioactive substances are as dangerous. Polonium-210 emits alpha particles when it decays. Alpha particles are very energetic but large and therefore cannot penetrate the skin. If ingested, however, alpha particles ionise particles in bodily tissue, harming the body and destroying internal organs." Mr Harper ended by saying: "I don't think that the polonium-210 news has any bearing on previous correspondence about nuclear tests and the NRPB reports of 1988 and 1991."

It's amazing that not only had the government-sponsored HPA (formerly NRPB, now Public Health England) admitted to the media that alpha radiation particles were extremely dangerous when gaining access to the body, now the same message had been confirmed by a politician advised by the Ministry of Defence. In some sort of 'good cop, bad cop' fashion, the Shadow Minister for Veterans ended by praising the efficacy of NRPB reports, which rely only on the effect of gamma dose readings and findings significantly biased by government-sponsored epidemiologists. Those acting as ministers have no idea what they are saying – and that applies also to the bureaucrats advising them.

This was amazing because, only two years previously at an Edinburgh Low Level Radiation conference, Dr Keith Baverstock, Department of Environmental Sciences, Kuopio University, Finland and former Head of the Radiation Protection Division for the World Health Organisation (Europe) from 1991 to 2003, delivered a little-publicised presentation entitled 'Science, Politics and Ethics in the Low Dose' in which he stated: "In 1983, it was decided to mount an independent epidemiological study of UK test veterans and the National Radiological Protection Board (NRPB) was funded to undertake the work by the Ministry of Defence (MOD). From a scientific point of view and contrary to the claims made by the NRPB, this shortfall [of accurate records, lack of dosimetry etc] raised a serious flaw in the methodology. The exposed and control populations can no longer guarantee to be free of bias. It is clear that the science and associated ethics have been perverted for political aims. It is sad that the NRPB, which should be an independent and technically competent body, was complicit in this process."

My Member of Parliament was now holding the post of Shadow Minister for Veterans and had found himself in the revolving door all ministers and shadow ministers in this role have faced since its inception in 1993. He had entered a post widely regarded by nuclear veterans as a poisoned chalice and appeared to have handled the mixed messaging extremely well, even though it gave political support to a causation of harm denied for almost six decades.

Three months later I was delighted to hear Mr Harper had been released from the post where the policy of denial of nuclear veterans' ill health is based firmly on the lie that alpha and beta particles are harmless; a policy ignoring the significance that veterans had inhaled and ingested such radiation whilst working in a radioactive environment for possibly months on end without respirators or any PPE.

Yet when it came to the Litvinenko case, scientists from the same government-sponsored and dysfunctional department had flown into a panic to admit that just an invisible-to-the-eye quantity of alpha radiation is toxic when gaining access to the body.

This is the fantasy world of policy enforcement my MP had entered into. Mr Harper, I'm pleased to say, went on to better things and served as Minister of Pensions and Chief Whip. In 2020, during the Covid-19 pandemic, Mr Harper led a number of backbench MPs in the Covid Recovery Group (CRG), whose

Principle 2 of 3 states: "It is time to end the monopoly on advice of government scientists and prevailing expert scientific opinion must be challenged by multi-disciplinary groups from outside government. Ministers should publish the models that inform policies so they can be reviewed by the public."

Perhaps there is hope for better days ahead for all in these troubled times – provided, of course, stated principles are actually acted upon.

Back in 2007, the stage had been set for political interference to weaken the progress of the AVGL as much as possible. The Rowland Study of 50 New Zealand veterans' blood by the advanced diagnostic technology of cytogenetics to detect changes in chromosomes (genetic damage) as a result of exposure to radiation on Christmas Island in 1958 was due to be released and then peer-reviewed in 2009.

In the middle of the Limitation Trial, an inquiry – Parliamentary Inquiry (Nuclear Veterans) PIq (NV) – was arranged to be held over two days 18-19 October 2007 with the stated aim of trying to achieve a settlement of claims with the AVGL, progressing forward. The timing appears to have been planned for only one reason – that is, to disrupt the progress of compensation claims.

This was a cross-party effort initiated by two Members of Parliament, Conservative MP John Baron and Dr Ian Gibson, a Labour MP. Their motives may have seemed helpful, particularly for Gibson, but the outcome was less so.

Roy Sefton, chairman of the New Zealand Nuclear Test Veterans Association, was unable to attend but he asked me, on his authority, to attend and represent the views of the NZNTVA. As a fellow member of the CVFI Action Executive,

Roy was as dubious as me about the agenda of the two politicians and emailed: "With the best will possible, whatever their motives it will have no effect against the resolute actions of the MOD and UK Government."

The Inquiry had printed and circulated an agenda that stated the Rowland cytogenetic study would be the subject of a full discussion on the second day, to include questions and answers to the panel. Many veterans, widows, press reporters and interested others had turned up to listen with rapt attention.

Dr Ian Gibson (Labour) had been out to New Zealand to speak to Professor Rowland and was very enthusiastic about the cytogenetic findings. His cross-party counterpart John Baron (Conservative) had recently become Patron of the BNTVA charity, which was still under John Lowe's chairmanship but with a widely diminished membership. It seemed a political fudge was in the making.

Just 12 days earlier, Kevan Jones, Minister for Veterans had written to John Lowe with regard to a meeting they had held. "Turning to the Rowland Study at our meeting, I was pleased that everyone at the meeting generally was in agreement with me. Any new work [cytogenetic testing] is not anticipated to tell us any more about a possible link between the participation in the tests and subsequent ill health."

It appears there is very little difference between the motives of political lobbying and grooming. The BNTVA was being groomed with biased opinion and, as later revelations confirm, promises of reward and recognition for complicity in agreeing a settlement of claims with no admission of liability by government.

The Ministry of Defence had set to work early to diminish the findings of the yet to be peer-reviewed Rowland study showing significant evidence of genetic damage. Five months or so before the Parliamentary Inquiry, the MOD circulated an analysis of the Rowland study, focusing on the clinical relevance of the findings.

The MOD analysis admitted that the study showed significant levels of genetic damage and that 50 blood-tested New Zealand nuclear veterans had also been compared with carefully matched controls who had not attended a nuclear test location. The MOD also acknowledged this study was the first of its kind. But then their analysis changed tone in order to sow doubts as to the study's efficacy. I've broken it down for the reader below, along with the thoughts of the CVFI on each point.

"The study was only on a limited population which makes it hypothesis-generating."

CVFI appraisal: This appears to be sophistry for verification if something is likely to be true – as used in the Black Report, NRPB etc. to enable significant findings to be dismissed by epidemiology as 'just a chance occurrence.'

"Ideally the next step would be replication on a bigger study group."

CVFI appraisal: This appears in effect to be saying the MOD had no control over the Rowland study, therefore wished to replicate it in order to ensure it is biased to give the 'right' answer to suit their policy of denial and kick it into the long grass, possibly for another six or seven years.

" The fact cytogeneticist Professor Rowland stressed the study just showed chromosomal changes and added he had made no clinical claims about the health status of the nuclear

veterans."

CVFI appraisal: This is a subtle way to deflect from the purpose of the study. Professor Rowland is not a physician, he is a cytogeneticist, so any comment on the health of veterans was not the remit of the study; it was only to detect genetic damage causally linked to radiation. Genetic damage is a causation of mutation but dependent on where breaks in the chromosomes occur, which varies from one individual to the next.

The MOD then summarised their analysis to say they were *"always open to new evidence of chromosomal change and will give careful consideration to the study, its implications for the health of nuclear test veterans and our responsibility towards them."*

CVFI appraisal: That is, if any new study is controlled by them in methodology and protocols the MOD, with biased epidemiology (as in the past), will then perhaps give consideration to the findings.

The MOD hoped their analysis would help groom the BNTVA into surrender. But it did not impress any of the 70% of non-member nuclear veterans and widows campaigning for truth and justice.

On the first day of the Parliamentary Inquiry we were treated to an interesting talk by Britain's leading cytogeneticist, Professor Rhona Anderson of Brunel University, London. This was virtually a sales pitch for Brunel University to undertake a large study of nuclear veterans. She praised the efficacy of the advanced technology of cytogenetics in detecting radiation damage. This study, in effect, would take several years to complete; the Rowland Study took six years from commencement to peer review. But Professor Anderson failed to mention it would not be fully independent of Ministry of Defence control, as was the Rowland study. If ever undertaken it would, therefore, inevitably be significantly vulnerable to bias in its final conclusions.

On the morning of the second day of the hearing, all who attended quickly found that the agenda topic they most looked forward to – discussion of the Rowland study – had changed. Instead, in contradiction to the fact that the MOD was said to have refused to attend the Inquiry, two doctors from the MOD's former contractual partner the NRPB (now HPA) appeared and promptly launched into a presentation of the 'virtues' of the discredited 1980s and 90s mortality studies, which had been perverted for political reasons to deny liability for nuclear test veterans' legacy ill health. Eyes glazed over and disbelief raged.

These epidemiological studies had been conducted without blood testing of nuclear veterans. Nuclear veterans who sought cytogenetic blood tests for decades had been denied them. The atmosphere was livid with the incredulity felt by those who attended. No time was allowed for a question and answer discussion about the 'crucial and pivotal evidence' of the Rowland study. It was a classic use of filibuster.

The only point I was able to address to the panel was that "As a member of the CVFI and on behalf of the NZNTVA, we did not come here to listen to a talk by the NRPB, we came to discuss the Rowland study." The clock was then run down on the Inquiry for the rest of the day by a member of the BNTVA giving a long rambling talk about the wind direction at Christmas Island during Operation Grapple in 1958. Only frustration prevented those who attended from falling asleep.

Then, at the end, the BNTVA charity chairman John Lowe, who, like the vast majority of the depleted membership was not a claimant of the AVGL class action, stood up and addressed the panel. "I'm not involved in legal action against the MOD but believe I should be paid £10,000 compensation."

The Inquiry panel was composed of Dr Ian Gibson MP and John Baron MP and also included Dr Julian Peto, an epidemiologist, as chairman. During breaks in the two-day inquiry, nuclear veterans observed Dr Peto going back and forth to the Ministry of Defence building opposite. Many made the assumption that the MOD, who were said to have 'not attended', were in fact constantly being kept up to date with progress.

The Rowland study was peer-reviewed in 2009 in a prestigious scientific journal. Later, Professor Rhona Anderson of Brunel University gave a second peer review report to Rosenblatts that, in her opinion, the study had used methodology and controls that were "conducted with meticulous attention to detail." As a cytogeneticist she would not, of course, comment upon clinical results, but only on the genetic damage indicated by exposure to radiation.

Over the next 12 months the BNTVA ceased to have any connection with the majority of nuclear veterans and their widows after they signed up to a political settlement of claims as a registered charity under the Patronage of John Baron MP seeking a fund of £25 million from government, without any admission of Ministry of Defence liability.

A few days after the Inquiry I received an email from John Lowe which complained "...at the start John Baron MP prevented me from asking most of the questions which I had prepared, thereby creating the belief the panel was on the side of the establishment and against the nuclear test veterans. I'm afraid this set the tone for the remainder of the two days."

In the eyes of campaigning nuclear veterans, this only discredited his performance further.

Within a year, John Baron MP, Patron of the BNTVA, in debate in the House of Commons with the Minister for Veterans, admitted: "This without doubt is a political problem." It appears to be a political problem Mr Baron had thought best suited by a political fudge and best sorted without admission of liability. This would end in complete failure because the MOD and the government would rather systematically and cynically dodge a settlement through a continued conspiracy of silence and bad faith until all nuclear test veterans are dead, forgotten and no longer a vexation and irritation to those who had betrayed them.

The verdict of the Limitation Trial came in June 2009. "Fallout is the prime causal link to the nuclear veterans' ill health and the Rowland cytogenetic study is crucial and pivotal evidence to allow all cases to proceed for individual claims."

A first victory for the AVGL. But one factor was not applied in Mr Justice Foskett's trial summary: the door had been left open for the MOD to appeal against the finding. This did not, however, prevent Susie Boniface from the *Daily Mirror* publishing a photograph of veterans and widows on the steps of the London High Court celebrating with a bottle of champagne under the headline prematurely proclaiming: "We did it!"

The AVGL nuclear veterans and their widows had cause to celebrate Rosenblatts' hard work – but only for a short time.

Before the BNTVA became a charity, the former justice-campaigning association had a legal secretary and an executive committee. As a charity, this administrative body had been swept away, replaced by trustees and a patron. All the former ethics and morality of the former association had changed.

The CVFI stressed at the time: "It is not a charity who has the prime consideration for the majority of nuclear veterans and widows; it is truth and justice."

Chapter 10: The Supreme Court, A Pyrrhic Victory and the Fight for Military Pensions

Mourn not the dead...
But rather mourn the apathetic throng
The cowed and meek
Who see the world's great anguish and its wrong
And dare not speak!
Ralph Chaplin, World War One poet, on the final page of
Robert Green's 'A Thorn in Their Side: The true story of the
shocking death of Hilda Murrell'

The success of the Atomic Veterans Group Litigation (AVGL) in the Limitation Trial in June 2009 was not the quick victory the MOD and UK Government had hoped for. The AVGL's 1,011 claims from nuclear test veterans and widows seeking compensation had not been knocked out by the MOD in a single blow. The use of the Statute of Limitations Act as a legal technicality had been roundly defeated by two decisive scientific truths.

With the Limitation Trial verdict's statement that "the prime causal link to veterans' ill health is fallout" and "the cytogenetic blood test study by Professor Rowland is crucial and pivotal evidence", two key factors undermining the MOD's defence had been judicially recognised. More importantly, this information had now entered the public domain. But like all truths regarding the hazards of radiation, as recognised by the 1956 Medical Research Council Report and debated in the

House of Commons, it was the antithesis of what the Ministry of Defence wanted the public to know.

Both key factors of evidentiary proof of the irradiation of nuclear test participants had long been considered game-changers, not only by nuclear veterans in the UK, Australia and New Zealand but by others globally, including peer-reviewed scientists who had taken an interest in radiation hazards. The whole motivation behind the formation of the CVFI was to get such science recognised by the veterans' legal team, headed by Neil Samson of Rosenblatts, who were starting from scratch, and use this evidence effectively in court. It was with an immense sense of pride, therefore, that a small forum of independent-minded veterans and others exchanging information between the UK, Australia and New Zealand had helped to obtain the science needed by the Atomic Veterans Group Litigation to enable onward progress towards a just and honourable settlement of claims.

The information had flowed in from many sources: independent radiation scientists' peer-reviewed papers; press reports in the UK, Australia and New Zealand, both scientific and political; archive documents, such as the 1956 Medical Research Council Report; Freedom of Information requests and so on. No part of the equation was ignored. Because, after all, this without doubt had been identified as a long-running political problem rather than one about the efficacy of the biological impact of radiation on the human body – despite it being common knowledge by now that radiation is indeed a toxic pathogen when gaining access to the interior of the body.

It was a huge relief that the hard work of Rosenblatts so far had paid off. However, by the new year of 2010, progress in the

AVGL's claims for compensation was balanced on a knife edge. It did not matter that a new government would be in place in May 2010; nothing would change. As affirmed in 1999, any help to nuclear veterans is seen as an 'unfriendly act' to government; in the eyes of government policy, helping nuclear veterans is something that must be undermined at any cost, be it tax payers' money or, if necessary, through an absence of ethics.

The AVGL's legal train, carrying the concerns of 1,011 nuclear veterans and widow claimants, had, between 2005 and 2009, reached a platform of success. But before it teetered again down the steep mountain track towards a Court of Appeal set for 4 May 2010, without brakes, and with no means of pulling the emergency stop cord or communicating with those in the engine, the claimants suddenly found they had lost their star barrister, Ben Browne QC. The loss was questionable, but perhaps it had its genesis two years earlier, around the time when the peer-reviewed New Zealand cytogenetic blood study had found that veterans who attended nuclear weapon test locations had a 300% higher level of genetic damage in their DNA compared to veterans who had not attended such locations. From that time on, every effort would be made to ensure the findings of this study could not be used or even referred to again in court by a star barrister such as Ben Browne.

The heavily biased Parliamentary Inquiry (Nuclear Veterans) PIq (NV) report of October 2007 recommended the MOD and AVGL should mediate a settlement of claims. In effect, this was to weaken the resolve of legal action for compensation. Meanwhile, even before the Inquiry, the BNTVA had consolidated their position of no longer being a campaigning association seeking justice by becoming a charity, recognised and supported by the Minister for Veterans, whose political patron sought a payment of £25 million without any admitted liability from the MOD for the ill health, premature deaths and genetic damage suffered by the AVGL claimants.

This all had indications of a throwback to 17th century imperial colonial times. That is, divide the natives into weakened positions of administration, gain a submissive ruler under your patronage and then take over all by rule and conquer.

From this time on, the CVFI and anyone associated with the AVGL claimants would be undermined and discredited as 'anti-nuclear' and 'a vexation'. In the coming weeks and months, such accusations escalated – and much of this came from the charity, which was controlled increasingly and submissively by non-veteran trustees and its patron, John Baron MP. A time arrived where seeking the truth had become a thorn in the side of the MOD and undermining the whole legal process had become the prime objective of the Ministry of Defence.

The two cross-party politicians who set up the Parliamentary Inquiry would both be dealt with. It is a salutary lesson of where the power exists in UK politics – and it does not rest with backbenchers on any issue ordained as government policy across party political lines. In seeking a £25 million donation for the charity of which he was patron, the Conservative MP, John Baron would end up being humiliated before the end of 2013.

The Labour MP, Dr Ian Gibson, who had travelled to New Zealand to speak to Professor Rowland and supported the efficacy of cytogenetic blood tests over the bias of easily manipulated epidemiological studies, would pay the penalty for attempting to help nuclear test veterans.

As an academic, Dr Gibson genuinely sought compensation for nuclear veterans and their widows, but he would be forced out of politics during the political expenses scandal of the time. Dr Gibson would be forced to resign as a backbencher whilst other politicians in ministerial positions, who had abused privileges significantly more, managed to survive. In what many perceived as a kangaroo court to cull backbenchers seeking the truth rather than following established bi-party nuclear veterans' policy, Dr Gibson was removed from office.

It therefore appeared that kangaroo courts did not only apply to nuclear test veterans' and widows' pension appeal tribunals, they were also used for politicians who, for whatever reason, had stood against a policy of government. It seems the party whips are not in place just to allow backbenchers to ignore the ideology of ministerial leaders, whichever party they are elected to represent. And yet, many of the electorate believe MPs have a duty to help their constituents with their genuine concerns.

This in fact was a message to politicians who had tried in any way to be of help to nuclear veterans. The BNTVA, on the other hand, had become a ministerial and government favourite purely as a result of their submission. Veterans who, for many years, had campaigned for justice within the BNTVA began to leave the association in increasing numbers as the charity fell under the influence of government and became further removed from the concerns of veterans.

Discontent within the BNTVA came thick and fast. For example, I received a copy of a letter written by Derek Fiddaman on 8 December 2008. Mr Fiddaman was a tireless campaigner who I had met in London on several occasions. He had retrieved many documents from the National Archives that proved helpful to the campaign for justice and had assisted with the AVGL legal case. Derek had served in the Royal Navy at Christmas Island and had suffered skin cancer for many years, having countless all-body skin grafts as an unwelcome badge of service. This was induced by the massive gamma radiation released from a nuclear bomb detonated while he was standing in the open, on deck, in only shorts and shirt and without any protective clothing. MOD officials had dismissed his cancer as "too much sunbathing".

Mr Fiddaman wrote to John Lowe, chairman of the BNTVA, that: "The membership has dwindled to approximately only 3,000 of which I am thoroughly ashamed only 130 or 230 (I've heard both figures) are actively involved in litigation. That does not say much for the fighting spirit or the interest you are generating in the membership.

"The government has said on many occasions that litigation is the only way for us to be heard and achieve some form of recognition. A silent membership will not achieve that. On the basis of the figures, the BNTVA is very much a minority voice in the courts, so my suggestion to you is that you let the people who are concerned and working on everybody's behalf get on with the task and stop interfering.

"Your constant mutterings about the anti-nuclear lobby are utterly ridiculous. I'm not surprised you have not replied to my resignation letter. That would be too polite, so please be informed that I resign as a member of the BNTVA forthwith."

This is typical of what many nuclear veterans faced within the charity as it became increasingly dominated by non-veteran trustees and with a politician as patron. At the time, it reinforced my view that action by a small forum of independent activists, free from political control, free from interference by people in any government-approved quango, was the only ethical and moral way to proceed to establishing the truth and justice.

The Court of Appeal hearings began shortly after the 2010 general election, which brought a Conservative administration to power under the leadership of David Cameron. Cameron had been referred to in some sections of the press as "the heir to Blair", so gaining power from the Labour Government did not herald any change in government policy towards the nuclear test veterans. Seamless transfers from opposition party to government had happened many times in the past and the policy against nuclear veterans' duty of care retained the same ethos of denial reliant on outdated and flawed advice to ministers. Politicians from all parties sang from the same devil's hymn sheet of misinformation.

Following the 2007 Parliamentary Inquiry (Nuc Vets) recommendations, the situation regarding compensation had been set in stone by a series of meetings, held behind closed doors, between the BNTVA executive and the MOD. This resulted in no compensation being paid to AVGL claimants on account of the BNTVA waiving any Ministry of Defence liability for exposure to radiation. Instead, a settlement would be made to the BNTVA as a charity.

Robathan was the first Minister of Veterans in a decade with military experience. He had served in the armed forces for some 18 years as an officer in the Coldstream Guards. However, this counted for nothing in the eyes of campaigning nuclear test veterans for the simple reason Robathan had not served at a nuclear test location and was, therefore, reliant only on the inherited advice of the biased and manipulated quasi-military standard issue document, the *SPVA Statement on Radiation Advice to Ministers*. That is, as with all his predecessors, Robathan ran his portfolio on the basis of a 'need to know' document, a sort of standard military instruction book of advice ideally suited to ministers who hadn't a clue about radiation but regarded the content with the same rapt attention as a military recruit used to following instructions from any person just one rank above them.

As a former Guards Officer, Robathan was an ideal candidate to follow the rule book and not allow any independent thought or empathy deflect from the mission at hand. Presumably if he had seen military service over several months at a nuclear weapon test location he would have been overlooked as a candidate for the portfolio. Almost certainly he would have been judged anti-nuclear or, possibly the worst transgression, liable to show empathy towards the position of the AVGL claimants who had been forced into litigation by successive governments.

In early statements, the new Minister for Veterans, with the usual party-political habit of petty point-scoring, claimed, "Labour had failed to protect armed forces personnel" and pledged himself "to be a minister who would stand up for soldiers past and present." Bravo. A fine way to rally the troops before ignoring their many concerns on behalf of desk-bound, radiator-hugging and indolent superannuated civil servants.

The lack of empathy in politicians never fails to amaze. Every Minister for Veterans since the inception of that poisoned portfolio in 1993 has failed to protect armed forces personnel and any who had empathy with them, or stood up for every soldier past and present, were quickly ejected through the rapidly revolving door. They can only be allowed to act with the World War One mentality of attrition that coined the expression 'Lions led by donkeys' – an ethos where loss of life is just an acceptable statistic. For many it is a dilemma: follow the advice or lose an increased ministerial salary and the ministerial car that goes with it.

So, news of Cameron's premiership and appointments made with regard to policy on nuclear veterans was treated with decades of scepticism by those nuclear test veterans still campaigning for justice; it did absolutely nothing to inspire confidence for the future.

Archie Ross had been a keen supporter of the CVFI's independent campaigning since its beginning in 2002. He served with the RAF at Christmas Island during 1957-8 and shortly after his return he developed cataracts after witnessing six nuclear bomb tests. In 1960, his daughter Julie was born with arm and chest deformities. Because he thought no government would do this to their own men, his suspicion that the bomb tests had caused his ill health and the genetic destruction of his family was held in check until the 1980s. It was finally shattered when he found a colleague he had served with at Christmas Island also had cataracts that could have been caused by radiation – and the biggest shock to Archie was that his former colleague had also had a deformed daughter, who died at birth.

From that moment he was a tireless campaigner for truth and justice, and an early member of the BNTVA. His comment about Robathan's 2010 appointment, published in the press, just said, in the very moderated tone of veterans of this era:

"After 50 years of politicians it would need something very big to happen for me to suddenly think things are going to change."

With regard to the Court of Appeal hearing at London's Civil Appeal Court, given the go ahead by PM David Cameron on gaining office, Mr Ross simply added: "It is disgusting what has happened. I will say this: David Cameron has pledged to clean up the House of Commons [after the MPs' expenses scandal] and the same needs to take place at the Ministry of Defence. They need to clean up their act so that the right thing can be done by people that have been exposed to radiation."

When Archie Ross died in 2015, his wife Chris followed up one of his last instructions and ensured his certificate giving cause of death as Chronic Lymphoid Leukaemia was published in the press for all to see. Archie's fight for a war pension had been turned down by the MOD because he had not gone to a war zone and fought in battle, and therefore had no entitlement to compensation or pension rights normally afforded to other servicemen or women injured in service to the nation.

New Conservative Prime Minister David Cameron wasted no time in showing his true colours. Just before Christmas 2009, five months before the general election, he used the assembled crew on HMS Ark Royal as a backdrop for a press release promising all servicemen a Military Covenant would be enshrined into law as soon as he had his hands on the levers of power. As Conservative Party Opposition Leader, he had initiated a Military Covenant Commission (MCC) with carefully contrived terms of reference hidden at the end of its carefully crafted launch document.

The continuation of the decades-long "It's a pity, but it cannot be helped" policy of denial had already been aided and abetted by Labour's Minister for Veterans, Kevan Jones, before the Labour Party lost the 2010 general election. The seamlessness of transfer of power enforcing this policy was well practised by both Labour and Conservatives over many years. The groundwork had already been laid for a bi-party deception.

Meanwhile, Cameron's Military Covenant Commission appeared to the public to be a benign initiative, a helpful look at the welfare of veterans to improve their overall duty of care by government. Cameron appointed a Shadow Minister for Veterans, Dr Andrew Murrison MP, a former Royal Navy surgeon officer, as political advisor for the Commission to frame the 'right' recommendations. This window dressing of a 'political advisor' just proved to be another example of putting a fox in charge of the henhouse.

The CVFI contacted and exchanged emails with Murrison over a period of time, stating that any recommendations to the MCC "would not be worth the paper written on unless nuclear test veterans are included in the Covenant and the duty of care recommendations are enshrined into law."

Among much else, we sent Murrison a copy of former Labour Secretary of State for Defence Dr John Reid's letter, written in 1993 when he was Shadow Labour Spokesperson for Defence. This letter stated the Labour Party principle was that a nuclear test veteran should be treated the same as any other member of the armed forces injured, disabled or killed in service to the nation.

This was a pledge of principle that the prime minister and barrister Blair quickly reneged upon when elected to power in 1997. When it comes to nuclear test veterans, both political party leaderships since 1952 need to join a circus as backward somersaulting clowns. Even the Liberal Democrats joined the pantomime of clowns when Nick Harvey MP became Defence Minister in the Conservative–Liberal Democratic coalition administration. Harvey immediately reneged on a witness statement in support of the AVGL litigation he had written for Rosenblatts, claiming now he was a minister he had been made privy to new information. We suspect he had either been told to shut up or had perhaps read a copy of the SPVA's biased advice to ministers with regard to radiation. We wrote to him asking what new information he had been made 'privy' to. But only silence was forthcoming.

Dr Andrew Murrison's email response to the Reid letter was short: "I find this all rather sickening." Sickening to Murrison, no doubt, because the massive backward somersaulting on this principle had entered the public domain? Or perhaps because Murrison realised himself to be just another stooge in the revolving door of potential Ministers for Veterans portfolio of continued deception?

This is only another footnote in the real history of this period but it's a toxic and poisonous reminder of the deliberate exclusion of nuclear test veterans from a duty of care and how close our democracy is to becoming noted internationally as unaccountable and irresponsible towards those who serve the nation.

So, on becoming Prime Minister, David Cameron told the press that despite his promise to enshrine a Military Covenant into law he had broken it on the advice of Ministry of Defence officials. This came as no surprise to nuclear veterans and their widows. Right from the initiation of Cameron's Commission in 2009, the covenant was impossible to be enshrined into law because it had already been agreed in the terms of reference used by the Ministry of Defence.

This concept of our democratic government is demonstrated in the following poem.

Ministerial Policy (Apologia and Advice)
by Lib Rowland Hughes, 1997

I'm one of the advisors and in case you're int'rested
I think I must tell you my int'rests are vested

And one of my jobs which I do every day
Is briefing the Ministers just what to say.

They're sometimes all right, and sometimes a mess
I keep in the background nevertheless.

If things turn out wrong they can always blame me
But I am anonymous as you can see.

So, pity the Minster, they're not to blame,
But neither am I, that's part of the game.

Hidden in the small print of the terms of reference of Cameron's dubious MCC launch document is the statement that "any recommendations of the MCC will only be made from existing Ministry of Defence budgets". It's a reference clearly designed to seal its fate by the bean-counting superannuated officials of the Ministry of Defence. This is a department known to campaigning nuclear veterans for decades as a government-financed administrative quango whose members are appointed by government with the powers of bias funded by unlimited taxpayers' money in excess of every other quango ever appointed in the history of Britain. Unless, of course, you go back to the court of Henry the Eighth in the 16th century.

The result of Cameron's MCC initiative was all predictably "rather sickening", as Murrison had opined when reading Reid's letter of similar broken promises. The MCC was merely a public relations exercise just before a general election to gain votes, with no intention of enshrining anything into law that may be helpful to nuclear veterans – or indeed to the naval ratings who had assembled on the deck of the aircraft carrier HMS Ark Royal.

But at least it was consistent with the inherited nuclear veteran policy seamlessly and sickeningly passed from one administration to the next, like an axe from one medieval executioner to another. That is, genetic damage to nuclear veterans is 'a pity, but it cannot be helped' and 'any help to nuclear veterans is regarded as an unfriendly act' by the British government.

So, with David Cameron as Prime Minister in 2010, nothing would change except the credibility of our democracy would be further diminished. For the AVGL and the BNTVA charity, they saw no gain either, and the government would also fail to resolve the matter. That is, except by attempting to rewrite history.

After the Limitation Trial verdict of June 2009, government lawyers had been undone and surpassed by the very able and winning barrister Benjamin Browne QC, who had been hired by Rosenblatts as counsel for the Atomic Veterans Group Litigation's 1,011 cases of nuclear veterans and their widows.

Within four months it appears dark forces, often talked

about, of the Ministry of Defence had struck to change the legal playing field to the government's advantage. A public announcement on 29 September 2009 by Minister for Veterans Kevan Jones MP stated that a settlement offer to the AVGL had been made but rejected by its counsel. Without any further detail, this statement was now widely – and some would say deliberately – pushed into the public domain.

A mediated settlement had been the recommendation of the Parliamentary Inquiry in October 2007 but, following its exposure as a manipulated fiasco, all recommendations to mediate had been swept under the carpet. This is because any mediated settlement would almost certainly be one on the government's terms because they had a reciprocal treaty obligation with Australia to avoid paying any compensation.

The Limitation Trial verdict had obviously put a mediated settlement back onto the MOD's agenda with perhaps some degree of urgency and panic. The Justice Foskett verdict of June 2009 had, in almost everyone's opinion, humiliated the MOD's lawyers. Everyone now wanted to know the truth of Kevan Jones' authorised settlement proposal because no details had been given about it in the press and Rosenblatts, who led the AVGL and had hired Ben Browne as their lead counsel, had stated no such settlement offer had been made.

On 14 December 2009, I wrote a letter to Kevan Jones on behalf of the CVFI Action Executive of Shirley Denson, Ken McGinley, Roy Sefton and myself, stating: "This issue is seen by veterans as a cynical attempt to drive a wedge between the nuclear veterans and our legal team."

Four days earlier, on 10 December, there had been a debate in the House of Commons where Shirley Denson's MP, Siobhain McDonagh, had put up a spirited support not only for

Shirley's struggle as a nuclear widow to get justice for her husband's radiation-induced suicide and her genetically damaged daughters and grandchildren, but also to get some sense with regards to the reports that there had been a genuine negotiation between the government and the AVGL and their legal team. Rosenblatts kept saying "Oh no there wasn't," so interest in the media regarding the questionable proposed settlement still persisted.

A later reading of Hansard on the debate suggested there may have been some talk about legal costs accrued by Rosenblatts of £9.5 million. But, as a result of the 2007 Parliamentary Inquiry, the unremitting 50 year-plus track record of government bad faith and much else, veterans could only trust Rosenblatts' view on this matter. Trust in the Ministry of Defence and the government had disappeared decades earlier.

We veterans and widows also wanted to know more about the episode that had removed the star of the AVGL's legal team, Ben Browne QC, from being any further help in the Court of Appeal, due in 2010. We wanted to know the truth about the Minister for Veterans' authorisation of a settlement proposal which had, in our view and the view of many, been motivated to separate the very able Ben Browne QC from further involvement in the case and had forced Rosenblatts to use a less experienced counsel in the coming appeal process.

In the meantime, the CVFI had expressed in writing to Rosenblatts our continued support for them despite what had happened. As with everything about the running of the Atomic Veterans Group Litigation train, it was now halted on a platform of success but still set to clatter once again down a steep mountain track, with no emergency cord for the claimants to pull and no one sure who was steering the engine.

Kevan Jones responded to the CVFI's letter in January 2010. He started by saying: "In the hope that it helps explain our situation…" This is a familiar phrase seen in countless letters from this portfolio over the years that rarely if ever help to explain anything. Probably because, as veterans have learnt over the decades, any help to veterans has been regarded as an 'unfriendly act' by successive UK governments since the Cold War. The framing of letters from this department over decades either begin or end with the same fatuous cliché.

The 'bending over to be helpful' remark by the flummoxed MOD barrister at the successful First Tier Freedom of Information hearing of February 2012 springs to mind in this context. Following from this, when their 'helpful' explanations are exposed as misinformation, what comes next is silence.

Kevan Jones then continued: "The MOD has attempted to settle this matter under the Alternative Dispute Resolution (ADR) process holding counsel to counsel negotiations. ADR is confidential between parties, but while continuing to respect the confidential process I can advise that on the 29 Sept 2009 I authorised a settlement proposal (although I cannot disclose the amount or any details in relation to it) which was conveyed to the veterans' counsel who was, of course, negotiating with the authority of and as a spokesman for Rosenblatts. I am unable to comment on subsequent discussions. I also cannot comment further on negotiations which are subject to confidentiality agreement. I am hopeful the renewal of meaningful discussions between parties can take place in coming weeks. If the matter cannot be settled the case will proceed to appeal."

His response was, significantly, devoid of what amount of

settlement had been made, something which was essential for the claimants of compensation to know. It all had the air of yet another behind-back-doors agreement that litter nuclear history to the detriment of any openness or honesty.

The CVFI believes Members of Parliament and the public are entitled to their own views on this matter. We expressed this belief in a letter following the Nuclear Test Veterans Debate on 29 October 2013 when the settlement of a £25 million donation was being discussed, to be placed under control of a quango of trustees and a political patron known as the BNTVA charity.

In 2013 a new Minister for Veterans, the Conservative MP Anna Soubry QC, would help shed some further light into the darkness about Kevan Jones' authorised settlement of claims in 2009 – possibly without knowing she had done so.

Meanwhile, Kevan Jones finished his letter to the CVFI Action Executive by saying: "The BNTVA is recognised by my department and it is with the BNTVA that the MOD and parliamentarians have engaged in recent years. Indeed, the BNTVA have written to me to disassociate themselves from your letter of 14 December. I do not believe therefore that your group [i.e. the Combined Veterans Forum International, representing the views of the AVGL claimants and Australian, New Zealand and Fijian nuclear test veterans] represents the views of the majority of nuclear test veterans and their families."

Of course the minister was delighted to only recognise the BNTVA and engage with them. The CVFI, on the other hand, was not a carbon copy of the BNTVA and from its outset in 2002 never intended to be. We had set out to be an antidote to their appeasement and were proud to be recognised as a thorn in the side of the MOD.

The words of Kevan Jones were a repetition of past history. Anyone who believed in a charity seeking a £25 million handout, without any admission of liability for the legacy ill health, premature deaths and genetic damage of those who took part in the nuclear weapon test experiments, against the majority views of all, could only be regarded as ridiculously out of touch or extremely biased.

Besides which, as a result of *Fissionline* Freedom of Information requests by investigative journalist Alan Rimmer, it revealed that the minister, in discussions behind closed doors on 29 October 2008 with the BNTVA chairman John Lowe and nuclear veteran charity officials Jeff Lyddiatt and Doug Hern, sold out the veterans.

That is, the trio of nuclear veteran charity officials agreed that instead of supporting the cytogenetic blood study of New Zealand's Professor Al Rowland, a health audit of surviving nuclear veterans would be undertaken. The minister drove home the point on which they surrendered: "The Rowland Report is already on the table and any new work is not anticipated to tell us anything further about any possible link between participation in nuclear tests and subsequent ill health."

In a separate clause to the 'surrender terms', the BNTVA ditched any further cytogenetic testing of veterans and agreed that a health audit would be better than more effective evidential blood tests. The assembled trio also all agreed with the minister that it was not possible to overturn previous war pension decisions that had gone against the veterans.

These now complicit and favoured nuclear veterans were

not labelled anti-nuclear. They had just signed themselves up to the pro-nuclear lobby and into a junior contractual partner role with the Ministry of Defence.

The exact words in the minister's letter about the CVFI being a minority representative view of veterans' opinions were also at the end of John Lowe's 2007 email to MP John Baron, patron of the BNTVA, when Lowe had complained, after the Parliamentary Inquiry fiasco, that he had been prevented from 'asking questions'.

By 2009, the remark from John Baron MP that the treatment of nuclear veterans is 'without doubt a political problem' had indeed become a problem when he had taken over the BNTVA and turned it into a quango run by trustees with an agenda to ensure no recognition or compensation would be given in settlement of the claims of nuclear veterans and their widows.

The labels 'vexation' and 'anti-nuclear' increasingly were used against those seeking truth and justice in the UK, Australia and elsewhere. During this time, from 2007 through to 2014, the anti-nuclear card was repeatedly shown to anyone supporting the AVGL case. Compiled from scientific peer-reviewed papers and other archive documents, the anti-nuclear charge against those seeking the truth is spurious and needs explanation.

The science of radiation damage to health and genetic damage is anti-nuclear. The nuclear industry is sustained primarily with a political motive of obtaining fissionable material for nuclear bombs. Independent scientists have calculated that more people have died prematurely from the activity of the nuclear industry than in two world wars. Genetic damage caused by the nuclear industry is passed to future generations and will take 500 years to work itself out of the human genome.

Following the success of the Limitation Trial, the history of future justice for the 30,000-plus nuclear test veteran 'indoctrinees' set in train by the 1952 task force that sailed to the other side of the world for the first UK nuclear bomb test now rested on a knife edge balance of deception. From the actuality of sowing seeds of death amongst young servicemen at Monte Bello Island to the seeds of doubt nurtured with regard to the AVGL's compensation claims, nuclear veterans were heading towards being airbrushed from history.

Surviving nuclear veterans' understanding of the questionable settlement offer of claims in 2009-10, from a legal source totally independent of Rosenblatts, is that the MOD sent an offer of settlement to the AVGL's counsel, Ben Browne QC, when he was away on holiday and therefore unable to consult with Rosenblatts. The MOD then released a press statement to say an offer had been made but not responded to. Since Rosenblatts had no knowledge that such an offer had been sent to Browne, this greatly embarrassed them in the media.

This caused a dispute between the solicitors and their hired star QC and resulted in Rosenblatts having to hire a new lead QC at short notice. This would be a new counsel without the acquired knowledge regarding the complex science needed to handle the forthcoming Court of Appeal hearing due to commence on 4 May 2010. This outcome enhanced prospects for the well-funded MOD legal team.

Sending a settlement offer to Ben Browne when he was away on holiday and was unaware of it, and not to Rosenblatts, for the attention of the AVGL claimant nuclear veterans and widows, sowed seeds of doubt. It confirmed the suspicions many held of 'dark forces' using an underhanded ploy: get rid of Browne from the Court of Appeal and therefore reverse legal judgements for the Ministry of Defence.

At the time, Rosenblatts assured the CVFI that no approach had been made to them of a settlement and we confirmed we had every confidence with the AVGL's legal team. We had no trust or confidence in the MOD version of events.

As mentioned above, three years later at a Nuclear Test Veterans Debate (NTVD) on 29 October 2013, the new Conservative Minister for Veterans, Anna Soubry MP QC, was asked about the questionable settlement offer said to have been authorised by Labour's Minister for Veterans, Kevan Jones MP. Anna Soubry's appointment at this time is interesting. As a Member of the Criminal Bar Association, she was also the first ever female Minster for Veterans in the never-ending revolving door of ministers to hold this portfolio. The debate was about the proposal to donate £25 million to the BNTVA under the patronage of John Baron MP, and possibly to ask why a barrister Minister for Veterans had been appointed.

The information she put forward in the debate, as with all her predecessors in this role, was inevitably provided by nameless officials within the MOD. From an account of the full debate she appeared to be playing an important part in building upon former Labour Veterans' Minister Kevan Jones who, in 2009, had stated: "The settlement I authorised was rejected by the lawyers involved. I am sorry, but I think that was the individual veterans' best chance of getting a large amount of compensation. The figures stretched to several million pounds."

Anna Soubry's response to this matter in the 2013 debate

was: "I know no details, but I have experience as a criminal barrister and know that every lawyer is under a duty to consult the client first. The client provides instructions and makes the decision. Perhaps the honourable gentleman and I should talk about these events after this debate."

From a layman's view, the above from a criminal barrister seemed perhaps a qualified comment on something many believed: that the settlement offer had a hint of criminality about it rather than openness and honesty.

In 2009 Kevan Jones, of course, did not consult the client – the nuclear test veterans and widows; he only stated that he had consulted someone (Ben Browne QC) who was leading the AVGL class action on their behalf. As a criminal barrister, Anna Soubry knew there was no legal relationship between a barrister and a client. If a settlement of claims had actually been made, then surely even at this belated date of 2013, the claimants had a right to know the figures involved. So did the press. It appears no settlement of claims for compensation had been made and only what appears to be a fraudulent and unethical deception had taken place.

This was a salutary lesson that brought home the fact: why ever take the words of a Minister for Veterans as being truthful or indeed helpful to those who serve the nation? After all, any help to nuclear veterans is regarded as an 'unfriendly act' by the United Kingdom government, a fact admitted in 1999.

The prime reason for the Nuclear Test Veterans Debate in October 2013 was to discuss a £25 million donation without liability to the BNTVA charity. Many had watched the debate live online, and had obtained and read the full 18-page Hansard transcript.

The CVFI sent an open email letter to all the MPs who took part in the debate. It was written by the Action Executive on behalf of all AVGL veterans supporting legal action against the MOD; that is, the vast majority who were not members of the BNTVA. It was also sent on behalf of Commonwealth allies of combined forces from Australia, New Zealand and Fiji who had participated in the weapon test experiments and who still sought accountability and responsibility for their service.

We stressed again that it was not a charity (the BNTVA) that was the prime consideration of the nuclear veterans and their widows through their claims; it was truth and justice. The donation of any monies into a benevolent fund stood the risk of not reaching those of individual entitlement. As an example, we mentioned the National Coal Board fund of some £1 billion to settle compensation claims of coal miners suffering illnesses like silicosis and chronic pulmonary disease after inhaling or ingesting coal dust. A great deal of this money proved difficult to claim by many aging coal miners (my father-in law being one of them) because of the complexity of the process, and much ended up in the pockets of trade unions and lawyers overseeing the disbursement.

As we had long suspected, without a meaningful Military Covenant the so-called "debt of gratitude" continually espoused by Prime Minister David Cameron was a set of empty words. This confirmed why, outside the bubble of the BNTVA charity and Westminster, the majority of surviving nuclear veterans and their widows had lost all trust in ministers and the government.

This lack of trust, induced by politically backward-somersaulting ministers, dates back many years. Since 1993 the political principle, supported by Labour, that the nuclear test veterans should be regarded in the same way as any other serviceman or woman injured in service to the nation had remained unchanged. The majority of veterans supported legal action because the government had repeatedly said it was the only way to settle this matter and was the only way to gain recognition and justice.

As patron of the BNTVA, John Baron MP was asking for £25 million for a benevolent fund without liability. This, in the view of the majority of veterans, was far too lenient in comparison to the many millions of pounds of taxpayers' money spent over 50 years or so by successive governments to prevent any settlement of claims. Meanwhile, reports in the press talk of annual bonuses for MOD officials over the last decade averaging around £30 million per annum. Clearly the way tax payers' money is being wasted to keep veterans out of court is unacceptable.

The reality is that nuclear veterans and their widows are no different to any other in a democracy in one respect: they do not appreciate being consistently lied to, as happened when ministers were advised to stick to the guidance of the SPVA Statement on Radiation, an outdated and biased document, which, when circulated amongst veterans and widows, received many forthright reviews.

The nuclear widow Anna Smith, whose husband Barry served at Christmas Island and died of pancreatic cancer in 2009, read the full SPVA document in 2010 and remarked: "You would get more sense if you went to your local newsagent and bought a copy of the *Beano.*"

John Baron's political fudge to get his charity a donation with no liability ended in humiliation. The CVFI agreed, however, with the BNTVA charity's patron when he said at the debate that "words are not enough" and added that "they are determined to see it through." Who was he talking about? What could Mr Baron have expected to have happened when he led a campaign and begged to see it through by appealing to the government's conscience when the MOD and UK Government clearly do not have one? The unique and hazardous service at the nuclear test locations actually undermined veterans' health and this is an embarrassment to successive governments.

Of course, the points made by the CVFI fell on deaf ears at the debate. Most who attended had obviously accepted the fact that the MOD only dealt with organisations approved by them. That is, organisations that agree with MOD and government policy. Non-government organisations (NGOs) with opposing views are *personae non gratae* and therefore viewed by the MOD and many in politics as a threat to democracy. The reverse is the fact. Independent groups are essential in a democracy, when needing to hold people to account.

Personae non gratae is a phrase I became familiar with when I worked in Saudi Arabia for British Aerospace for three years during the late 1970s. The Latin phrase is applied to any person the totalitarian regime believes has broken their laws. For example, drinking alcohol, singing Christmas carols, dressing in public in clothing deemed inappropriate by government, driving a car as a woman, being involved in a traffic accident and not paying blood money etc. Any persons infringing these diktats are removed by the authorities of this totalitarian state as unacceptable people – *personae non gratae* – and expelled from the country. I never allowed it to be applied to me. Draconian views can be avoided. While I was there, I never drove a company vehicle and always insisted on a Saudi driver in order to avoid the possibility of paying blood money if I was involved in a motor accident.

But the way the nuclear test veterans and widows are treated by the authorities in the UK, in a democracy, bears little difference to the ideology of the totalitarian regime of Saudi Arabia.

In May 2010, the MOD began an appeal against the verdict of the Limitations Trial – going against the 'crucial and pivotal' evidence to allow all 1,011 claims to proceed to High Court trial, and once again drawing upon a bottomless pit of tax payers' money.

The Verdict

"We did it!"

Celebrating the High Court Limitation Trial decision allowing over a thousand Atomic Veterans Group Litigation (AVGL) cases to proceed with compensation claims, 9 June 2009.
Sent to the author courtesy of Susie Boniface, *Daily Mirror*.

Chapter 11: The Limitation Trial Appeal, Supreme Court and Military Pensions

"The treatment of the nuclear veterans is
'without doubt a political problem'."
John Baron MP, Patron of the BNTVA charity
in a House of Commons debate, 2008

In November 2010, the MOD was handed down a successful judgment in its appeal against Mr Justice Foskett's High Court verdict of the 2005-2009 Limitation Trial. This was based on the spurious preconceived argument from the MOD that the AVGL cases would not succeed.

In the Court of Appeal, the MOD ignored the prime causal link between fallout and cytogenetic blood test evidence. Their lawyers then regressed to science of causation based on the epidemiology of significantly biased statistics, without cytogenetic blood tests. Their case in fact regressed again to rely upon old, outdated, biased and discredited studies from the 1980s and 90s. Added to this, in Australia, a similar epidemiological study, without blood tests by Adelaide University in 2006 and using methodology based upon the UK's NRPB studies of death certificates, was used to help discredit the need for further cytogenic blood tests.

Expert witness for the MOD, epidemiologist Professor Kenyon, was flown in from Australia to help sow seeds of doubt in judicial minds about mortality epidemiological statistics. Another expert, cytogeneticist Dr Firouz Darroudi, stated the veterans would not be able to prove causation and sowed doubts on the efficacy of the peer-reviewed New Zealand Rowland study. Both MOD expert witnesses were merchants of doubt to wreck advances made in the understanding of science.

Freedom of Information questions in 2012 revealed Dr Darroudi was the senior cytogeneticist for covert MOD cytogenetic blood testing of 18 nuclear veterans in Holland in 1990. This clandestine study, at the University of Leiden, was secretly commissioned by the MOD and went unpublished. Dr Darroudi, used as an expert witness to undermine the "crucial and pivotal" evidence of Professor Rowland's independent New Zealand study, had acted without disclosure of his previous knowledge of the blood testing of nuclear veterans. He should have been excluded from being a reliable and suitable witness.

As shown earlier in this book, epidemiology had already been exposed as an obsolete and discredited method of denial of exposure to radiation. Yet it has been the preferred method used by the MOD and government since the 1980s because it can be easily biased and manipulated to achieve the 'right' answers for political reasons. The independent cytogenetic blood analysis by Professor Rowland of New Zealand, double peer-reviewed and totally free of interference by the UK MOD, showed significantly that nuclear veterans have 300% more genetic damage that any serviceman who had not attended a weapon test location.

Being independent of MOD/government control in nuclear health studies is crucial to avoid bias in cases where those in judgement have no in-depth knowledge of the science of causation from inhaled or ingested ionised radioactivity and are therefore easily misled.

Compared to cytogenetics, epidemiology is a useless application of science to show genetic damage. The peer-reviewed Rowland study used cytogenetic blood testing, which has been acknowledged and used clandestinely since the 1960s by the UK government, who have kept silent about their findings. This advanced diagnostic technology actually shows, at a cellular level, genetic damage – that is, the mark of radiation from nuclear bomb testing – in the translocated chromosomal DNA of nuclear test veterans.

The MOD had cytogeneticist Dr Darroudi as an expert witness at the Court of Appeal to discredit the Rowland study. If the AVGL's QC Ben Browne had been in court to cross-examine both Kenyon and Darroudi, the outcome would undoubtedly have been different.

This use of expert witnesses of dubious bias against the science continued throughout the litigation from 2005 until 2014. Truth is not proven in history when the legal process is heavily weighted against claimants. Events in the background are a more reliable historic indicator. In totalitarian states, the legal process is controlled by the dictator to ensure nothing is allowed to undermine government policy or ideology. Here the same applies when the legal process is not conducted on a level playing field for claimants.

In 2011, Professor Al Rowland, then aged 65, was honoured with an award, equivalent to an OBE, from Her Majesty The Queen for the ground-breaking efficacy of having discovered significant genetic damage in the New Zealand naval ratings who sailed under the fallout of UK nuclear bombs at Christmas Island in 1958.

The citation published in 2011 for Professor Rowland's award is for research the UK government ignored and dismissed. It's an award for research the UK government would not allow to take place openly for the benefit of nuclear test veterans and their families. Science always has to be controlled by the MOD to be accepted as evidence. This undermines all trust.

The citation for Professor Rowland specifically mentioned the blood testing and mFish assay work on the nuclear veterans. On receipt of the award, he stated: "It's recognition from the establishment that my research is credible, and I hope this honour will add some weight to the veterans' cause."

In an exclusive report for the *Daily Mirror* on 12 June 2011, Susie Boniface succinctly summed it up: "The scientist whose research into Britain's nuclear test veterans was rubbished by the government has been honoured for his work by the Queen. Professor Rowland led a ground-breaking study which proved men present at the atomic blasts in the 1950s were left with serious genetic damage which could have caused the legacy of cancers and rare diseases they now suffer from.

"Faced with a multi-million pound pay out, the Ministry of Defence tried to damn his work, insisting the research proved nothing. This has left thousands of veterans fighting a lawsuit for compensation. Dozens have died waiting for it to come to court. His pioneering research led New Zealand to accept that its men were harmed and they agreed to pay for treatment.

"Professor Rowland has been made an Officer of the New Zealand Order of Merit and will receive his medal from the Queen's representative, the Governor-General, later this year. An MOD spokesman said: 'We do not accept the findings.'"

The MOD's statement of denial is one of a department

immersed only in scientific papers that are pro-nuclear and protectionist. The MOD only recognises papers that ignore advances in the understanding of the hazards of radiation to any persons occupationally or otherwise exposed. Burying heads in the sand is, for political purposes, to avoid accountability and responsibility. The MOD is also ignoring the joint findings of eminent biologists and physicists in the 1956 Medical Research Council Report on the hazards of radiation to man.

Historically, this appears similar to the Luddite rioters of the 19th century, who smashed industrial machinery in order to preserve an existing state of affairs that had become obsolescent and less productive. Huge misunderstandings in science regarding radiation damage to health have taken place since the dawn of the atomic age. In contrast to the Luddite mentality of the MOD, the United States, Russia and China have given recognition and financial benefits to their nuclear test veterans.

The MOD and UK Government's biased and obsolete SPVA 'advice to ministers' document was judicially ignored in the Limitation Trial verdict in June 2009 by hard focus on advanced nuclear scientific reality.

In the words of Ben Browne, the QC leading counsel for the successful Limitation Trial, "The MOD should have known the claimants were exposed to radiation, failed to take reasonable care for health and safety from both external and internal radiation, failed to consider the aftermath of the tests, failed to account for accumulated radiation dose, allowed claimants to enter into zones of radioactive fallout or contamination, failed to provide adequate PPE to claimants, failed to take measures to ensure seafood caught and known to be contaminated by radiation was not consumed, failed to take account of weather patterns before and after detonations, film badges did not measure nor were capable of measuring alpha and beta particles potential levels for inhalation or ingestion."

All the above still stands the test of time. Ben Browne's citation cannot be dismissed; it is all fact.

Browne affirmed that cytogenetic blood testing evidence in the Limitation Trial had shown genetic damage in nuclear veterans. This is evidence of the causation of legacy ill health and yet, by various acts or omissions in evidence regarding this, the MOD had shown negligence.

In simple terms, the QC explained this advanced technology shows the destruction or derangement of the molecular integrity of the human chromosome, straws of chains of tens of thousands of genes, by energy absorbed from ionising radiation. This is the causation of a wide range of illnesses.

The above is the winning scientific case on known advances in science. From now on the Ministry of Defence's sole intent with expert witnesses is firstly to ignore, dismiss and diminish the fact that fallout is the prime causal link to the ill health of nuclear veterans, and secondly, to undermine the double peer-reviewed and world-acclaimed Rowland Study, rated meticulous in all detail by the UK's leading cytogeneticist Professor Rhona Anderson of the UK's Brunel University, and applauded by the United States' leading cytogenetics expert David Brenner, Higgins Professor of Radiation Biophysics at Columbia University Centre for Radiological Research, New York, as findings 'the UK Ministry of Defence do not accept'.

Without a counsel with the experience and understanding of

science that Ben Browne QC had, the AVGL's case was gradually pushed over the edge of the steep mountain legal rails by the MOD's Treasury Solicitors. An air of untouchability and arrogance now crept into the Treasury Solicitors at court hearings. It was, as always, not a case of who knew the scientific truth; it now became a case of 'he who pays the piper calls the tune'.

The tune to be called incessantly until the end of the legal proceedings was now one of attrition against the truth rather than of seeking justice; attrition by a well-funded government legal team of barristers to ignore or prevent the AVGL's evidence being heard or, if heard, to do the best they could to cast doubt upon it. But by doing so, they would still not win the case with any clear or safe margin. By doing so, history will judge them harshly.

The feeling amongst veterans was that this legal reversal and delay had done nothing to assist the MOD's credibility as an employer. For the AVGL legal team, it would have to be a case of doing better next time and hoping evidence of fallout and diagnostic genetic blood testing would be allowed to be included in evidence to get the truth back on track to a just and honourable settlement of claims.

Harking back to the eminent and uniquely knowledgeable US President John F Kennedy, in 1963 when he signed the atmospheric atomic bomb test ban, in addition to his comments on the impact on unborn children he also said: "A war today or tomorrow, if it led to nuclear war, would not be like any other war in history. A full- scale nuclear exchange, lasting less than 60 minutes, with weapons now in existence, would wipe out more than 300 million Americans, Europeans, and Russians as well as untold millions elsewhere. And the survivors, as

Chairman Kruschev warned the Communist Chinese, 'the survivors would envy the dead.' For they would inherit a world so devastated by explosion and poison and fire that today we cannot even conceive of the horrors. So let us try to turn the world away from war. Let us make the most of this opportunity, to reduce tension, to slow the perilous arms race, and to check the world's slide toward final annihilation. This treaty can be a step towards freeing the world from the fears and dangers of radioactive fallout."

And yet, in the Court of Appeal verdict of 2010, 'the fears and dangers of radioactive fallout' known to President Kennedy and all nuclear powers since 1945 was totally and conveniently ignored. The appeal focused only on gamma radiation and ignored alpha and beta fallout which, when inhaled or ingested, act as internal emitting radiation to damage blood, tissue, organs and bone. Crucial and pivotal parts of evidence were not considered and would continue to be ignored.

The views of surviving nuclear veterans, their widows and families are rooted in the biological actuality of the health and genetic damage they, their children and grandchildren have suffered every day over decades.

The rejection of a mediated settlement of compensation claims and the desperation and indefensibility of continued legal delaying tactics continued, firstly, with the Limitation Trial to strike out all cases; secondly, by reverting the evidence of the prime causal links of illness back to epidemiology; thirdly, by ignoring the Rowland study as if it had not happened whilst continuing to disingenuously undermine it; and fourth and finally, by withholding radiation levels at nuclear test locations etc. All this deception carried on.

But there is much, much more to come to tarnish the MOD and UK Government's reputation as a responsible employer of young members in the armed forces.

Before the end of 2010, in November, an Inquiry report was slipped out to the media virtually unnoticed. It coincided with the marriage of HRH Prince William to Kate Middleton and therefore received only a line or two in passing in obscure scientific or other intellectual publications. Naturally and conveniently, the Inquiry report escaped notice of all the mass circulated popular tabloid press.

The report, by Michael Redfern QC, which had taken three and a half years to complete, had 655 pages of investigation into the post-mortem analysis of tissue and other body part samples at nuclear facilities over many decades. (See also Chapter Five.)

The Redfern Inquiry focused on the removal, without family consent, of blood, tissue, organs and bone from deceased nuclear industry workers and, as mentioned in an earlier chapter, similar clandestine post-mortems had been carried out on nuclear test veterans (as noted in the Redfern Report, pages 89 and 90).

The admitted purpose of the removal and analysis of body parts from nuclear veterans, as with nuclear industry workers, was reported to be for medical research and in case of future claims by bereaved family members. This Inquiry report is confirmation of the ethos not only to avoid possible compensation claims at a future date but also of the lack of ethics that underpinned the 1956 top secret document on biological experimentation at Maralinga. In the 1956 biological studies, nuclear test veterans were exposed to fallout to assist in an understanding of the genetic effects of inhaled or ingested radiation, to help the nuclear industry develop protective clothing and respirators for nuclear workers.

The Redfern Report put the NRPB (who produced the epidemiological studies in the 1980s and 90s) and the MOD at the heart of controlling post-mortem analysis at nuclear facilities. The NRPB, now renamed Public Health England, together with the MOD are listed in the Redfern Report as being assisted by scientists and doctors from the NHS, Medical Research Council (MRC), the Atomic Weapons Establishment (AWE) and assorted other doctors, pathologists and coroners. But a reading of this report puts the Ministry of Defence as the sole arbiter at the centre of this spider's web of clandestine study into radiation damage to persons exposed to radiation.

The sad, despicable fact here is a betrayal of trust. A betrayal of anyone potentially exposed to ionising radiation. While the UK Government and MOD has refused cytogenetic blood tests to UK nuclear veterans which could have indicated, as in Russia, cancers and other genetically induced disease (by a diagnostic technology known and used covertly by the UK Government since the 1960s), they have been engaged in the clandestine desecration of nuclear workers' and veterans' bodies, without family consent, for medical research for decades. These activities have all been done 'for government eyes only'.

The unnoticed Redfern Inquiry report shows political leaders and officials have no interest in a duty of care towards nuclear veterans whilst they are alive, no interest in detecting genetic damage (chromosomal aberrations and translocations) and, therefore, no interest in giving veterans or their children the possibility of early remedial treatments.

It also shows that their only interest in the nuclear veterans is when they are dead. This lack of ethics and morals has also been replicated in Australia and dates back to the 1956 biological investigations at Maralinga and also to the 1956 Medical Research Council Report on the hazards of radiation to man, followed by the bilateral treaty in 1993 to work together to avoid compensation.

The above clandestine research does, however, fulfil the remit of the Medical Research Council's recommendations. That is, research into the genetic damage of nuclear weapon test fallout was agreed would take a hundred years to be fully understood. Research has continued since the nuclear weapon tests in the 1950s and 1960s and probably explains why the UK is more highly competent in genomic sequencing and other science involved in the human genome. But none of the benefits are admitted – and, of course, none are linked in any way to the sacrifices made by the nuclear test veterans and their families.

At the end of 2010 my wife Dawn, who has followed every twist and turn of the nuclear veterans' quest for justice since 1975, said to me: "Perhaps this is a good time for us to take a break from the nuclear issue, and visit my sister and cousins' families in Australia again. It would also be a chance to visit your old school friend Steve." This was former RAF apprentice Steve Rawlings, who lived with his wife Sue in Hervey Bay.

This is typical of the patient, practical and loving support I had become used to since I married the daughter of a Forest of Dean coalminer and engineer. Dawn's father died in 2008 from chronic obstructive pulmonary disease and silicosis; her mother, who worked at a Gloucester aircraft assembly line during the Second World War, died in 2009. My wife has accompanied me on frequent trips to London and Australia and she has as much knowledge as me – in fact, possibly even more – about the nuclear test veterans' and families' fight for justice and the betrayal involved.

My father served in the infantry – Wiltshire Regiment – throughout the Second World War and in Palestine and in Korea. He always said: "Whatever you do in life, always stand up for truth." This ethos was echoed by my mother, who stood by his side throughout the turbulent years of his armed forces service and when they retired. This generation upheld a sense of duty that is sadly missed today. It should not be an outdated concept because truth and duty are essential for any civilised democratic society.

Today's politicians increasingly appear to lack any regard for truth and duty, both values my apolitical parents drummed into my head at an early age. Senior politicians and those officials advising them today profess to be acting in the 'national interest' but very often they are acting in their own mutual self-interest to avoid accountability. This is demonstrated particularly with regard to settling the claims of nuclear test veterans and their families by implementing a policy of avoiding responsibility by pouring unlimited amounts of tax payers' money down the drain whenever deemed necessary.

So, before the end of 2010, and with these facts continuing to emerge from the ongoing Atomic Veterans Group Litigation, we booked a five week visit to Australia, returning to the UK on 29 March 2011. As I write this in 2021, during a period of over a year in Covid lockdown, it's with regrets no doubt shared by many that such ease of travel will never, ever return. The future of travel will be a 'new normal' – but I hope politics will also see a change to a 'new normal', in a positive way, because a return to pre-Covid political business as usual will be a tragedy.

Travelling along the east coast of the Australian continent between Sydney, Brisbane and Hervey Bay with no news or thoughts of the ongoing nuclear veterans' scandal in the UK was sheer bliss. But, on 11 March, while with friends in a country social club near Hervey Bay, the usual ambiance of joy and laughter was suddenly halted by urgent television network reports showing graphic pictures of the unfolding Fukushima nuclear accident.

Panic was etched on the faces of those Australian officials and politicians who were interviewed as they rushed to reassure the Australian public with the familiar cliché: "There are 'no worries'." The reports continued: "We can assure you the radioactive fallout from Fukushima is not, we repeat, is not heading towards the east coast of Australia. It is heading towards the west coast of the United States. The US Pacific fleet in the area is making urgent changes in direction as a precautionary measure."

Well, that's alright then, mates. The Australian officials and politicians falling over themselves to reassure the Australian public about the hazards of fallout from Fukushima had moved positively forward in openness and honesty. Compared to the generation of politicians who ignored the fallout from the 1950s atomic bomb tests at Maralinga – the known hazards of which the former Australian Prime Minister Sir Robert Menzies had lied about being of 'no conceivable injury to life and land of Australia' – it showed how times change when the truth has become a consensus view of politicians, when it suits them.

It was with some interest that we returned to the UK, where we were updated on the AVGL's claim progress. In our absence, the tone of communication from Prime Minister Cameron and in letters from other ministers had changed dramatically since the beginning of the litigation. Until the Court of Appeal verdict in November 2010 the MOD's repetitive mantra had been: "The only way veterans can settle this matter is by litigation." Now it had changed to an equally repetitive and insincere prime ministerial edict fed to David Cameron by MOD officials: "The government is extremely grateful for the service given by nuclear test veterans during the Cold War to help secure the safety of the nation."

In my mind, when reading this revised epitaph of ultimate betrayal in letters from the Ministry of Defence and others in government, I was carried back to my childhood days in post Second World War Britain, paying five pence (in today's currency) to go to the Saturday morning children's film show at the local cinema, where we booed the baddies and cheered the goodies, especially in the many cowboy and Indian films that were mass entertainment favourites at the time.

These films often showed a US cavalry officer or US Government official sharing a 'pipe of peace' with the leaders of the Indian tribes. Such encounters inevitably ended with the Indian chief looking directly at the camera, knowing his tribe was about to be forced off their land to live in a segregated reservation on poor land, and simply saying: "White men speak with forked tongues."

This seems an apt analogy for the political quango takeover of the BNTVA charity from 2002 to 2008 and what subsequently flowed from it. From 2011 the nuclear veterans and their families found the "extremely grateful" prime ministerial statement by Cameron meant the beginning of being airbrushed from history, like Bullingdon Club champagne corks after a night out.

In a Prime Minister's Questions (PMQ) session in Parliament over the meaning of 'official recognition' of nuclear veterans, an increasingly desperate John Baron MP, patron of the BNTVA, found the "extremely grateful" thanks expressed by Cameron did not mean anything approaching a full and honourable settlement of nuclear veterans' claims under a meaningful Military Covenant enshrined into law. Instead, it meant the eradication of the history of nuclear veterans' service to the nation, with even the term 'nuclear test veteran' being deleted from history.

Prime Minister Cameron's "extremely grateful for the service given by nuclear test veterans during the Cold War to help secure the safety of the nation" resulted in 'gratitude' of no compensation, no military pension and no medals of recognition.

The 'heir to Blair' reference made about Cameron by some sections of the press on his election can even be applied to his disastrous foreign policy. Blair invaded Iraq in 2003 on the false pretext of Saddam Hussein's non-existent weapons of mass destruction and the tragic death of whistle blower Dr David Kelly. Cameron, along with the French president, did the same in Libya, ousting Colonel Gaddafi. As happened in Iraq, Libya was reduced to an ungovernable basket case of rival warring factions that still exists today. Both episodes left a vacuum for the jihadist, nihilistic ISIS to wreak murderous havoc and exacerbate the flow of homeless refugees to flood into Europe.

Cameron then ended his political career by promising that, whatever the result of his Brexit referendum of 2016, he would accept "the will of the people". When the will of the people did not agree with his preference to remain in the EU he immediately reneged from any duty to negotiate a settlement of the electorate's desire to become a self-governing independent sovereign nation. Cameron resigned and ran from Prime Ministerial office, just to show how unsuitable he was to have held the honour in the first place.

It is against this background of political and legal mayhem that the nuclear veterans found they were being airbrushed from political history as 'anti-nuclear' and 'a vexation', simply for seeking truth and justice. But, from 2014, the true history of the veterans' betrayal continued, built upon the prejudice and contempt shown towards them from the very first atomic bomb, detonated on 3 October 1952.

After the Appeal Court verdict of November 2010, the AVGL, led by Rosenblatts, took their case to the Supreme Court in July 2011, where a panel of three law lords ruled in favour of the claimants proceeding with their claims. The MOD appealed this verdict and Rosenblatts pushed on again.

In March 2012, again at the Supreme Court but with a panel of seven, the law lords ruled four to three against the nuclear test veterans' and widows' claims. A narrow one vote margin delivered a questionable verdict that "the nuclear veterans have no chance of success and are unable to prove causation of their ill health, premature deaths and genetic damage." It was an astounding and unbelievable failure of reality.

The Treasury Solicitor's team of barristers were in full flow in the final hours of the final day as they dismissed fallout as just low dose, low level radiation. It was shocking to have to sit and listen to this repetitive nonsense. The Rowland study, admitted to have shown genetic damage, was diminished by saying it had no clinical impact on health. All utter nonsense. Again, expert witnesses for the AVGL were denied access to give evidence.

The subject of causation was effectively prevented from full court examination by this narrow verdict. The Supreme Court ruled in favour of the MOD that the claims were time-barred. They declined the action to proceed under statutory discretion and stated, misguidedly, on the science of causation: "The veterans would have great difficulty proving a causal link between illnesses suffered and attendance at the tests."

On the final day of the hearing the Treasury barristers repeatedly petitioned the seven law lords that fallout radiation was 'only' low dose, low level radiation and therefore, by inference to the non-scientific minded, of little or no consequence to the health of individuals exposed. Nothing is further from the known scientific truth. But four of the seven judges lapped it up.

I listened to the judgement in disbelief. I had my doubts whether the Treasury barristers would have agreed to partake of a cup of tea from a pot containing only a miniscule, invisible to the eye quantity of what they had disingenuously and mistakenly referred to as 'only' a low dose, low level of radiation of little consequence. That is, low dose, low level particles of ionised nuclear bomb fallout. But they were already internally irradiated and inebriated by the deception of their own misguided verbosity.

As for the time-barring of case by case AVGL claimants, this had already been noted by many supportive politicians and others as a disappointing verdict because the case seemed to have gone against the veterans on a technicality relating to the time the irradiation took place. The decision was wrong, and a major setback for the families. The fight will go on and is backed by the Scottish Parliament (although, as you'll discover later, as a devolved administration the Scottish Parliament has no authority in this matter).

My feelings reflected the consensus of opinion amongst the veteran and widow claimants. The causal link to ill health, premature deaths and genetic damage had not been allowed to be fully cross-examined in an open court with expert scientific witnesses acting on the claimants' behalf.

The unsubstantiated confusion over the inhalation and ingestion of fallout had enabled successive government-sponsored scientists and political leaders to avoid accountability and responsibility to provide a duty of care to any person exposed, whether militarily or occupationally, to this type of ionising radiation.

All of the above give reason to support the fact that the Supreme Court verdict of March 2012 was a gross injustice in need of future correction. The narrow verdict supports the fact that, since 1952, the MOD and successive UK Governments are conducting a deliberate policy of exclusion against the interests of loyal servicemen. It is a war of attrition conducted under a conspiracy of silence until the last nuclear test veteran and his widow are dead.

However, the fight for justice was still alive in the real world.

At the end of the Limitation Trial in June 2009, Ken McGinley, the BNTVA founder, who had successfully led an association campaigning for justice for 17 years until being ousted by a new hierarchy of veterans committed to collusion with the Ministry of Defence, received the following accolade of praise from Mr

Justice Foskett: "He was an engagingly frank and open witness who had lost none of his combative instincts that had obviously led him to be a champion of those he felt had been short-changed by various governments over the years. There will be many who, over the years, have achieved the highest of offices in countries throughout the world about whom the same could be told."

Mr McGinley lobbied for and set up a Nuclear Veteran Debate, through Christina McKelvie SNP, Member of the Scottish Parliament, in November 2011. During this year we had also lobbied the devolved Scottish administration to find laboratories abroad and independent of UK Government/MOD control to conduct cytogenetic blood tests on Scottish nuclear test veterans. Scotland seemed a good possibility for achieving this step forward. The Medical Research Council, Western Hospital, Edinburgh had already demonstrated, through cytogeneticist Dr H Evans, that Scotland had the expertise to conduct such studies successfully.

Ian Anderson, the Scottish international advocate and attorney at law, based in New York, who has been legal advisor to the CVFI since 2002, wrote to the then Scottish Health Minister, Nicola Sturgeon MSP (who later became Scottish First Minister), asking for cytogenetic blood testing to be done on all Scottish nuclear test veterans. Ken McGinley and David Whyte were amongst many veterans who were willing to have this done – independent, of course, of MOD control. Any tests would be extremely useful to the AVGL, led by Rosenblatts, if they were needed in court hearings.

Health Minister Nicola Sturgeon turned down the request for cytogenetic blood testing, saying that Scotland had no remit to carry out such testing because it was a reserved authority for the UK Government in London. This confirmed our belief that the Westminster Parliament (i.e. ministerial leaders and officials) were the final arbiters in the matter of radiation-induced genetic damage diagnosis.

We thought the Scottish administration's response a disappointment, particularly because the tiny independent parliament of the Isle of Man, a parliament with Viking heritage that predates the UK Westminster Parliament by several hundred years, had awarded every nuclear test veteran resident on the island compensation of £8,000 in 2007.

At the time, our enquiries found such studies could be done – at great cost – in the US by eminent scientist Dr David Brenner. But the logistics of getting a dozen or so aged nuclear veterans to New York in person within a limited timeframe was extremely complex and very expensive, taking into account air fares etc. Rosenblatts could not help with the £40,000+ cost as they were themselves already fighting a war of financial attrition against UK Government lawyers floating on a tsunami of unlimited tax payers' money.

In a motion framed by Christina McKelvie MSP, the November 2011 debate in the Scottish Parliament produced overwhelming support from all speakers for justice in the AVGL's case. One speaker said it was amazing that the Westminster Government could find £100 billion to renew the Trident nuclear missile system but not even a fraction of 1% of that huge sum to settle nuclear test veterans' claims.

But the supportive sentiment was not binding on the Scottish Parliament to act upon. Interestingly, in this respect, all speakers in the debate were members of the Scottish National Party (SNP). Labour, Conservative and Liberal Democrat members of the Scottish Parliament did not contribute to the debate. It appears the power of party whips changes many things in the UK's tribal democracy. It may offer some reason why Scotland is intent on becoming independent of domination by Westminster. But not everything you wish for is necessarily an answer. Leaving the UK union to become a vassal state of the European Union appears not to be a solution, because of the bureaucratic EU Commission's wish to erase individual nation states' sovereignty into oblivion through the sclerotic diktats of centralised Brussels commissioners.

We had hoped the SNP MPs in the UK Parliament would raise the issue but the 'tartan army', as they were often described in parts of the UK media, that had descended on London and occupied benches in the House of Commons remained silent on the issue, although they were noisily active on other matters. The SNP, now under leadership of First Minister Nicola Sturgeon in the Scottish devolved parliament, were now primarily focused on seeking independence for Scotland and joining the European Union. One has to wonder what stance an independent Scotland would take over the undoubted and unresolved political problem of the nuclear test veterans. The answer is unfathomable because under the rules of the military–industrial game it appears, at least to the minds of the Westminster Government, that any help to nuclear test veterans would be, as with New Zealand, regarded as an 'unfriendly act'.

Nuclear veterans, however, remain extremely grateful to Christina McKelvie MSP for her motion for the November 2011 debate and her support and interest in the nuclear test veterans' betrayal.

Meanwhile, the accolade given to Ken McGinley by Mr

Justice Foskett following the Limitation Trial verdict and the drain on the BNTVA charity membership led many nuclear veterans to call for his reinstatement to the association. The now weakened non-campaigning organisation acted swiftly and quashed any attempts to revive the failing membership.

The BNTVA Executive Committee wrote to Mr McGinley in the most disrespectful terms: "We received an anonymous membership fee on your behalf, together with a request that you be reinstated as a member. This would carry conditions. 1) A full and unreserved apology in writing to the Executive Committee and an apology to the members of the association, to be read out at the next AGM. 2) A letter from you undertaking that you would not at any time attempt to seek nomination to the Executive Committee. 3) Your application would have to go to the floor for a vote at the AGM."

Ken McGinley told *Fissionline* editor Alan Rimmer: "I knew nothing about this, and I had no intention of returning. But if I did, they expected me to grovel to join the organisation I had founded. What sort of people want to humiliate fellow human beings like this?"

This was news to me until I read it in *Fissionline*. But the answer to Ken's question seemed obvious. The sort of people doing this were people who were living in fear and desperation of being run by the Ministry of Defence and trustees who had no empathy for the concerns of the nuclear veterans and their families, who were paying them annual subscriptions. This would not end well.

In the same issue of *Fissionline,* Alan Rimmer wrote: "Shirley Denson and Dennis Hayden have helped keep the spirit of Britain's nuclear veterans alive through many dark and lonely years. Working virtually alone from their homes they have single-mindedly taken on the government and MOD as well as informing the public with well-judged criticism and comment about the conduct of the nuclear bomb tests. Mrs Denson, the widow of an RAF 'sniffer plane' pilot, and Mr Hayden, a Maralinga veteran, were concerned the BNTVA was going in the wrong direction and voiced their misgivings to the charity. The response from the Board of Trustees astonished them. The following extract from a two-page response sets the tone: 'Having considered your communications which contain a high degree of ignorant statements drawn from sparse grasp of facts … your absurd stance as a rag-tag group of Sunday afternoon revolutionaries seeing conspiracy in every shadow, looking only to the past, confrontationally, and exceedingly selective of facts is not one that any of our members could share any part of...'"

I remember receiving the letter, but it went quickly into a bin marked 'Avoid the negative influences of other people'. However, I'm pleased Alan Rimmer kept a copy of this missive and mentioned it in *Fissionline* because it's part of the history of this period, where insults and intimidation had begun to take over from logical thought. The description 'rag-tag group of Sunday afternoon revolutionaries' appealed to me as a badge of honour, much like the German Kaiser Wilhelm II's description of the British Expeditionary Army in World War One as 'this contemptible little army'.

The above set the tone for the years following the 4:3 verdict in the Supreme Court in March 2012, about which Roy Sefton, in his capacity as chairman of the New Zealand Nuclear Test Veterans Association, wrote to Prime Minister David Cameron to outline his concern at developments in the UK.

He expressed the view that the self-appointed position of the BNTVA being the prime body to represent UK veterans was incorrect and undemocratic. He explained that the NZNTVA/BNTVA had once stood shoulder to shoulder and had lent assistance to each other, as they did at the nuclear weapon test sites, but now, due to a change in leadership, they had changed direction, which no longer allowed for consultation between the two. Mr Sefton referred to the BNTVA's 2014 AGM, where a policy was revealed to disassociate themselves from the NZNTVA and, in his opinion, with those campaigning for justice for nuclear veterans in Australia and Fiji.

He then focused on the narrow Supreme Court verdict, won by only one vote, and said: "I believe this is too close to say that justice has been served. I note that all of the court hearings included opinion from both sides on the Rowland Study findings of significant elevated chromosome damage. The Rowland study was downgraded by the UK Government because it failed to provide evidence on the health conditions that chromosome translocations may cause. The fact is the study researchers were not medically qualified to give such detail. That responsibility was presumed by the NZNTVA to be left to government.

"The New Zealand Government set up a 'Ministerial Advisory Group on Veterans Health', chaired by Professor John Campbell of Otago University. A group of six academics of the group, and invited scientists, disregarded all previous publications and peer reviews of the Rowland study. They started afresh to review all aspects of the research.

"On 23 December 2010, Professor Campbell advised the NZ Government of the Advisory Group's conclusions, which in part stated: 'The Massey University mFISH study results do provide evidence that the nuclear test veterans were exposed to ionising radiation. The clinical consequences of this, if any are not known.'"

Roy Sefton added: "The Rowland research has therefore been subjected twice to vigorous scientific investigations. There can be no doubt about the scientific integrity of the Rowland research. It must be concluded that the very same factors that radiologically affected the NZ veterans, irrespective of their country of origin, also affected all of the veterans who took part in the UK nuclear test programme. Professor Rowland is strongly of the opinion that the veterans are to this day carrying active contaminants within their bodies. They must have suffered various types of cancers and ill health which has resulted in earlier deaths and chronic health conditions, and the situation has existed right up to the present. Additionally, Dr Rowland considers abnormal damage to the chromosomes has the ability to cause cancer and other health problems. Indeed, some well-known health conditions can be identified as due to chromosome abnormalities."

Mr Sefton concluded his letter to Prime Minister David Cameron to say: "It can now be concluded those who attended nuclear test locations suffered chromosome damage. Legal arguments against this finding can now be ignored. The Supreme Court verdict by only one vote against veterans' and widows' compensation claims has every ground to be ruled as invalid. A settlement of claims should proceed and Rosenblatts' costs should be cancelled. Additional assistance to compensation that can be offered to UK veterans and widows should also be investigated and encouraged."

Several days after Roy sent this letter, I asked him if he

knew about his own cytogenetic assay results. He said he had been shown them on a monitor by Professor Rowland and the translocations and derangements in his chromosome strands were clearly all over the place, in line with the 300% significant abnormalities of the 50 analysed New Zealand veterans. He added that Professor Rowland was unable to tell him what legacy health issues the multicoloured, fluorescent, in situ hybridisation of his chromosomes showed, because in all veterans analysed the breaks and translocations were many, and varied from individual to individual, so the degree of widespread legacy ill health and illnesses would also vary from individual to individual.

I agreed with Roy that the genetic damage was a Sword of Damocles hanging over the heads of all those who attended the nuclear weapon test experiments from 1952 to 1967.

In January 2021, just three days after I started to write this book, Roy died at his home in Palmerston, New Zealand.

When his New Zealand navy frigate sailed under the fallout of nuclear bomb testing at Christmas Island in 1958, Roy was the youngest rating in the warship's crew. He ended his career as a Chief Petty Officer with legacy ill health from the bomb tests. He will forever be remembered as young man who stood without protective clothing on the deck of a radiation-contaminated ship in a Cold War experiment. From the great sadness of his loss, he leaves a legacy for all seeking truth and openness that independent science, free from government control and interference, is as much needed today as it was at the beginning of the atomic age in the 1920s.

Roy Sefton's tireless campaigning and political handling of the situation shows New Zealand stands head and shoulders above the United Kingdom and Australian governments in ethics and morality when it comes to the unresolved political problem of nuclear test veterans' betrayal.

About a year after Roy Sefton sent his letter to Prime Minister David Cameron, the UK Minister for Veterans, Anna Soubry MP QC, stated in a House of Commons debate on 29 October 2013: "I do not believe that our [war pension] record is shameful." This was the same debate (covered in Chapter Ten) where she had attempted to shed light on Kevan Jones' questionable authorisation of a settlement of claims for AVGL claimants following the Limitation Trial verdict of June 2009.

This 'honourable' lady would appear to believe anything she was told by the pen- pushing superannuated officials of the UK Veterans Agency without looking at the truth. She was ill advised and/or lying. It is just a case of pity another minister, she's not to blame, but neither are her advisors. That's the name of the game.

It's questionable ethically that, as a QC, she had not looked into how other nations treat their nuclear veterans to find the reality rather than the fiction of the matter. But old habits die hard. From 2016 she became a voice in Parliament attempting to overturn the will of the people's referendum vote to leave the European Union. She had obviously grown used to the ideology that rule by bureaucratic diktat was preferable to independent thought. At the next general election she lost her seat; she denied nuclear test veterans their rights, and I believe justice was duly served upon her.

Veterans Affairs New Zealand (VANZ) has a 'presumptive list' of 20-plus cancers which, if suffered by a veteran, entitle him to a War Disability Pension. A widow of such a deceased veteran can claim a Surviving Spouse's Pension under the same entitlement. Both these claims are not subjected to any investigation or tribunal. They are granted automatically and attributed to nuclear weapon location service.

Pension payments to nuclear test veterans in New Zealand are handled quickly. This ensures other war pension payments from armed forces personnel are not delayed by waiting for settlement. Nuclear veterans' children also have a similar entitlement for a number of health conditions. All New Zealand nuclear veterans who served at Christmas Island are classified as having given War and Emergency Service. This classification means that "if the claims panel cannot determine that the claimant's ill health is due entirely to factors unrelated to service, the claimant must get the benefit of the doubt."

Added to the above, the Special Services Medal (Nuclear), created and approved by HM The Queen, is available to all New Zealand veterans who served at UK nuclear weapon tests.

And these New Zealand nuclear veterans, who served at the Christmas Island bomb tests, stood shoulder to shoulder with UK allied veterans.

Anna Soubry, like all her predecessors as UK Defence Minister, has been badly advised by MOD officials and bureaucrats about a non-existent Military Covenant that ensures a shameful record of war pensions and other duty of care towards those who have loyally served the nation. They are all walking within the same ill-advised bubble of lies and deception.

The UK's treatment of their nuclear veterans is a national scandal, the worst in the world, even compared to Russia and China. It is a disgrace that lowers our standing as a democracy in the world.

This without a doubt 'political problem' is set to be revealed as even worse.

Chapter 12: MOD Propaganda, Government Controlled Committees and Quangos

"I am not an expert; my role is to implement the functions of government."
Senior career civil servant Dame Lin Homer,
Head of HM Revenue and Customs, when questioned by MPs
of the House of Commons Public Accounts Committee

This book is the true history of thousands of young servicemen who were deployed to UK experimental atomic tests sites in the 1950s and 60s without being told the truth of the resultant dangers to their health and that of their offspring. This is not the sanitised version being airbrushed from history by government officials. What's been deployed, to avoid a duty of care, is misinformation, control of science and committees of officials whose only purpose is to implement the functions of government policy against the interests of nuclear test veterans and their families.

Propaganda has been a weapon of war ever since conflicts began between nations. It's no surprise that the ideological struggle of the Cold War would resort to propaganda being used extensively by both sides. Truth is said to be the first casualty of war by use of propaganda. This doctrine has been meticulously applied both during and since the Cold War.

However, propaganda – the organised promotion of information to assist or damage the cause of potential enemies – takes on an entirely different code of ethics and morality when applied against a country's own servicemen who loyally served the nation.

Up until the early 1960s the Ministry of Defence was referred to as the War Office. The change of name may sound less belligerent, but that does not prevent the Ministry from taking *offensive* rather than *defensive* action on occasions which may not entirely directly impinge upon the defence of the nation. This happened in 2003 with the Iraq War, because policy is often bound into allied action perhaps deemed to be in the national interest.

With regards to the service given by nuclear test veterans, the MOD used propaganda against the 30,000-plus cohort of young men who loyally served the nation in defence of the realm. This is probably the most unfathomable betrayal and deception through the use of organised misinformation, and it will interest historians for years to come. It is perhaps born out of Cold War paranoia that weapons of mass destruction are a hazard not only to opposing forces but also to the bomb recipients, as shown in the 1945 bombing of two Japanese cities, followed by the legacy ill health of by-standing civilian populations down wind of the nuclear fallout. Those at the sharp end of nuclear bomb testing experiments, the nuclear test veterans, significantly fall under the term of reference known as 'collateral damage' when applied to the above.

Of course, the new nuclear weapons of war had to be tested by the scientists and generals. They needed servicemen without adequate protection or respirators for logistics, engineering and the actual experiments. They also needed civilian scientists with respirators and better body protection to act as a control group to monitor the effects of being with or without protection.

This was an arrangement that suited the 1952 'chewing gum and shoestring' task force that sailed to Monte Bello Island, off the northwest coast of Australia, in 1952. Adequate personal protection equipment to protect the men from acute gamma radiation and the more insidious particles of alpha and beta radiation in the inevitable fallout was a luxury deemed too expensive and impractical for persons working, living and breathing in such a toxic environment for the long periods necessary to complete this hazardous duty.

Knowledge of the effects of the bombing of Japan had already flagged up a legacy of increased leukaemia within six years of exposure to fallout. Also, genetic damage to children conceived during these years was noted. The 1956 Medical Research Council Report confirmed all this and indicated the precariousness in which the servicemen were placed.

But nothing could be changed. Power and prestige rested upon the nuclear bomb test experiments. The prime ministerial edict "It's a pity, but it cannot be helped" became the callous propaganda of the day. Mirrored by the Australian Prime Minister's statement that "no conceivable damage to population or land will result from nuclear bomb testing," it ensured the propaganda regarding fallout hazard was bilateral between two democratic nations.

The MOD commenced its decades-long message of propaganda to ensure radiation was thought of as harmless and that the only hazard from atomic bombs was the massive heat released at the time of detonation.

So, why did the MOD follow this sanitised propaganda campaign to deny a duty of care to the men who took part in the UK nuclear weapon test experiments?

The answer is in the accumulated archive records of

nuclear test veterans in the UK, Australia and New Zealand; that is, the three main allied contributing nations of servicemen who participated. The answer is in press reports over the decades, and in the actions of successive UK governments since 1952. It's in the many peer-reviewed scientific papers about radiation hazard. It is actually underpinned by the genetic damage of nuclear test veterans. The motivation, however, has puzzled many members of the public for years.

The doctrine of denial dates from the 1950s, when the then UK Prime Minister Sir Anthony Eden wrote in an internal memo: "It is a pity, but it cannot be helped," when warned about the genetic hazard to the servicemen from atomic bomb testing. The overarching motive appears to be the power and prestige to be gained through nuclear weapon possession, the huge potential profits of an emerging nuclear energy industry and the elevation of politicians to a permanent seat on the security council of the United Nations.

Draconian powers existed during the Cold War to impose the Official Secrets Act and 'D' notices for decades as gagging orders on those who participated; to control science with regard to the causation of legacy ill health; to have the ability to deny cytogenetic blood testing for persons potentially exposed to ionising radiation; and to repeat the lie that it was in the national interest that radiation levels at nuclear weapon test locations should not be disclosed.

The above powers needed propaganda to deny the prime causal link of inhaled and ingested fallout by measuring only gamma radiation released when an atomic bomb exploded, to ignore the more insidious alpha and beta fallout ionised particles, to only recognise scientific publications and peer-reviewed research that agreed with the policy of denial, and to pass a strong message that nuclear test service is not active conflict with an enemy and is therefore deemed in principle to be ignored as eligible for injury, disability and pension entitlements etc.

As time progressed these elements of propaganda began to manifest in many other ways and adjust to the needs of government. By the end of the 1950s they were supported by the international agreement behind closed doors between the ICRP, which backed the nuclear industry, and the World Health Organisation (WHO). The WHO was gagged from commenting on any radiation-linked deaths globally. The 1993 bilateral treaty between the UK and Australian governments agreeing to work together to deny compensation was also a prime necessity as litigation became inevitable.

Control of science became a prime motivation. The propaganda of the MOD has been blatantly pro-nuclear and protective of the nuclear industry. Those seeking the truth of the hazards of radiation exposure, or seeking information necessary to process claims for disability or pensions – nuclear test veterans, their widows, and expert witness scientists –were referred to as 'anti-nuclear' or a 'vexation', or were even intimidated.

The experiments carried out on men with and without any protection were to assist the nuclear industry with developing PPE for nuclear industry workers. The control of scientific research also came under the political control of the MOD. (See earlier chapters and below.)

Archive records and other data demonstrate that the key evidence used by government representatives at pension appeal tribunals was the SPVA *Radiation Policy Statement for Advice of Ministers*, which relied on significantly biased and obsolete scientific papers weighted heavily against the truth. This virtually led to the setting up of what have become known to veterans as 'kangaroo courts' to deny access to a duty of care.

All the above is just a brief overview of the subject of how propaganda has been used to deny nuclear test veterans' and widows' claims. The secondary motive of the use of propaganda is to save the MOD budgets the cost of enshrining into law the principle that nuclear veterans should be treated the same as any other veteran injured, disabled or prematurely deceased by radiation-induced legacy ill health in service to the nation. It is because of such propaganda that this entitlement is not attributed to service because the servicemen were not in face-to-face conflict with enemy forces in a battlefield situation. The mixed-messaged doctrine is that it is acceptable to step on a land mine and have your legs blown off or be shot through the shoulder or head by an enemy sniper, but to be injured, disabled or die prematurely as the collateral damage of inhaling or ingesting fallout from your own weapons, which you have been deliberately exposed to, is not regarded as entitlement for a duty of care.

Underpinning all MOD propaganda is the control of science and the use of government committees known as 'quangos'. That is, government-appointed committees headed by, and with, appointed long-time career civil servants or academics who often have no in-depth knowledge of the subject matter to which the committee has been appointed. This is helpful because their sole aim is "to ensure the implementation of the functions of government." This places protectionism before the need of often necessary policy change, and lets ministers off the hook.

The use of dodgy civil servants and other appointed

stooges to remove responsibility from ministers has been suspected by nuclear test veterans and their widows for many years. But it is only in recent years it has become self-evident truth. Nuclear veterans found the key factors of science and the route of causation of legacy ill health has been deliberately downplayed or ignored, and suspected dodgy dealing. How the mechanism for this unethical practice worked had always been a bit of a mystery.

However, explanation came in a full-page article by this book's author in *Fissionline*, the International Bulletin of Nuclear Veterans and Families (issue 43, April 2016) entitled 'Dodgy Civil Servants Let Ministers Off the Hook', which commented on a report published in national newspapers at the time. The following is extracted from the article.

"Career senior civil servants, posing as so-called experts, enable political leaders to deny truth and justice and indulge in subterfuge. Take one recent example of so-called experts advising MPs: Dame Lin Homer, Chief Executive and Head of HM Revenue and Customs (HMRC) for the past four years was hauled before MPs of the Commons Public Accounts Committee. Backbench MPs asked the lady questions about the reported lenient taxation of large corporations by HMRC.

"Dame Homer's failure to answer questions was supported by this long-term civil servant's incredulous (even to the MPs on the public accounts committee) excuse: 'I am not a tax expert. I don't think I would regard myself as a deep expert and I don't sit on any hearings.' The Dame added that her role as Head of HMRC was 'to implement the functions of government.'"

This is a revealing admission of public interest as far as tax payers are concerned. The report by the CVFI continued:

"Dame Lin Homer's words (and the words of other so-called government experts) bear a striking similarity to the incredulous testimony of the MOD's Dr Anne Braidwood, as reported in *Fissionline* issues 20 and 21 of 2014, when cross-examined by the AVGL's legal expert, Neil Sampson, during the Stubbs Ionising Radiation Tribunals [for Military Pensions].

"Dr Braidwood, as expert witness for the MOD, despite her role as Senior Medical Adviser to the MOD's Service Personnel and Veterans Agency (SPVA) Statement on Radiation to Chiefs of Staff, the Secretary of State, Defence and other Ministers, said she had 'no idea' that radiation could enter the body of servicemen through cuts or abrasions in the skin, or whether the prime causal link [to premature deaths and legacy ill health etc] of inhaled or ingested low dose low level fallout was even recorded.

"Dr Braidwood treated all questions by nuclear veterans' legal expert Neil Samson in the same manner: 'I am not the government's leading expert on anything.'"

Just as with senior career civil servant Dame Lin Homer's "I don't think that's my expertise," Dr Braidwood's testimony omitted one common truth with her fellow 'expert' at the Head of the HMRC. That is, the role of both these senior civil servants, and many other career civil servants, is "to implement the functions of government." The actual truth of what is happening is therefore deflected from ministerial responsibility.

This of course means deflecting any blame from ministers, even to the point of not answering questions liable to possibly incriminate. The role of Dr Braidwood and other civil servants at the MOD is well known to veterans to be to give advice to the prime minister and their ministers in order to ensure loyal servicemen who participated in the nuclear experiments are denied any duty of care, as obligated by a non-existent military covenant. The same negative ethos also applies to any other person potentially exposed to radiation, occupationally or otherwise.

In the case of the HMRC, the Public Accounts Committee of MPs attempting to ensure huge superannuated corporations are not treated more leniently than the rest of taxpayers, this is a matter of national interest for small businesses and the wider tax-paying public. However, the vested interests appear to be upheld by government-appointed quangos to let ministers off the hook and continue policy as normal, even if change is needed.

Following the derailment of the AVGL's legal quest for compensation in 2012 and military pensions hearings where MOD expert witnesses, such as Dr Braidwood, deflected accountability by not answering questions on behalf of the MOD, expert witnesses for veterans were also being prevented from giving evidence at Pension Appeal Tribunal hearings.

The MOD and UK Government had, through the attrition of unlimited taxpayers' money, depleted Rosenblatts' funds to the extent that they could no longer continue with litigation. In 2014, Neil Sampson had proved in his questioning of the MOD's 'say nothing – keep silent – deny everything' expert witness Dr Braidwood and others that money counts more than the truth. The bedrock of civilised society and our democracy was being undermined.

By 2017 the BNTVA had been totally infiltrated and taken over as an associate of the Ministry of Defence. The organisation diminished further as a charity into a quango of a few nuclear veterans, a mere token to keep the BNTVA name as a shield of past respectability, with trustees administering a fund falsely said to be for use of nuclear veterans and their families.

The chairman, John Lowe, had surrendered all policy-making to the MOD in 2008 and a political patron and trustees had been appointed, many of whom had been given honorary awards to match that given to Professor Rowland. In 2010 Lowe was replaced by the son of a nuclear veteran, Nigel Heaps, with Jeff Liddiatt, a veteran of Maralinga, waiting in the wings to take over when the need or time arose.

The government, using Libor fines given to big banks for malpractice in setting bank interest rates, handed some millions of pounds to the BNTVA. But by 2016 Mr Heaps had left the BNTVA to set up BH Associates with a non-veteran, Stephen Bexon. BH Associates was set up as a services company to manage the money but it soon became apparent that the money was not going into a fund for nuclear test veterans, widows and families; it was going to a new MOD-controlled fund which was renamed the Aged Veterans Fund and was available to about ten nominated armed forces charities.

All this happened between 2015 and 2019 as part of the Armed Forces Covenant Trust, headed by Melloney Poole OBE, a career academic and solicitor directly under the control of the Ministry of Defence. It all seemed appropriately above board and in accordance with charity rules.

About £430,000 was allocated to Brunel University for a Nuclear Community Charity Fund (NCCF) chromosomal study led by Professor Rhona Anderson and with the agreement of the new chairman of the BNTVA, Jeff Liddiatt, at the end of 2018. Professor Anderson had made a sales pitch for a cytogenetic study on nuclear test veterans at the Nuclear

Veterans' Parliamentary Inquiry set up by MPs John Baron and Dr Ian Gibson in November 2007. (See Chapter Eight.) This was the inquiry that deliberately avoided discussion of the peer-reviewed New Zealand study showing 300% elevated genetic damage in exposed veterans, even though this question and answer discussion was on the agenda for the second day.

The Combined Veterans' Forum International (CVFI) and others had been concerned for some time about possible dodgy methodology and protocols being used in any Nuclear Community Charity Fund (NCCF) chromosome study. These concerns were confirmed to me when I received an invitation, via my GP, to take part in the study. I had no qualms about Professor Anderson as a cytogeneticist, but was concerned that epidemiologist Professor Julian Peto, who chaired the fiasco of the 2007 Parliamentary Inquiry, was named on the NCCF chromosomal information sheet as the coordinator and collaborator of the study. This was unacceptable in view of Peto's biased chairmanship of the inquiry and his close ties with the MOD.

There were many other reasons to regard the efficacy of methodology and protocols of the study with some suspicion. Nuclear veterans understand, from our accumulated archive records, that for many years the benefits of UK research into cytogenetics has been used by successive governments not for the benefit of early diagnosis and remedial treatments of radiation damage in veterans, their children and grandchildren but for the eyes of government academics only. We consider this a key failure of the MOD and successive governments. The MOD has – not openly and transparently but almost always in a clandestine manner to avoid any accountability – treated nuclear veterans as research subjects.

Historic records confirm our lack of trust in government is primarily due to epidemiologists who in the past have "perverted government-funded mortality studies for political reasons," (Dr Keith Baverstock, 2004) and also denied cytogenetic studies (such as that by Professor Rowland in 2009) to maintain the bias that ill health is not attributable to radiation exposure. And all this is funded, by the way, with tax payers' money.

Although I was invited to join the study, as a married nuclear veteran without children the methodology of the study excluded me from taking part. The study was for trios comprising veteran, spouse/partner and conceived children. It claimed to be taking a 'meticulous' control path by using 50 trios of military families – who had no connection to nuclear test locations. The information document also stated: "We need blood samples from both parents to determine whether any chromosomal changes in the child are also seen in the father and mother."

This is a gift for epidemiologists to cast doubt on the findings, which has been their historic role over past decades with regard to nuclear test veterans. The conclusions of the findings of any cytogenetic report with this epidemiological involvement would dilute the findings of the most heavily irradiated; that is, the most genetically damaged nuclear veteran fathers, who, in any case, were almost all dead and therefore unable to take part. Those still surviving today are inevitably the ones who had less exposure to radiation and therefore have less genetic damage. The study also excluded the nuclear fathers who died in the 1950s and 60s or within 15 years of returning from nuclear test sites.

Then there are those young men who were rendered sterile

by the radiation, many of whom are now dead and buried, as well as those who committed suicide. All are, conveniently for the MOD, unable to participate in the study.

The above begs the question: would the NCCF study include children born before their father commenced nuclear test service and compare them with siblings born after he returned?

All the above is convenient for the named epidemiologist coordinator and collaborator of the study to muddy the conclusions. Page 4 of the NCCF Information Sheet (regarding the benefits) states: "We cannot promise that taking part in this study will help you, but your participation will give valuable information."

This single sentence explains it all!

It would be the perfect epitaph for the gravestones of veterans who loyally served the nation during the Cold War; an epitaph that would confirm the men were and remained experimental subjects, even unto death. The 'valuable information' will, of course, be of no benefit to them or their families.

The science of cytogenetics and those who work in it, such as Dr DH Evans of the Medical Research Council, Edinburgh in the 1960s onwards and New Zealand's Professor Rowland in 2008, deserve far greater appreciation for the truth they and others are revealing with regards to genetic damage in persons exposed to radiation in the past.

Historic archive documents have shown that, as the years go by, every time epidemiologists get involved in the conclusions it is shown they are lying.

The NCCF study is yet another case of 'whosoever pays the piper calls the tune' – at vast expense to the tax payer, of course, and with absolutely no benefit to nuclear test veterans and their families.

The study invitation included a 9-page Information and Consent Form giving details of the purpose, the organisation and the methodology of the study. I sent a 10-page critical analysis of the study to Professor Rhona Anderson at Brunel University, together with six pages of supportive archive references.

My critique concluded: "Nuclear veterans have good reason historically to believe any evidence of genetic damage found by cytogenetic means will be ignored and diminished by epidemiologists. The only beneficiary of research will be government to add to the results of all previous studies undertaken on veterans since the nuclear weapon tests. This also includes admitted removal of organs, bone and tissue in clandestine post-mortems on deceased nuclear veterans."

The CVFI received no response from Professor Anderson to my critique, but we did not expect any, purely on the basis of historic silence being appropriate in such circumstances.

The critique was copied to the new chairman of the BNTVA, Alan Owen, former chairman Jeff Liddiatt having left the charity shortly after signing the agreement for the NCCF study.

Jeff Liddiatt, from Bristol, was sent to Maralinga in 1959-60 to take part in the notorious minor trials. He was only 19 years old. He later became a leading member of the BNTVA, under the chairmanship of John Lowe and during its downward spiral to a non-campaigning, neutered charity after 2002. When interviewed by Australian author Frank Walker for his book *Maralinga*, published in 2014, Liddiatt said, quite simply, but accurately: "What did the bastards do to us? We are like ghosts. We shout in the dark, but they don't see us, they don't hear us. They pretend we are not there. We were just working-class squaddies, so we didn't count. The senior officers and scientists were all given awards and medals and made knights and lords, but we in the ranks got nothing. All we got was a legacy of it in our blood and genes. They hope those still remaining will die sooner rather than later. That way, there will be no one left to bother them."

This is a somewhat late admission of the folly of Liddiatt, Doug Hern and other committee members' support for BNTVA chairman John Lowes' 2008 sell-out appeasement to the UK government and the MOD's nuclear veteran policy of denial.

Between 2005 and 2013, Rosenblatt solicitors of London entered into litigation with the UK Government to get a settlement for nuclear veterans and their families. During talks, Defence Minister Kevan Jones and several MOD officials met with the BNTVA leadership. This signalled the end of the association's long proactive 'All We Seek is Justice' campaign. Ken McGinley's seventeen years of BNTVA leadership for truth and justice was now replaced with abject surrender; that is, the BNTVA leader offered appeasement along the lines of 'If we say you are not liable for the ill health and premature deaths of nuclear veterans and their families, will you, by an act of grace, be kind to us?' The government must have laughed their socks off.

Like much else in Alan Rimmer's *Fissionline*, the bulletin for nuclear test veterans and their families, the minutes of this meeting were released after Freedom of Information requests. Seventeenth century colonial rules of divide and conquer, backed by unlimited money, were now at fever pitch.

The lure of possible honours and medals had proved too powerful for many to resist. Still, as they say, everyone is entitled to see the truth of the matter eventually. For Jeff Liddiatt, his part in this was perceptively noted by nuclear veterans and their widows who were engaged in the litigation.

The rank and file membership of the BNTVA during these febrile years mid-2000 onwards was not being listened to. The leadership had been hijacked to the point of becoming a compliant vassal of long-intended government policy to avoid any payment of compensation to surviving veterans, their widows and families.

Government policy towards the nuclear weapon test location participants had been commonly noted as 'a policy to deny everything until all surviving veterans are dead'.

A 'grace and favour' settlement without an admission of MOD liability rather than a continuation of the campaign for compensation, justice *and* an apology evolved from 2001. This was a betrayal of everything BNTVA fuonder Ken McGinley worked for from 1983 to 2001.

The fact remains today that any veteran seeking evidence about this period of our history to support their claim is labelled as a 'vexation' for asking questions. The true vexation, of course, is the government's refusal to answer questions.

The timing of the 2008 MOD/BNTVA meetings could not have been better for damaging the nuclear veterans' campaign for justice. A cytogenetic study of nuclear test veterans had been completed in New Zealand and the conclusions of peer-reviewed evidence showing the men had 300% more genetic damage than men who had not attended a nuclear weapon test location was due to be published in 2009.

The new chairman Alan Owen gave an account of his early days at the BNTVA in issue 58 of *Fissionline* in October 2019. We must thank investigative journalist and editor Alan Rimmer, whose experience in these matters has been crucial in establishing the truth.

Mr Owen said he went along to his first meeting of the BNTVA and walked away with the chairmanship and the promise of an MBE. This was an eye opener for all who had tirelessly campaigned for truth and justice for nuclear test veterans since the founding of the BNTVA by Ken McGinley in 1983. The new chairman told Alan Rimmer just what a shambles of ethics was taking place: "I was brought in as a stooge, but they chose the wrong guy." He added: "I could have been a mass murderer for all they cared, just as long as I shut down the veterans... It happened so fast, of course I was flattered. But then I thought, hang on a minute. What is this all about?"

At this time, the veterans had just been awarded £6 million of Libor funds. But instead of going to the BNTVA, which had made the application, the money went to a new organisation called the Nuclear Community Charity Fund (NCCF). This became a regular occurrence – money said to be intended for veterans was moved around by the BNTVA to the Aged Veterans Fund, to the NCCF, anywhere that suited the government, whose purpose was to make sure it benefitted anyone but the nuclear veterans. This is just one of many reasons why Alan Owen ultimately resigned as chairman of the BNTVA.

Mr Owen said: "I knew nothing about this organisation. Like everyone else, I thought the cash was for the nuclear veterans so when the BNTVA put out a post asking for trustees,

I thought I could help so I put in an application. I got a letter saying, 'Yes, the board has accepted you. Come to our AGM. You can attend our first meeting and see what's going on.' So I went there the night before the main AGM for a board meeting. Most of the trustees were there and Jeff Liddiatt, the chairman, said he was going to be stepping down and they wanted me to be their new chairman.

"I was shocked. This was my first meeting. I now believe there was a plan to neutralise the BNTVA as a campaigning organisation. And I believe I was being set up to be the fall guy to carry out the plan. I sat down with all these people I hardly knew, and we were barely four minutes into the meeting when I was asked would I like to be the chairman.

"I thought, 'They cannot be serious.' They knew nothing about me; all they had was my CV, which could have been a pack of lies. I could have been a mass murderer for all they cared.

"I was so taken aback that I refused to take it on. I asked them how they could possibly ask me to take on such an important post. I said I only went along because I thought I could help with their IT systems. That's what I went looking for. But they said not to worry. They would set me up as a chairman designate and I would shadow Jeff Liddiatt for a year.

"They said it was because of my background in running an IT company for charities. Because of that they insisted that I could bring something to the board. So I became the chairman designate. When I rang my wife to tell her, she didn't believe it. She thought it was crazy.

"I decided to do some research. I read a couple of *Fissionline* articles and was disturbed by them. They raised my doubts about the way the BNTVA was being run.

"The next day I met Nigel Heaps, a former BNTVA chairman, but now acting as a special advisor to the NCCF charity. He was scathing about *Fissionline*. He told me not to approach Ken McGinley, a *Fissionline* board member. He said, 'Don't go anywhere near him. You need to talk to the French. That is where the future lies. Don't talk to the Americans; they are a waste of space.' Finally, he assured me all would be well. He said to me, 'Don't worry about a thing. You'll be all right. We'll even get you an MBE as well.'

"I spoke to other members. They too had been told to stay away from *Fissionline*. Everyone was apparently told to stay away from it. 'Don't go near it.' There was a lot of worry about *Fissionline*.

"I sat for a couple of days thinking, do I really want to do it? I was shocked and flattered. But then I decided to give it a go; that I would throw time at it. My father, who served on Christmas Island with the Americans as part of Operation Dominic, always told me to do the right thing. He told me to stand up for what you think is right. If you get it wrong, put your hands up and say 'Well, I got that one wrong.'

"I was told there was nothing to worry about taking on the job as chairman and everything was above board. But I wanted to find out for myself. I looked at everything that was online, like *Fissionline* articles, like emails I was receiving from members, and it slowly dawned on me that something was wrong. It seemed to me that the BNTVA was slowly being strangled. Worse, I realised it was being eradicated.

"The members were not even called nuclear veterans anymore. They were being called Aged Veterans. But I believe their position is unique; there is a big difference. It was all wrong, so I decided to do something about it. We stepped up the campaign for medal recognition, and we were making progress; and we are actively helping members in their fight for war pensions. I read the interview [by Alan Rimmer of *Fissionline*] with Melloney Poole, the head of the Aged Veterans Fund. She gave explicit assurances about the Libor cash, assurances that turned out to be hollow.

"I believe the deal was that the £6 million Libor funds would only be released if nuclear veterans gave up campaigning. I believe that because as soon as we announced we were going for medal recognition, I was thrown off one of the committees I had been co-opted on to oversee the health studies. I realised then that I was just brought in as a stooge. But they chose the wrong guy to allow the BNTVA to sink into obscurity and to be airbrushed from history."

Alan Owen is a man of high principles. The prospect of becoming another appointed academic whose sole purpose in life would be 'to implement the functions of government' to enforce policy against the interests of all he believed in is a red line of principle he would not cross. But many have crossed that line throughout the UK's nuclear scandal, where the power, prestige and profit of the few ignores the collateral damage of the many.

Many succumb to the lure of honours and medals, just as Napoleon had recognised as a totalitarian dictator when he created mayhem rampaging through 19th century Europe. But Alan Owen was having none of it.

Mr Owen's reference to the word 'stooge' to describe the hollowed-out wreckage of the former vibrant BNTVA veterans' association that once campaigned for justice echoes eminent biologist Professor Alex Haddow in 1951. Professor Haddow used the term 'stooge' to describe answers from government-sponsored committees of physicists regarding his and other eminent biologists' many concerns with regards to the hazards of radioactive fallout from nuclear bomb tests. Professor Haddow went on to say the physicists of the Atomic Energy Authority (AEA) were only providing the 'right' answers in a 'conspiracy of silence' towards the concerns expressed from his branch of science, which is primarily interested in life rather than the death of individuals.

Mr Owen's comment that nuclear test veterans are being "airbrushed from history" is now an established fact. In 2019, CNN reported that all data held in Australia with regard to radiation levels at UK nuclear test locations was being deposited in a new archive in the far northern tip of Scotland, where it will be unavailable for access by nuclear historians for an unspecified number of years. In addition, the term 'nuclear test veteran' has been replaced by 'aged veteran' rather than 'unique veteran of hazardous service to the nation'.

It is almost reminiscent of 1930s' Germany's anti-Semitic burning of books and the final solution of the holocaust. To rewrite history in the manner of a totalitarian state rather than face up to the mistakes of past politicians and bureaucrats is an affront to civilised society and democracy.

Control of science by the MOD plays a major part in airbrushing history. This has impacted negatively upon independent-minded scientists and other academics who have stood up to science rather than the dogma of government scientific manipulation.

Since 2002, Professor Chris Busby has stood up against successive governments as the UK's leading independent expert on low dose, low level radiation as the prime causal link to ill health and premature deaths in persons exposed, occupationally or otherwise, to inhaled or ingested internal emitting ionised radiation.

Professor Busby was blocked from giving evidence during the AVGL case hearings and in War Pension Appeal Tribunals. Scientific papers such as his meticulously researched *Meteorological records, airflow and other factors affecting fallout from British nuclear bomb tests at Christmas Island in 1957-9* (2010), co-written with independent academic Dai Williams MSc, were barred from being heard in court. As expert witness of data for the nuclear veterans, scientific secretary to the European Committee on Radiation Risk, a committee member of the Committee Examining Radiation Risk from Internal Emitters, founder of the Low Level Radiation Campaign etcetera, and as the author of two scientific books and much else internationally, Dr Busby has consistently been intimidated.

In an article in *Fissionline,* issue 58, October 2019, Dr Busby said he had been arrested after his home in Cornwall was raided by bomb squad officers. He was later released without charge amid claims the raid was politically motivated. Speaking after his arrest, Dr Busby said: "I was arrested for no good reason last September and put into handcuffs and thrown into cell on a completely trumped-up charge about manufacturing explosives for which there was absolutely no evidence whatever. The police broke into my house without a warrant and carried out all sorts of actions which were strictly illegal."

Dr Busby added: "The MOD know they are losing, and that is what is worrying me a bit because the most dangerous animal is the animal that is cornered or wounded."

When commenting about a case carried over from the War Pension Tribunal hearings of 2016, Dr Busby said: "I have brought two very eminent expert witnesses and am acting as a representative of a veteran who died of pancreatic cancer. The MOD called Dr Anne Braidwood who wrote a report. But unfortunately for them in 2013 Dr Anne Braidwood had admitted under oath she wasn't an expert on anything. So I had written to the judge saying you can hardly allow the MOD to use this woman as an expert witness when she herself says she isn't one. So this case is still hanging in the air."

What is worrying MOD officials in all of this is the truth. Professor Busby has fought and won many cases for nuclear veterans. But control of science is not limited only to scientific experts such as Professor Busby. Politicians also come under the same intimidation, as demonstrated through Michael Meacher MP's initiative, the CERRIE committee in 2003 (see Chapter Eight), and when Dr Ian Gibson MP's attempt to get recognition for the Rowland study in 2007 was brushed aside.

The fact of the matter is that since the 1956 Medical Research Council Report and the 2009 peer-reviewed Rowland cytogenetic study, when it comes to science the MOD has increased the pace of taking everyone into a dark abyss of a lack of morality, ethics and humanity.

After seventy years and multi-millions of pounds spent by the MOD to deny justice to nuclear test veterans and their families, all they have achieved is a narrow, inconclusive Supreme Court verdict by a majority one vote; that is, a 4:3 verdict from seven law lords.

Kicking a long-running political problem into the long grass in the hope that it will disappear is an unresolved waste of taxpayers' money. But the truth, and the concerns of nuclear test veterans, won't disappear. Since 1952, the MOD has only succeeded in shining a bright light into the darkness of institutional collusion and bad faith.

For nuclear veterans and their families, their concerns about legacy ill health and premature deaths have not been settled honourably or justly. They have been betrayed. There are too many skeletons in too many cupboards, and this cannot be airbrushed from history despite ongoing attempts to do so.

Coming out of the 2020-21 Covid pandemic as a self-governing, independent sovereign democracy should be an opportunity to settle the concerns of past history and move forwards to a more open, honest and brighter future.

All that politicians and government officials need to do is follow the example of the monarchy and put duty and service above all else.

Australian Treaty Series 1993 No 40

DEPARTMENT OF FOREIGN AFFAIRS AND TRADE

CANBERRA

Exchange of Notes constituting an Agreement between the Government of Australia and the Government of the United Kingdom of Great Britain and Northern Ireland concerning Maralinga and other Sites in Australia

(London, 10 December 1993)

Entry into force: 10 December 1993

AUSTRALIAN TREATY SERIES

2. Subject to paragraph 3 below, the claims referred to in paragraph 1 are any claims whatsoever which the Government of Australia or any person, natural or legal, may have, now or in the future, arising out of any act, matter or thing done or omitted to be done by the United Kingdom or its servants or agents in relation to the carrying out of nuclear tests or experimental programmes by the United Kingdom at the sites in Australia or in relation to the decontamination and clearance of the sites.

3. The Government of the United Kingdom shall indemnify the Government of Australia in respect of all claims which arise out of the death or injury of any person and which -

(i) are referred to in paragraph (c) of the 1968 Memorandum, or

(ii) result from nuclear tests or experimental programmes at the Monte Bello Islands in respect of which the cause of action occurred before 27 June 1956.

4. The Government of Australia shall indemnify the Government of the United Kingdom against any loss, costs, damages or expenses which the Government of the United Kingdom may incur or be called upon to pay as a result of any such claims by any person, natural or legal, as are referred to in paragraph 2 above.

5. If a claim covered by paragraph 3 or 4 is made, the Government against whom, or against whose representatives, a claim is brought shall inform the other Government of the claim prior to the commencement of proceedings or as soon as possible thereafter. The Governments shall consult at the request of either of them on the conduct of the legal proceedings arising out of the claim and on the manner in which the claim may be settled.

6. In relation to a claim for which the cause of action occurred prior to the date of entry into force of this Agreement, references in paragraphs 2 and 4 above to any person shall not include a person who was at the time when the cause of action occurred a member of HM Forces or a person employed by the Government of the United Kingdom for the purpose of working on the sites. This paragraph has no application to members of the forces of the Commonwealth of Australia.

The Betrayal

The bilateral UK–Australia Treaty to work together to deny any claims arising from the death or injury of any person employed at nuclear test locations, in particular members of HM Forces or any person employed by the UK Government. This treaty was agreed in December 1993.

Conclusion: The Truth will be Judged by History

"If the Ministry of Defence had stopped telling lies about the nuclear veterans the nuclear veterans would have stopped telling the truth about the Ministry of Defence."
The Combined History Archive of Nuclear Veterans.
Adapted from The Deal, a campaign speech in 1952 by
Adlai Stevenson (1900-1965), former US Vice President

As a political bastion of freedom, democracy completely loses the trust of the people when it fails to stand up for the truth.

When referring to the political 'deal' in a 1952 campaign speech, former US Vice President Adlai Stevenson said that if someone stopped telling lies about you then you would stop telling the truth about them – and this is an accurate summary of the Ministry of Defence's failed nuclear veterans policy.

An undemocratic negative culture and attitude of lies, misinformation and bad faith towards those who loyally served the nation underpins the historic content of each chapter of this book. All combined armed forces participant nuclear veterans from Britain, Australia, New Zealand and Fiji underpin a legacy of genetic damage, serious ill health and premature deaths as a result of the loyal service they gave to the UK's Cold War experimental military programme. Worse still, the legacy of the nuclear weapon test experiments has been passed to the nuclear veterans' children and grandchildren.

Successive UK and Australian governments (backed by a premeditated treaty obligation and prime ministerial edicts) have deliberately lied about this in order to avoid accountability and responsibility.

Without truth, trust is lost and democracy is weakened and undermined.

The fate of the nuclear veterans' health was sealed politically right from the beginning. The United Kingdom and Australia, the two main participating nations of the bomb tests from 1952, both embodied the same negative culture and attitude about the known hazards of fallout. That is, ignore it, deny it and forget it.

Well, although it was seen politically as "a pity, but it cannot be helped," the legacy ethically and morally could and should have been helped.

The Australian Government had an opportunity in 1985 to redeem themselves from the negativity. The Royal Australian Commission (see Chapter Six) returned to Australia with a 615-page report and seven recommendations after the UK had left a legacy of radioactive contamination behind following the closure of bomb testing locations in 1967. The Commission's report was dismissed by the senior British QC who suggested it all "a fuss about nothing".

It did not take long for the Federal Australian Government in Canberra to reconfirm the undemocratic negative culture and attitude towards the servicemen who participated in the nuclear tests. Money was a greater priority for the pen-pushers of Canberra than the genetically damaged Australian servicemen who participated. They were callously abandoned to their genetically damaged fate.

A 25-page Federal Government Cabinet document dated 31 July 1986 and entitled *Handling of Recommendations of Royal*

Commission on British Nuclear Tests in Australia Overview Submission no. 4158, Decision no. 8091 (ER) states, under the heading 'British Interests' on page 18: "While the British Government will continue to minimise its obligation to clean up the sites, its final willingness to pay in whole or part will depend on both a mix of legal and moral argument, and on the extent of the clean-up insisted upon. The British have also stated their concern that if personal compensation awards are opened up, precedents will be set for compensation of their own nuclear veterans.

"There is a connection between the compensation and clean-up issues only in as far as restraint by the Australian Government on this compensation issue may assist the negotiating climate when it comes to seeking recovery of clean-up costs."

The decisions made in the document were overseen by Senator Gareth Evans QC, Minister for Resources and Energy.

The truth of the genetic damage to the health of Australian veterans and their families was ignored; it was politically and expediently swept under the carpet, as was any legal or moral principle.

This brought a return to the days of the cosy toxic agreement between Sir Robert Menzies and the UK Government of the 1950s to totally ignore the nuclear test veterans' legacy ill health, genetic damage and premature deaths and deny any possible compensation to be paid to them, in exchange for money to clean up the radioactive contamination. This was the foundation for the bilateral treaty in 1993, a treaty of lies undermining the truth about radiation hazard. It was a cost-saving measure that undermined the democratic principle of providing a duty of care for those who loyally serve the nation.

The inescapable fear about compensation payments created the deliberate, breath-taking duplicity and lack of openness and honesty politically enforced against nuclear test veterans and their widows from that date on by both the UK and Australian Governments. For New Zealand and Fijian participants, it appears, as minor nations of little comparative economic or financial value, they were both forced out on a limb of their own to fight for justice. No sense of Commonwealth unity, recognition or care was considered.

The New Zealand Nuclear Test Veteran Association leader Roy Sefton independently achieved recognition and pensions for the nuclear veterans from the New Zealand Government. That is, from a New Zealand democracy which undoubtedly has a higher moral and ethical sense of duty towards nuclear test veterans than the bilaterally treaty-obligated UK and Australian Veterans Agencies, who lack any appreciation for those who served the nation during the Cold War.

The positive culture and attitude shown by the New Zealand Government is a credit to democracy and has been demonstrated throughout the 2020-21 Covid pandemic. New Zealand Prime Minister, Jacinda Ardern, has an emotional empathy for people that's sadly lacking in the UK and Australia. This enlightened democratic leader has been rightly praised for New Zealand's handling of the pandemic.

When asked by the press to explain her firmness and decision-making authority in handling the pandemic, she said: "I think one of the sad things that I've seen in political leadership is – because we've placed over time so much emphasis on notions of assertiveness and strength – we have assumed that it means you can't have those other qualities of kindness and empathy. We need our leaders to be able to empathise with the circumstances of others; to empathise with the next generation. The world doesn't need a whole lot of massively thick-skinned politicians; they do need people who care."

From truth comes trust. This is a salutary lesson in democracy for both the United Kingdom and Australia. Nuclear test veterans have learnt from experience that kindness and empathy do not sit well with the UK and Australian Governments' track records of dealing with the health concerns of anyone. The combined archive history of UK nuclear bomb testing held by UK, Australian, New Zealand and Fijian veterans shows clearly that the UK and Australian Governments' policy towards veterans who served at nuclear test locations is to betray them, use them, abuse them and then finally abandon them for political reasons to save costs and protect vested financial interests in nuclear mining and industry.

The New Zealand Prime Minister's comments in 2020 are interesting with regard to the culture and attitude of the UK towards the New Zealand nuclear test veterans' service at Christmas Island. It is shown to be one of imperial colonial disdain. One of Prime Minister Ardern's closest political colleagues, who stood in for her during maternity leave, just happened to be Winston Peters, a former leader of the New Zealand First party, who in 1999 was warned by the British High Commissioner to New Zealand that any help to nuclear veterans would be regarded as an 'unfriendly act' by the UK Government.

Mr Peters was said to be unimpressed. Justifiably so,

considering the extent of the knowledge of the truth about the science of radiation hazard that was widely available at the time; in fact, since the bombing of Hiroshima in 1945.

Roy Sefton, chairman of the NZNTVA, was extremely fortunate to have the support of politicians of such high moral and ethical integrity. Mr Sefton's attempts to get justice for the New Zealand and Fijian servicemen who took part in the UK's Operation Grapple series of nuclear bomb tests on Christmas Island succeeded despite the UK and Australian bilateral treaty. They succeeded despite Australia and the UK ignoring the efficacy of the peer-reviewed Rowland study and the bilateral obsession with significantly flawed epidemiological studies biased to give the 'right' political answer without blood testing the veterans.

In early 2020, Australian and New Zealand nuclear campaigning sources were excited that the plight of Fijian servicemen who took part in the UK nuclear tests would be raised at the Commonwealth Heads of Government Meeting (CHOGM). But in the event only the manipulated and biased records of the UK and Australian Governments were relied upon or listened to. It came as no surprise when the Fijian petition for recognition of claims fell on deaf ears.

The lack of any response or empathy for the Fijians was best summed up by a CVFI contact since 1965, with many years' experience of southern hemisphere politics, particularly in Australia, who said the CHOGM is regarded in Canberra as 'Chaps Holidaying On Government Money'.

Despite this 'couldn't care less' snub from the CHOGM, the small Fijian Government has made a one-off payment to their veterans for service at the UK nuclear weapon tests. But no recognition or thanks has ever been expressed by the UK Government, in whose service these Commonwealth allies were employed.

The Covid-19 pandemic has been a great leveller. It has shown that democracies in the west are miles apart from each other in terms of openness and honesty on the issue of public health concerns. Airborne pathogens, whether manmade or naturally occurring, are treated with varying degrees of ambivalence when it comes to personal protective equipment (PPE) for front line services. This does not bode well for the future – unless politicians begin to empathise with the concerns of future generations.

"Science can only be trusted if it is pursued with the most rigorous procedures that guarantee freedom of bias." These words were spoken by Michael Meacher MP, Environment Minister in 2004 with regard to a committee he set up specifically to publish all views of radiation hazard – including those of independent experts. Mr Meacher was sacked for his unique initiative. This committee appears to have to be controlled by government because only the 'right' political consensus can be tolerated.

However, in recent years Members of Parliament are beginning to speak against the control of science and the way policy decisions are decided in a more enlightened, open and honest way. It's a positive change that would be most welcome in the context of the UK's nuclear scandal and also in all areas of science.

For example, Mark Harper MP, a former Conservative Shadow Minister for Veterans, Minister for Pensions and Chief Whip, and now on the back benches in the Boris Johnson government, has shown a positive culture and attitude towards government's questionable control of science. In November 2020, when setting himself up as chair of the Covid Recovery Group (CRG) of some 70 MPs, with Steve Baker MP as deputy, Mr Harper launched the group with 'three guiding principles' by which the government should move forward in the future.

This had been prompted by a continuous lockdown policy of blanket restrictions that many feared would push the UK economy into an abyss following months of poor decision making and ministerial responses to government-appointed science advice, the lack of PPE, a poor 'track and trace' system, an 'open border' policy and mixed messaging to the public. Despite bungling attempts by the government, the problem has only been solved by science independent of government-controlled committees; that is, the hard work and expertise of scientists has provided the vaccine solution that lets ministers off the hook.

The CRG's first principle was that the government must undertake and publish the full cost–benefit analysis of the restrictions on a regional basis. This was so local MPs had a chance to make balanced decisions. Although this is not directly linked to the government's failed veterans policy, it is a breath of fresh air, taking power away from the centralised control of Westminster.

The second principle was that it is time to end the monopoly on advice of government scientists. This is a positive statement, the likes of which Mr Harper could not have expressed as a minister, and definitely not while he was wearing the straitjacket of scientific bias as a Shadow Minister for Veterans.

The third principle was about improving track and trace

during the pandemic; a laudable concern, but secondary in the long term to the second principle i.e. the priority is on ending 'the monopoly of government scientists', particularly where public health is concerned.

Another example, this time in the context of the constant 'revolving door' of those who have served any time as a Minister for Veterans, is the April 2021 sacking of Johnny Mercer MP. As with all others before him handed this politically poisoned post of misinformation, he would only remain in post if he followed the MOD's official scripts, which left no room for independent thought or any intention of ever actually helping veterans. Mr Mercer was sacked by a text message because he independently followed a point of principle.

The day before Mr Mercer was sacked, the government watered down a controversial bill dropping plans that made it harder to prosecute soldiers for historic war crimes. To give this context, terrorists who had committed planned and premeditated murders during what was known as 'The Troubles' of the 1970s were given immunity from such prosecutions following the Northern Ireland Peace Agreement. British soldiers were not given any immunity for shooting terrorists during this conflict. They have, as a result, been hounded through the courts for years.

Later, Mercer referred to Boris Johnson's 'Veterans Pledge', signed in 2019 when Johnson was running for prime minister, and accused him of breaking a promise to not abandon the troops to legal action against them. Mercer said: "Perhaps nothing embodies this more than what we are asking our veterans in their 70s and 80s to relive, through endless investigations and inquests into events 50 years ago in Northern Ireland. We have abandoned our people in a way I simply cannot reconcile.

"Whilst endless plans and promised solutions are mused, veterans are being sectioned, drinking themselves to death and dying before their time because the UK Government cannot find the moral strength or courage we asked of them in bringing peace to Northern Ireland, in finding a political solution to stop these appalling injustices."

This is not a direct comparison to the betrayal of nuclear test veterans, but the same negative culture and attitude is applied with regards to ignoring the obligation to provide a duty of care.

Mr Mercer's sacking was followed by a Downing Street spokesman saying: "The Prime Minister has accepted the sacking of Johnny Mercer. He thanks him for his service." This short, callous dismissal matches the insincerity of previous and devious prime ministers saying they are 'extremely grateful' for the service given by nuclear test veterans during the Cold War, followed by ignoring any accountability or responsibility for their sacrifice. It is classic, politically expedient double standards of betrayal.

Of his time in post from July 2019 to April 2021, Mr Mercer has stated, regarding the Ministry of Defence as a department: "It is the most distrustful, awful environment I have ever worked in. It is a cesspit."

This is an extremely accurate and truthful account of the Veterans Agency of the Ministry of Defence, and Mercer's words are another indictment of a dysfunctional ministry in need of radical reform.

Politicians in the UK are misled on a daily basis by official briefings filled with naïve contradictions of actual fact. Officials believe they can mystify science to a degree where they are enabled to appear in authoritative control of scientific truths of radiation hazard, when in reality they have lost control.

What are the prospects for the future? On 24 December 2020, following publication of the first Global Health Survey of nuclear test victims, Alan Owen, former BNTVA chairman and founder of LABRATS International, said: "The descendants of the nuclear testing programme continue to struggle daily from the health effects of nuclear testing. This must be addressed. Further research into the health of the descendants is desperately needed. The research needs to include analysis of the mental and physical health conditions being experienced by extremely high levels of the atomic family."

In an age of mass communication, people in a democracy are no longer prepared to be patronised by officials or politicians. It is no longer credible to use biased dogma which is uneducated in or unable / unwilling to accept advances in science that have taken place in the 76 years since Hiroshima.

The days when medieval bishops and popes suppressed people who followed the science that the earth orbited the sun in opposition to the dogma that the earth, like the church, was the centre of everything are long over. Except in the Ministry of Defence and governments.

Suppress the truth and you banish all trust.

The negative ethos of advice handed to politicians by the MOD scientists and officials is riddled with inaccuracies and obsolescence. Their advice is based on propaganda that is leaking like a rusty old bucket. They have failed to grasp the truth that they have been overtaken by an understanding of the hazards of radiation, acknowledged across both biological and physicist sides of radiation consensus since the 1956 Medical Research Council Report.

The term 'negative culture and attitude' of the Ministry of Defence was coined by Shadow Conservative Minister Gerald Howarth in February 2005. This was said at a Porton Down debate into the illegal killing of Leading Aircraftsman Ronald Maddison in nerve gas experiments. Nothing appears to have changed since then, apart from the fact that ministers have allowed themselves to be put into a deeper hole of deception through following the advice of senior career civil servants.

Negative advice still impacts upon the welfare of the electorate's sons and daughters entrusted into the MOD's care today. This is unacceptable in the 21st century.

On the strength of career civil servants' performances to date, political appointees to the Minister for Veterans post both in the UK and Australia have clearly been exposed as unknowledgeable enforcers of policy against the interests of past, present and future veterans.

Political judgements and decisions are more often than not biased through lack of independent or rational thought. Without radical thought or change, our armed forces will continue to have to function without designated military hospitals, without adequate equipment, in ever decreasing numbers and while being consistently under-valued by supine officials and politicians who are still locked into the 'systems analysis' and 'game theory' devised by Cold War nuclear strategists. Added to this are the often cost–benefit saving algorithms used in science today to frame policy that often lacks common sense.

Without radical change, those serving today or enlisting

tomorrow, like past veterans, will be forced to sue future governments in order to gain an entitled duty of care for themselves, their widows and, if radiological weapons are involved, for their genetically damaged children. Such is the current arrogance of desk-bound officials who brief ministers who legislate the policies that affect every young person motivated to enlist to serve the nation.

The current ethos allows politicians to continue to betray our armed forces personnel. It's just not good enough.

The ethos still apparent today that "it's a pity, but it cannot be helped" evolved because too many politicians and officials, through their own sheer apathy, blindness, greed, incompetence, misguided adventurism, ignorance and lack of common sense, have placed all men, women, children and future generations in a trap.

It is a trap that has not changed since the First World War ethos of treating servicemen as mere cannon fodder to feed insatiable weapons and egos.

Access to information through the Freedom of Information Act is prevented when gaining access rights to personal information required as evidence – as demonstrated by nuclear test veteran David Whyte in his 2012 First Tier FOIA case in February 2012 (see Chapter Eight).

Mr Whyte has explained what will be faced by any questioner using the FOIA. He says: "When making a question, ensure you have all the pertinent facts pertaining to the subject. It is not unknown for the MOD to request further information, or to be more precise of requirements. The format best used is the 'What do they know' format; the information requested can be seen by all users of the web.

"The most famous excuse for not answering is, 'We do not have this information.' It is amazing how much information has been lost (or hidden) by the authorities. This shows a gross lack of administration within the Ministry of Defence.

"I would say the next best excuse is, 'It would cost too much to get this information.' It would appear that each request is given a certain amount of funds in order to obtain the information; if it appears they would go over this amount they say they cannot give an answer.

"On occasion, they will say the request is 'vexatious' and refuse to answer. At this stage you are well aware that you have struck a raw nerve, and they have been informed by the unseen backroom boys not to answer. If you continue to press them for a truthful answer, you will be banned from making any further requests.

"They will only answer the questions they wish to answer; all others are labelled vexatious. They are not accountable to any person and make up their own rules as to which information they give."

Before the master of spin Tony Blair left office, he had enacted the Freedom of Information Act and stated "nuclear veterans should receive some help from government." But was this the first empty posturing from a prime minister who left a legacy of bending the truth? Was he belatedly seeking redemption?

People in power only indicate help for veterans when seeking election or when leaving office. Whilst in power, they do absolutely nothing. Several years after leaving office, Blair, who many believe led the nation into an illegal war with Iraq in 2003, admitted publicly the enactment of the FOI Act was possibly his biggest mistake. But not to worry: as nuclear veteran David Whyte explained above, senior career civil servants soon render any regrets with caveats to ensure the function of government policy remains unchanged.

In summary, the Veterans Agency statement that there is no peer-reviewed evidence to support the nuclear veterans' claims of legacy ill health, genetic damage and premature deaths being attributable to exposure to radiation is a corruption of the scientific truth.

The current prime minister's recent statement that the government is "extremely grateful" for the service of the nuclear test veterans through the Cold War is an insincere and hollow corruption of the truth of recognition for their unique service to the nation.

In 2021, the statement from the Veterans Agency and the lack of any radical change in government policy are a misuse of the English language, a misuse of taxpayers' money and an abdication of any principles.

The reality is there are far too many nuclear skeletons in far too many government cupboards falsely and expediently marked 'official secret' and in the 'national interest'.

Airbrushing the nuclear test veterans' decades of betrayal from history through presenting a sanitised official government version and burying the truth in a deep depository in the far northern tip of Scotland, with no access to nuclear historians and the public, is their final solution to a political programme that has been found to be a disgrace.

Burying the truth and rewriting history is worthy only of a totalitarian state, not any credible democracy.

The 4:3 Supreme Court verdict is an unresolved legal verdict –

unresolved despite the huge amount of taxpayers' money used against nuclear veterans since 1952 to ensure a level playing field for litigation was weighted in the government's favour. The Atomic Veterans Group Litigation from 2005 to 2014 was denied access to evidence needed and much evidence was denied presentation by veterans' expert witnesses in court. Money wasted by the Ministry of Defence showed nothing has been scientifically proved to deny accountability and responsibility for the legacy ill health, genetic damage and premature deaths of the nuclear test veterans.

Even after the use of propaganda, withholding of 250,000 or more documents from AVGL lawyers, burial of AWE and other records not to be accessed by nuclear historians or media for unspecified years, current attempts to foist a sanitised version of nuclear test veterans' service into the nation's history, denying access to radiation levels at nuclear test locations etc., the efforts of all this undemocratic activity by superannuated officials has failed.

The global atmospheric nuclear bomb test programme from the 1940s to the 1970s by nuclear powers is a historic scandal of deliberately ignored fallout radiation hazard. This will always be a fact.

In history, nuclear bomb testing is the only development of a weapon of war where benefits have been measured in power, prestige and profit for the few at the cost of the deliberately ignored legacy ill health, genetic damage and premature deaths of the many.

The United Kingdom's atrocious treatment of its nuclear test veterans will not end until it is admitted, recognised and apologised for. Until the claims are honourably and justly settled for the nuclear veterans, their widows and genetically impaired offspring and a meaningful armed forces covenant is enshrined into law, it will remain the UK's nuclear scandal.

This book is the true history of the betrayal of all British and Commonwealth servicemen who participated in the UK nuclear weapon tests from 1952 to 1967. It is a betrayal that undermines our democracy.

It has been written in memory of them all.

To Contaminated Carelessness

The winds that blew across this ancient ocean floor
did not sow
Sycamore seeds on Blighty air.
These winds sowed seeds of death to poison and penetrate
almost everywhere.
Young men thrust by duty upon these hostile irradiated
shores were
Innocent, trusting, unaware.
Those who sent them
Knew this then.
They know this now
And still don't care.

*Written by the author, Dennis Hayden with knowledge
gained by 2005 with the help of from UK, Australian and New
Zealand veterans.*

Useful Reference Sources and Recommended Reading

The author is extremely grateful and humbled by the sources of data and archive documents acquired by nuclear veterans, investigative journalists, scientists and others from the 1980s onwards. Without this acquired source information, this book could not have been written.

Readers and others will find there is much more of relevance, particularly for nuclear historians. Only lack of space excludes other sources.

The true history of the betrayal of nuclear test veterans of the UK test experiments is therefore well supported by science, archive documents and other evidence that will inevitably be added to in the future.

History can be changed by governments; however, the truth cannot – and that is a democratic freedom and a right.

ATOM: Quarterly publication of worldwide news for the atomic family. Can be ordered from www.labrats.international. Essential reading for anyone wishing to keep updated with current news related to atomic test survivors.

BANDASHEVSKY, Yuri. I.: *Medical and Biological Effects of Radio Caesium Incorporated in the Human Organism* (2000). A comment on Chernobyl fallout as a cause of cardiac arrest and deaths in children. The scientist was placed under house arrest for disclosing a truth the authorities would rather have remained hidden.

BAVERSTOCK, Keith: *Science, Politics and Ethics in the Low Dose* (2004). A presentation in Edinburgh by former head of the World Health Organisation (Europe). This low level radiation conference was a critique of the 1980s and 1990s NRPB studies of nuclear test veterans' mortality as being "perverted for political reasons".

BERTELL, Rosalie: Eminent cancer research scientist, expert witness to US Congress and author of *No Immediate Danger: Prognosis for a Radioactive Earth* (The Women's Press, 1985)

BERTELL, Rosalie: *Testimony to the US Senate Committee for Veterans Affairs* (1998)

BLAKEWAY, Denys & LLOYD-ROBERTS, Sue: Joint authors of *Fields of Thunder: Testing Britain's Bombs* (Unwin Paperbacks, 1985)

BUSBY, Chris: Britain's leading independent expert on low dose, low level radiation. Author of *Wings of Death: Nuclear Pollution and Human Health* (Green Audit Books, 1995)

BUSBY, Chris: CERRIE committee members' *The Cerrie Minority Report* on the Sacking of Michael Meacher, Environment Minister (Sosiumi Press, 2004); the blocking of independent scientists views on the dangers of inhaled and ingested 'internal emitting' radiation once inside the body.

BUSBY, Chris, with BERTELL, Rosalie; SCHMITZE-FEUERHAKE, Inge; SCOTT CATO, Molly; and YABLOKOV, Alexei: ECRR Recommendations of the *European Committee on Radiation Risk, Regulators Edition: Brussels by Green Audit – The Health Effects of Ionising Radiation Exposure at Low Doses for Radiation Protection Purposes* (2003)

BUSBY, Chris: The Eva Adshead Appeal Tribunal (2002) A victory by expert witness Professor Busby when Scientific Secretary of the ECRR using the *European Committee on Radiation Risk – Health Effects of Ionising Radiation Exposure at Low Level for Radiation Protection Purposes*, published in 2003.

BUSBY, Chris and DE MESIERRES, Mireille: *British Nuclear Test Veterans Association Child Health Study Preliminary Analysis* (2007). This showed significant genetic damage in the children and grandchildren of nuclear veterans. However, the BNTVA did not persist with this line of direct challenge to the government because by this time the leadership had embarked upon a policy of cooperation with the MOD in the hope of achieving an act of grace settlement instead of supporting efforts of the AVGL in seeking compensation.

BUSBY, Chris and WILLIAMS, Dai: *Meteorological records, airflow and other factors affecting local fallout from British nuclear tests at Christmas Island in 1957-9* (2010). A report that was blocked from being presented in court.

BROWN, Kate: US nuclear historian and author of *Manual for Survival: A Chernobyl Guide to the Future* (Allen Lane

Penguin Books, 2019). The author makes a direct link to Chernobyl fallout evidence that would "blow the lid on the massive radiation released from weapons-testing during the Cold War", pointing to the need for cover-up.

CABINET–IN–CONFIDENCE (1986): *Federal Australian Government Canberra documents, Decision No's. 8342 and 8342 (AER)*, some 37 pages dated 31 July 1986. These papers show details of the radioactive contamination left at Maralinga and Emu nuclear test area and the Atomic Energy Research decision to exchange compensation for nuclear test service personnel and others for the cost of removing radioactive contamination. This formed the basis of the bilateral Treaty of December 1993 for Australia and the UK to work together to deny any accountability or responsibility for nuclear test veterans' and families' claims.

ECRR Lesvos Declaration (2009) by 17 eminent radiation experts from 10 nations which included two pivotal points: 1) the ICRP risk model on radiation exposure is significantly flawed, and 2) every person has a right to know the degree of exposure and the health consequences of such exposure. A shift in the growing consensus of opinion.

EVANS, H.J.: Cytogeneticist for Medical Research Council, Western Hospital, Edinburgh; author of paper *Radiation Induced Chromosome Aberrations in Nuclear Dockyard Workers* (1979). A report on a 10-year study which found even at low dose exposure the men showed significant chromosomal damage and this increased as dose of radiation increased. Dr Evans wanted to carry out similar blood testing on nuclear test veterans but was blocked from doing so by the Ministry of Defence.

FOSKETT, Mr Justice: High Court Judge for the Nuclear Veterans Limitation Act Trial which was seized upon by MOD as a delaying tactic against the Atomic Veterans Group Litigation led by Rosenblatt Solicitors of London. The trial verdict (June 2009) was successful, due to the "prime causal link" being fallout radiation and the Rowland cytogenetic blood tests being "crucial and pivotal evidence". Nothing has changed since that date.

GOFMAN, John: *The Environmental Impact of Nuclear Power Plants* (1976). This is an examination of some criticisms of those in opposition to the nuclear industry which sparked Gofman's comment: "The nuclear establishment is conducting a war against mankind."

GREEN, Robert: Cold War fleet air arm bombardier/navigator in nuclear Buccaneer aircraft and author of *A Thorn in Their Side: The Shocking Death of Hilda Murrell* (John Blake, 2013). The book gives details of other persons harassed, intimidated, assaulted or worse for challenging the power of the state.

HADDOW, Alex: Eminent biologist and director of the Chester Beatty Research Institute, Royal Cancer Hospital, London. His 1951 letter to the Director of the Atomic Energy Authority (AEA) first showed the schism existing between biologists and physicist regarding the truth of radiation risk to the human body. He wrote: "It will become increasingly difficult to counter those who already believe that there is some sort of conspiracy of silence."

LITVINENKO, Alexander: Died in 2006 of alpha radiation poisoning. Former NRPB scientists admitted inhaled or ingested alpha particles are an extremely hazardous pathogen if entering inside the body – a fact of radiation denied as applicable to nuclear test veterans living, working and breathing in areas of alpha and beta radioactive fallout.

MARTLAND, Harrison: His post-mortem examination of the US Radium Corporation 'dial painters' in 1929 is the earliest recognition that inhaled or ingested low dose, low level radiation causes lethal and toxic poisoning once lodged inside the body.

MILLIKIN. Robert: *No Conceivable Injury* (Penguin Books, Melbourne 1986) The story of the Australian/UK atomic alliance and cover-up.

MILITARY COVENANT COMMISSION, 2008–2010: A cynical initiative of David Cameron prior to the 2010 general election under the banner "They are doing their duty. Are we doing ours?" This was a pre-election initiative promised to be 'enshrined into law' but predictably reneged upon when Mr Cameron became Prime Minister in 2010.

PETRUCCI, Mario: Freelance writer, physicist and resident poet at the Imperial War Museum. *Heavy Water – a poem for Chernobyl* (Enitharmon Press, 2004)

REDFERN, Michael (QC): *The Redfern Inquiry Report into*

Tissue Analysis at Nuclear Installations (2010). The 600-plus page Inquiry admits organs, bone and tissue is removed and analysed from deceased nuclear industry and nuclear test veterans, without family consent, for medical research and in case of future claims by families.

RIMMER, Alan: Editor of *Fissionline: The International Bulletin for Nuclear Test Veterans and Families.* Investigative journalism of the highest order with over 60 bulletins accessed worldwide free through the internet. fissionline@gmail.com. Try to get back copies of these bulletins; they are essential reading for anyone interested in the history of the nuclear test veterans' struggle for justice.

RIMMER, Alan: *Between Heaven and Hell* (Kindle, 2012). A book with detailed analysis giving detail of the selfless courage and dignity of thousands of nuclear veterans and their families over many decades. Also reference the children yet to be born who will be paying the price in decades to come.

ROWLAND, Al: Cytogeneticist of Massey University, New Zealand. His paper *Elevated Chromosome Translocation Frequency in New Zealand Nuclear Veterans* was ruled "crucial and pivotal" evidence in the London High Court, June 2009, yet ignored and undermined by the biased preference of the UK Government and MOD for statistical studies of mortality that do not involve blood testing and are not capable of showing radiation damage.

SAWADA, Shoji: Emeritus Professor of radiation biology paper *Cover-up of the effects of internal exposure by residual [*

fallout] radiation from the atomic bombing of Hiroshima and Nagasaki (2007). The title explains all. On the strength of this paper, some victims of nuclear bomb fallout radiation in Japan have won legal claims.

Service Personnel & Veterans Agency (SPVA): Radiation Policy Appraisal (2010) The CVFI showed that the document used to advise ministers and tribunals is biased and contains only scientific papers that support the policy to deny radiation risk from fallout. No mention is given with regard to the efficacy of cytogenetic blood testing. All conclusions of advice given to ministers are based entirely upon epidemiological statistics, which are shown to be significantly flawed and biased.

SUTCLIFFE, Charles M. S.: Economist and author of *The Dangers of Low Level Radiation* (Avebury Books – published by Gower, Aldershot, Hants, 1987). This book focused on exposure of the overlooked radiation risk from inhaled or ingested radioactive particles. The author wrote the book in 1987 based on studies published from the 1970s that indicated the risks from low level radiation are considerably higher than official estimates. He compiled it for Berkshire County Council following their concerns about discharges of radioactive liquids by the Atomic Weapons Research Establishment (AWRE) into the River Thames.

TICKELL, Oliver: *Toxic Link: the WHO and the IAEA. A 50-year-old agreement with the IAEA has effectively gagged the WHO from telling the truth about the health risks of radiation* (*Guardian* report, 28 May 2009).

WALKER, Frank: Investigative journalist and author of *Maralinga: Our Secret Nuclear Shame and Betrayal of Our Troops and Country* (Hatchette Australia, 2014). Very informative and packed with information about the Australian servicemen and their nation's betrayal.

WOOMERA BABIES: This research was decided in 1957 at a meeting held by the UK Atomic Energy Research Establishment on 24 May. An edict under file reference DEFE 16/808 set out the means by which the people of Australia would be used as guinea pigs. Australia was chosen to be the research laboratory for finding out how much strontium-90 had been absorbed in human bones from fallout. It is an act of covert research still denied by the Federal Australian Government. Over 22,000 babies, infants, teenagers and young adults were defiled for research.

Printed in Great Britain
by Amazon

21935523R00175